Praise for *A MIN*

"Drawing on a multitude of contempla
book is full of wonderful ideas for mindfulness practices for each day of
the year that lift us out of the treadmill of the automatic pilot."
—Prof. Paul Gilbert, PhD, OBE, author of
The Compassionate Mind and *Living like Crazy*

"They show us how to incorporate small, simple, but meaningful
changes toward mindfulness/presence in our own and our clients'
lives. A welcome and practical addition to any clinician's toolbox!"
—Kevin T. Kuehlwein, PsyD, coeditor of
Cognitive Therapies in Action: Evolving Innovative Practice

"This book is meant to be read one breath at a time. It will slow you
down—in the best of ways. More importantly it will allow each step that
you take to carry you at a more healthy and a more savoring pace."
—The Rev. Dr. Charles Lattimore Howard,
University Chaplain of the University of Pennsylvania
and author of *Pond River Ocean Rain*

"This book is a gift! Here are two real people who have made
a deep connection in their own lives. Out of that they are
offering us riches from their experience."
—Bishop Alison White, Diocese of York, Church of England

"*A Mindful Year* is jam-packed with entertaining, thought-provoking
insights and creative invitations to be mindful as you go through
your day, every day, for an entire year...A wonderful book."
—Joel Minden, PhD, clinical psychologist and author of
Show Your Anxiety Who's Boss

a
mindful
year

a
mindful
year

365 Ways to Find Connection
and the Sacred in Everyday Life

Dr. Aria Campbell-Danesh
and Dr. Seth J. Gillihan

**BLACK
STONE**
PUBLISHING

Copyright © 2019 by Dr. Aria Campbell-Danesh and Seth J. Gillihan, PhD
Published in 2019 by Blackstone Publishing
Cover and book design by Sean Thomas

Printed in the United States of America

First edition: 2019
ISBN 978-1-9825-0183-9
Self-Help / Personal Growth / Happiness

1 3 5 7 9 10 8 6 4 2

CIP data for this book is available
from the Library of Congress

Blackstone Publishing
31 Mistletoe Rd.
Ashland, OR 97520

www.BlackstonePublishing.com

For Marcia, Lucas, Ada, and Faye,
with love and affection.
You are the sacred I find in everyday life.

—Seth

For Emma and Alfie.
You remind me to find the joy in the little things each day.
Your enthusiasm for life (and dog walks) is unending.
All my love.

—Aria

FOREWORD

When my colleague Dr. Seth Gillihan asked me to write the foreword for *A Mindful Year*, I was immediately excited to read it. Seth told me that he and Dr. Aria Campbell-Danesh, a British psychologist and cherished friend of his, had written to each other for a year, taking turns sharing a mindful message for the day, on good days and bad. As I read, I had a strong sense that the daily messages they'd written to each other were like having a friend, guru, and psychologist all rolled into one—and always available! Not only are Aria and Seth whip smart, they're emotionally engaged and engaging, too—something each one of us can use in a friend and companion.

In modern life many of us feel scattered. Our weeks are so busy that it's difficult to find time to take a step back—to get a thirty-thousand-foot perspective on the decisions we make. Often we feel disconnected from what's important to us, guilt about whether we're maximizing every opportunity, and regret about getting hung up on things that, in the long run, don't really matter.

Perhaps you have a sense that you're not living your life to the fullest and feel powerless to break the pattern. Maybe you gravitated to this book because you're going through a difficult time, you're worn down by adulting, and you'd like some psychological support to prop you up. Maybe you're embarking on an exciting project and need some stress relief to cope with its emotional ups and downs. Or maybe you just feel stagnant and want to introduce an element of spontaneity to energize and motivate yourself. If you can relate to any of these hungers, you'll find them satisfied by the insight and nurturing in this book.

In *A Mindful Year*, there's one short passage for you to read each day—a format that makes each daily message manageable to digest and easy to take with you. The entries will help you feel more content, peaceful, grateful, courageous, and grounded—and less empty, irritable, anxious, and envious. You'll feel more in tune with your inner and outer worlds—your thoughts, feelings, goals, and relationships.

There will be times when you read an entry and it's immediately obvious how the insights it contains apply to your current life. There will be a lot of days when the message seems to come at just the right time, which speaks to the universality of the themes covered. There will be other days when nothing springs to mind as you read. But taking the time to ponder how a less-obvious principle applies to you as you move through your day might even lead to a delayed "aha moment." Sometimes reading an entry may even help you recognize a strength you didn't realize you had or an area of life in which you're already experiencing a deep sense of connection.

Reading *A Mindful Year* is like having a conversation with the most mindful, brilliant, and emotionally accessible psychologist-friends you can imagine—which is, in effect, exactly what it is. If you've ever wanted instant wisdom at your fingertips, you'll find that here. Take a mindful moment and see for yourself.

—Dr. Alice Boyes

PREFACE

SETH: Aria and I met in the fall of 2010 when I was on the faculty at the University of Pennsylvania. He was a visiting student from the University of St. Andrews in Scotland and took my psychology seminar called Anxiety and the Brain. He was a standout. It was evident from early in the semester that there was something unique about him. He related easily to his classmates and seemed to be as kind as he was bright. I never knew a harder-working student.

ARIA: On more than one occasion, Seth and I would talk after class as we left the building together. I'd ask him questions related to the syllabus, and we'd end up discussing various areas of psychology. We clearly enjoyed each other's company and shared a mutual respect. I had recently cofounded Mindfulness at Penn (MAP), the University of Pennsylvania's first mindfulness group, and mindfulness became a strand in our conversations.

SETH: Once the class was over, our roles as professor and student began to fade. Aria and I became friends. We shared many lunches together on our breaks. There was never enough time to talk, and our meals together always ended too soon. I dreaded his departure at the end of the school year as he returned to St. Andrews.

ARIA: On two occasions, Seth kindly invited me to have dinner at his house. Spending time with him and his family formed some of my fondest memories of my time in the States. Seth and his wife, Marcia, obviously loved each other dearly and welcomed me so warmly into their home. Baby Ada had recently been born, and Lucas was a hilarious little boy. We had so much fun together, sharing food, playing games, and laughing. I remember thinking that if one day I had a family unit like this, I would be a very fortunate man.

SETH: During our times together, I felt what I've often sensed about Aria: that he brings out the best in others. In the short time I'd known him, he had encouraged me to pursue my hope of making a major career transition and had fostered the growth of my nascent mindfulness practice. I had an intuition that he would continue to be an important part of my life in ways I couldn't identify at the time. It was with great sadness that I said goodbye to him when he moved back to the UK in May 2011.

ARIA: Over the next three years, Seth and I would email one another and occasionally Skype. It would have been easy to lose touch, but in the time that we'd spent together, we'd formed a close connection. It seemed as if it would have been a great disservice to our friendship to let it pass. Every time we did speak, even if months had gone by, it was as if we were back at Penn catching up on a lunch break over a falafel wrap.

SETH: When I was invited to Aria's wedding in the summer of 2014, I knew I had to go. My whole time in the Newcastle area felt magical—the small retreat many of us stayed in, the meals we shared together, the labyrinth we walked in the cool of the morning, the small roads I explored alone that traced the rolling hills around Newcastle.

ARIA: The fact that Seth traveled around 3,500 miles to be present at my and Emma's wedding meant more to me than I explained to him at the time. Actions like that always speak louder than words. Having breakfast at the retreat house together on the morning of my wedding, sharing memories, and taking photographs with some of my closest friends was the perfect start to the most significant day of my life.

SETH: The pouring rain on the day of the wedding couldn't dampen the joyous celebration in the old church where Aria and Emma were joined in marriage. It was hard not to cry as I looked at the two of them while I gave a reading from St. Paul's letter to the Colossians: "Above all, clothe yourselves with love, which binds us all together in perfect harmony."

ARIA: During the wedding service, there was a strong sense of unity in the church. I felt as though we were all parts of a larger body. Seth's reading was moving; he spoke each word with love and sincerity. What struck me about the passage was how much attention we can place on how we look and dress physically while giving so little to the clothes we wear spiritually. I connected with the image of clothing ourselves with our values each day.

SETH: Everything about the wedding weekend came together to provide a deep sense of connection—to the people around me, to each experience, to a sense of ease and contentment, to my two kids and very pregnant wife back in the States. I knew it couldn't last forever, yet I had to wonder: Why not? That deep feeling of connection to what matters—was it possible to foster it outside the context of a picture-perfect wedding in the English countryside?

ARIA: The day after the wedding, we took a long walk together with my family through the fields and forests around Emma's parents' home. Seth and I stood on a hill as the light grew longer and talked about our shared sense of connection to what we cared about most: family, simplicity, and service. We wondered together if it's possible to maintain and even strengthen our connections to the people and the passions closest to our hearts—especially during times of difficulty, distraction, and discontent. We vowed to one another to find out.

INTRODUCTION

When economics professor Richard Easterlin turned his attention to the study of happiness in the 1970s, he found a surprising paradox: while real incomes in the United States had grown in the preceding decades, happiness levels had flatlined. And while happiness often has little to do with our external circumstances, too many of us focus our time and energy on our financial progression and other outward markers of "success," while neglecting our emotional and spiritual development.

Recent technological advances have led to another paradox: although we're more connected than ever by the internet and social media, we're missing a true sense of connection to the things in life that provide us with meaning and fulfillment. Somehow we've lost our way, prioritizing financial and technological progression over our mental, emotional, and spiritual health.

This book is an invitation to find your way back to a deep sense of satisfaction and connection. For one year, starting on January 1, the two of us wrote to each other every day, taking turns as we composed 365 practices drawn from mindfulness and cognitive behavioral therapy. Each practice highlights a principle that encourages greater connection to the most important aspects of our lives.

You'll get the most out of this book if you read an entry each day as there will be a sense of continuity and connection that deepens day by day. Each entry is also written to stand alone, however, so feel free to pick the book up anytime you have a moment for quiet reflection. We do encourage you to make enough time to be able to engage with the reading and not feel rushed.

Over the course of the year, we return time and again to the themes that inspired us to embark on this journey together: compassion, authenticity, love, and simplicity. At the end of each entry is an invitation to pull the practice into your life in a meaningful way—an invitation you can choose to accept, decline, or modify. The important thing is to find what works for you.

We found these practices to be life changing over the course of the year as we dealt with major health issues, deaths, and nearby terrorist attacks as well as the ordinary ups and downs of adult life. Our mutual encouragement and daily mindfulness practice helped unearth the sacred over and over, on good days and very difficult ones.

We now invite you to join us in these practices and connect on a daily basis to what you value—to what truly matters. We wish you a year of learning, growing, and connecting, each day, to what inspires you.

JANUARY 1

Begin doing what you want to do now. We are not living in eternity.
We have only this moment, sparkling like a star in our hand and
melting like a snowflake. —MARIE BEYNON RAY

Hello, my friend! Happy New Year!

The dawn of the New Year heralds an opportunity to reflect on the year that has passed and look ahead to the upcoming one. How are you feeling about the last twelve months, with its ups and downs, peaks and troughs? It's incredible to think that the next 365 days will bring undiscovered joys and challenges.

As the days, weeks, months, and years roll into one another, it becomes ever more apparent that our time on this earth is short and precious. As easy as it is to take for granted, what a gift it is to be alive! It would be tragic to reach the end of life having missed out on the parts that mattered most. Let's do what we want to do now. Let's live this life to its fullest. This is a new year, a new day, and a new opportunity to reconnect to whatever we value most.

INVITATION

Take a moment to consider the following questions:

Looking back over the past year,

- What have been the high and low parts?
- In what ways have you grown and developed?
- What parts of your life are you grateful for?

Looking to the year ahead,

- What qualities would you like to cultivate?
- Who would you like to spend more time with?
- What would you like to spend more time doing?

This is your time. You deserve to have a meaningful and fulfilling life. I'm excited to embark on this journey with you.

JANUARY 2

You are always standing in the middle of sacred space, standing in the middle of the circle…Whatever comes into the space is there to teach you.
—PEMA CHÖDRÖN

One of the biggest challenges to connecting with what's most important to us is the feeling that we "should" be doing something else—even when we're doing exactly what we need to be doing. We might spend our entire day never really *doing* what we're doing as we try to get through *this* activity so we can move on to "what's really important."

Of course, the idea of what we "should be doing" is often a moving target. I find myself rushing through my morning routine to get out the door and to my office, only to rush home at the end of the day, resenting even the time it takes to move from one place to the next. It often feels like there's somewhere else I should be, and it's always ahead of me, just out of reach.

How refreshing it is to remember that all we can do is what we're doing right now—that that's everything. We can allow ourselves to be fully in our experience, whatever that may be. We can find rest there.

You can find rest when you're brushing your teeth, eating a meal, doing laundry, or standing in line at the grocery store. Right now, as you're reading these words, you can rest in this moment of your life—a moment unlike any other and as real as any other. Never again will you have exactly this experience. This is it.

INVITATION

Notice today when your mind is running ahead of where you actually are. Whatever today brings, remember that you can abide in the present—starting right now.

JANUARY 3

In your everyday life, you have always a chance to have enlightenment.
—SHUNRYŪ SUZUKI

Life is full of the ordinary. We have everyday chores, tasks, and routines that need to be completed. The trash needs to be taken out, dishes have to be washed, and the dog has to be walked.

At some point in our culture, the ordinary became "not enough" and "success" became equated with the exceptional. Each moment, though, contains within it the opportunity for enlightenment. Enlightenment is awareness: becoming mindful of the present moment and what you're doing, feeling, and thinking. If you're feeling frustrated and thinking, *I wish my partner was taking the trash out*, enlightenment is becoming aware of this—acknowledging it, observing it.

What if we came to see the ordinary in a different light? For our ancestors, the everyday—hunting, foraging, cooking—contributed to their survival. Nowadays, this link to the essential and sacred is often lost.

With awareness, we have a choice. We can find ways to appreciate the present moment and to see our situation with fresh eyes. We could, for instance, choose to view emptying the trash, preparing a meal, or washing the dishes as a way to show our love and to be a caring partner, parent, or child.

INVITATION

Notice when difficult thoughts and feelings arise, particularly when you feel or think that you should be doing something else. See if you can perceive your situation in a new light and discover the meaning that lies hidden in your everyday actions.

JANUARY 4

The more directly one aims to maximize pleasure and avoid pain, the more likely one is to produce instead a life bereft of depth, meaning, and community. —RICHARD M. RYAN, VERONIKA HUTA, AND EDWARD L. DECI

Most of us want a life of maximal comfort and minimal pain—what Aristotle called a "hedonic" focus. The guiding question from a hedonic perspective is, Which actions will bring me the most pleasure? Seeking pleasure directly, however, often has paradoxical results. For example, if we avoid the physical discomfort of exercise, we'll come to feel the greater pain of disuse.

Aristotle described an alternative approach that instead asks, "What should I do in order to live well?" Choices based on this question lead to a life of eudaemonia, a Greek word that describes meaning and connection to what we most value. Almost anything worthwhile involves some degree of discomfort, so it takes conscious planning and effort to override our focus on short-term pleasure and make choices that promote eudaemonia.

Fortunately, a eudaemonic approach does not mean giving up all earthly comforts. Ironically, the eudaemonic way of life is the surest path to a life of true pleasure. By seeking comfort, we lose it, and by giving up comfort, we find it.

For myself, it can be as mundane as recognizing times when I'm putting off refilling my water because I don't want to get up. The simple act of rising from my chair to get more water breaks me out of my "Stay Comfortable" default mode but makes me more comfortable in the long run.

We all want to enjoy our limited days on this earth. When we plan our actions such that we'll know we've lived well—for this minute, this hour, this day—we can keep finding the sacred in our everyday lives.

INVITATION

Today, look for even small opportunities to choose living well over immediate comfort or pleasure.

JANUARY 5

Mindfulness gives you time. Time gives you choices. Choices, skillfully made, lead to freedom. You don't have to be swept away by your feeling. You can respond with wisdom and kindness rather than habit and reactivity. —HENEPOLA GUNARATANA

At this time of year, many of us will have New Year's resolutions that involve eating healthily, being active, stopping smoking, or cutting down on alcohol. Even when we know what is good for us, facing urges and unpleasant feelings often seems to be the hardest part.

We usually try to ignore and suppress difficult feelings. But as anyone who has ever tried *not* thinking about a white bear knows, the paradox is that the more we try to avoid feeling or thinking about something, the stronger it grows.

If we don't fight thoughts, feelings, and cravings, what can we do? We can observe them. We can watch them with openness and curiosity. We can notice them as they come and go. This is mindfulness. Rather than reacting automatically and habitually, using observation we can respond more skillfully—more deliberately—taking action in line with our values and the good life.

INVITATION

Today, my friend, acknowledge any thoughts, feelings, or cravings that you have. Rather than fighting them, simply try to observe them. You don't have to resist or be swept away by your feelings. Use this sacred space you've opened by observation to then take action in the direction of your goals.

JANUARY 6

The really important kind of freedom involves attention and awareness and discipline, and being able truly to care about other people and to sacrifice for them over and over in myriad petty, unsexy ways every day.
—DAVID FOSTER WALLACE

I t's easy—sometimes too easy—to feel irritated at people whose actions create inconvenience—for example, the man who hits the up button just as the elevator doors are closing, forcing you and your fellow passengers to wait what feels like an eternity in elevator time. But these petty grievances erect a barrier between us and others. It's hard to feel compassion for people we see as annoying and selfish.

We've also all had times when we've decided to cut an inconsiderate person some slack or even extend kindness toward them. Caring for others by choosing to let go of minor irritations is truly "unsexy." Most of the time, you are the only one who even knows the choice you've made, and the alternative. How much nicer it feels to let go of that sense of being treated unfairly. We might even feel a sense of connection to the other person, since we've probably done the same thing ourselves.

How can we move beyond our knee-jerk irritation toward others? One of the most effective ways is to question the stories we tell ourselves to explain another's behavior. Maybe that person speeding past you isn't a jerk but is trying to avoid being late to pick up her kids from day care. Checking our assumptions makes it easier to drop our sense of indignation. It might even allow us to see ourselves in the other person, fostering a sense of compassion instead of condemnation.

INVITATION
What if, just for today, we cut everyone a break? As we interact with the world, we can decide in advance to let the little things go. We might consider it an act of love—not just for others but also for ourselves.

JANUARY 7

I am an old man and have known a great many troubles,
but most of them never happened. —MARK TWAIN

The future is unknown. The human brain, however, is hardwired to seek certainty. Through an evolutionary lens, certainty is survival. Being able to predict future events increases our chances of living to pass on our genes.

Uncertainty can be uncomfortable and even distressing. When we struggle to determine the outcome of an event, the mind becomes extremely active in order to predict the future and achieve certainty.

Our minds have a tendency to fall into certain thinking styles. An upcoming exam creates worries about failing. A changing economic landscape ignites concerns about job security and financial ruin. Getting older feeds fears of ill health. This is what the brain does. It catastrophizes about worst-case scenarios. It seeks certainty by imagining possible stories about the future.

The devil does not lie in our brain's capacity to construct stories or consider catastrophes. The brain's ability to make predictions is both unavoidable and adaptive. In fact, it contributed to your very existence on this earth right now. Liberation, however, is found in becoming aware of the impact of the stories, predictions, and thoughts that you hold. Are they distressing you, overwhelming you into paralysis, or stopping you from richly engaging in the activities that you enjoy with the people you love? Or are they empowering you, allowing you to make the most of each day, and helping you to prepare for the future, whatever that may be?

INVITATION
Notice any stories that your mind creates about the future. Become aware of the impact these predictions have on you right now. What thoughts will help you best appreciate this moment and live the life that you want today?

JANUARY 8

God loves to feel things through our hands.
—ELIZABETH GILBERT

We depend so much on these bodies we inhabit. Take a moment to look at your hands. You know these hands well—"like the back of your hand," as the saying goes—and yet they've changed throughout your life. They were tiny and wrinkled when you took your first breath, when you grasped the finger of your mother or father. They've grown as you have, getting stronger and more skilled. Your left hand might bear a ring that symbolizes an eternal joining with the one you love. These hands tell your story. In many ways, they have written it.

Your hands are miraculous, responding to your thoughts: *Open*, and they open; *Close*, and they make a fist—your very own telekinesis. Consider all the things these hands allow you to do: hold a baby, blow your nose, push a broom, hug a friend, wash the dishes, hold your head in grief, put on your pants, lift a fork, massage sore muscles, type on a keyboard, feel the pulse of your beating heart—to name just a few.

There is great power in our hands. We can deliberately pay attention to them, noticing their movements, their sensitivity to touch, the connection they make with our physical world. Like the breath, we can always return to our hands to ground our awareness in the moment, perhaps feeling gratitude for their exquisite design.

INVITATION

As you go about your day today, notice your hands, both what they're doing and the sensations they transmit to your brain. May your hands serve others and communicate love.

JANUARY 9

When an archer is shooting for nothing, he has all his skill.
If he shoots for a brass buckle, he is already nervous.
If he shoots for a prize of gold, he goes blind or sees two targets—
. . . .
His skill has not changed. But the prize divides him.
He cares. He thinks more of winning than of shooting—
And the need to win drains him of power.

—CHUANG TZU

Goals are important. They give us direction. If we become too absorbed with the end point, however, not only do we miss out on the joy of the moment, but we also handicap ourselves. We tighten up with the pressure and make it less likely that we'll reach our destination, especially if it's important to us.

Today I was out on a marathon training run. I suddenly realized that for most of my run I'd been distracted, thinking about an upcoming race and imagining possible outcomes. Something struck me. I was so fixated on my goal that I was missing out on the pleasure of running right now. Rather than focusing on the outcome, we can focus on the process. Rather than becoming consumed with winning, simply try your best. The beautiful, profoundly simple but often overlooked truth is that we can only ever try our best. When we remember this, the pressure of expectation begins to lift, and we're free to enjoy the present moment.

INVITATION

If you notice that you're feeling gripped by your goals, including New Year's resolutions, try holding them a little more lightly. Focus on the *process* of what you are doing and *simply try your best*, held safely and warmly in the knowledge that this is all that you can do.

JANUARY 10

Love is found in the things we've given up
More than in the things that we have kept
—RICH MULLINS

L ove seems to be about letting go. Love is apparent in the simple act of giving up some of our bread to share with another. Love is found in foregoing other relationships to be with our partner. Love is missing out on sleep to care for a child or a parent. Love is letting go of the internal voice that continually berates us for not being enough.

In a more general sense, real freedom is often found in the things that bind us: committed relationships, consistent work, sobriety, an ethical code. I recall not long ago being very aware of what I was missing out on by being a parent of three young kids. Then I considered what it would be like—what it *had been* like, in truth—being on the other side, being desperate to be a parent and not knowing if it was possible. In that moment a great feeling of gratitude completely eclipsed any sense of sacrifice.

Maybe in some way we're always behind bars, choosing one kind of freedom that in another way binds us. Love leads us to one side of the bars or the other based on what we're willing to give up for what we care about most.

INVITATION
The value we attach to our deepest connections is never more apparent than when we remember what we've willingly given up for them. Today, consider how love is expressed in your life through the things you've given up—and what you've gained in return.

JANUARY 11

Getting to the top is nothing. The way you do it is everything.
—ROYAL ROBBINS

R oyal Robbins is a pioneer in the rock-climbing world. He shaped history by making groundbreaking ascents in Yosemite without hammering pins into the rock surface in order to preserve its natural features. For Robbins, there was more to the process than the outcome.

There are different routes and ways to reach a coveted destination. We can get there ruthlessly, by overpowering others or simply ignoring their thoughts and feelings, but there is of course another way: We can live each day connected to our values. We can work toward our goals, however ambitious, with integrity and authenticity. We can treat every person the way we would like to be treated. The difference that this can make to an individual, a team, and the working atmosphere is astounding. We can still achieve all that we desire, whether as small as buying a cup of coffee or as meteoric as building a global business, by treating others with appreciation and respect.

INVITATION

Consider these three questions:

- What type of person do you want to be?
- How would you like to be remembered?
- Who do you admire?

These questions will help you discern the qualities that are important to you. Try writing your answers down somewhere you can access easily, perhaps in a note on your phone or on a small piece of paper you can keep in your purse or wallet. Throughout the day, bring these values to mind. Take a few slow, deep breaths. With each out-breath, say each value in your head or whisper them. Smile a little. Allow them to fill your body, to live in the present moment, and to guide your actions.

JANUARY 12

There is no more appropriate prayer which a man can offer than that his heart may have such a unity of purpose, and that nothing may be allowed to interfere with that one supreme purpose.

—ALBERT BARNES

I n considering how we reconnect with each other, the idea of simplicity, even unity, is a recurring, almost universal one. A singularity of purpose is captured in the psalmist's plea "Unite my heart"; in the Buddhist notion of "Drive all blames into one"; and in the proverb "Let your eyes look straight ahead...Do not turn to the right or the left."

Aria's wedding weekend is one of the times I've felt most grounded and connected. There were very few distractions, and I was able to focus on the people and the events of the moment—the meals together with other wedding guests, the walk in the labyrinth on the morning of the wedding, the beautiful ceremony. There was nothing to do other than what we were doing.

What if connection has as much to do with removing distractions as it does with pursuing some specific activity or way of thinking? On a recent trip to the ER with my six-year-old daughter, I decided for some reason to resist the impulse to take out my phone while my daughter dozed and we waited for the doctor. With my phone off, I was able to connect with a deep sense of gratitude for my daughter and her health. The space we were in became sacred.

INVITATION

Consider for a moment what purpose unites your passions. As you move through your day, notice things that compete for your attention and could pull you away from that unity of purpose.

JANUARY 13

To find yourself, lose yourself in the service of others.
                                        —MAHATMA GANDHI

It has been said that we can give ourselves the pleasure of pleasing ourselves and we can give ourselves the pleasure of pleasing others. I can eat a peanut butter brownie and feel good. I can also share the brownie with my friend Gary, who also loves peanut butter, and feel good. On the surface, one act appears more honorable than the other. Both situations make me feel good. This insight is the great leveler.

There's a temptation in life to see other people's actions as selfish and our own as altruistic: "They're out to get what they want for themselves," whereas, "I'm doing this for the benefit of others." But we all act in our own self-interest, even if it's to feel good or to know that we're doing the right thing. We gain something by giving, and when we acknowledge that, the veneer of superiority dissipates. We realize that we're neither better nor worse than anyone else.

Where does this leave us? I would say *give*—give generously and abundantly. Help others, and in doing so, lead a happier life. Find fulfillment in sharing your time, efforts, and wealth with those in need. Notice the pleasure you receive from giving and celebrate this! At the same time, be aware of how easy it is to climb onto a moral pedestal. See the common humanity that binds us all by recognizing that like everyone else, we too are serving ourselves.

INVITATION

Serve others today, especially in small ways: hold the door open for someone, let a car out in front of you, buy the person sleeping on the street a cup of coffee, offer to help at work or home. Enjoy the gift of giving!

JANUARY 14

The best years of your life are the ones in which you decide your problems are your own. You do not blame them on your mother, the ecology, or the president. You realize that you control your own destiny.

—ALBERT ELLIS

Each of us is responsible for caring for the person whose skin we inhabit. This uniquely intimate relationship means we are best positioned to be the caretakers of our own well-being. As such, no one can make us feel happy or unhappy unless we let them.

And yet when we're feeling discontented, it can be very easy to blame it on the cold rain, a frustrating situation, or the uncertainty that surrounds an important decision. It's easy for a sense of resentment to creep in, the feeling of getting a raw deal, that happiness would come *if only life would cooperate.*

How freeing it is to realize that happiness is a choice—and one that is always available! Happiness isn't contingent on everything working out our way, however we may define that. Conditional happiness is fragile and leads to clinging to "good" things—and fearing that we'll lose them.

This is not to suggest that we should never experience the sadness of loss, anger at others' inconsideration, anxiety about the future, or any other human emotion. It's about recognizing when we're clinging to stories that get in the way of a happiness that is ours for the taking. A basic contentment is your birthright, and it's available right now.

INVITATION

When anything threatens your peace of mind today, remember this: "Only I am responsible for my happiness."

JANUARY 15

The most important relationship in your life is the relationship that you have with yourself. Who else is with you at all times?
—DIANE VON FÜRSTENBERG

As humans we're extremely good at being hard on ourselves. We hold rules and standards for the way that we look, think, feel, act, and interact. And when we fall short of these benchmarks, we can come down on ourselves like a ton of bricks, hurling internal abuse and insults.

Self-criticism often develops as a protective mechanism. Our brains are wired to protect us. The ability to discern when our actions might expose us to danger is adaptive. Self-criticism, however, can easily tip from constructive communication into destructive dialogue.

If we want to be our own source of care rather than condemnation, the first step is to become aware of our inner voice, particularly during those moments we are charged with hostility rather than warmth. The second step is to acknowledge that our mind is just trying to keep us safe, even it if may be hurting us more than it is helping. The third step is to speak to ourselves in a way that will uplift and inspire.

INVITATION
When you notice an inner critic speaking, acknowledge that it's trying to help. Then ask yourself, What would I want a good friend to say to me?

JANUARY 16

Real fearlessness is the product of tenderness. It comes from letting the world tickle your heart, your raw and beautiful heart. You are willing to open up, without resistance or shyness, and face the world. You are willing to share your heart with others. —CHÖGYAM TRUNGPA

Our default mode seems to be self-protection. This stance is apparent in our physical posture as we hide our hands in our pockets or cross our arms over our heart. We can also foster conditions that prevent opening, like being overscheduled or indulging resentment. And yet these defenses, whether physical or psychological, only feed our fear, our sense that we *need* to defend ourselves.

Fearlessness, on the other hand, comes from a willingness to be vulnerable—to let the world in. This might seem like a position of weakness, but in fact, it connects us with our strength. For example, on the flight to England for Aria's wedding, I was holding on tight, mentally, and scared the plane might crash. I desperately wanted to see my kids again and meet my unborn baby girl. When I accepted the uncertainty about my safety, my fear vanished and I felt expansive, and deeply connected with the ones I love.

It can be surprising, too, the things that open our hearts. It may be a song, or a sunrise, or truly seeing a loved one. It's like suddenly stepping into a cool stream that's always available, and it's often closely tied to gratitude, both following and leading to a deep awareness of all that we have.

INVITATION
If there are times today when you find yourself feeling closed off, see if it's possible in that moment to allow your heart to open, even a little.

JANUARY 17

Twenty years from now you will be more disappointed by the things that you didn't do than by the ones you did do. So throw off the bowlines. Sail away from the safe harbor. Catch the trade winds in your sails. Explore. Dream. Discover. —H. JACKSON BROWN JR.

As men and women approach the end of their lives, pangs of sadness tend to accompany their thoughts on certain aspects of their pasts, including the following:

- Working rather than spending time with loved ones
- Losing touch with once-close friends
- Being in a relationship longer than they wished or giving up on one too soon
- Being too concerned with others' opinions
- Missing opportunities because of fear or a lack of confidence
- Worrying too much and taking life too seriously

As well as big regrets, such as having an affair or not reaching out to someone before they died, people often talk about "little things," like saying "I love you" or going to watch their child's sports games. What if it's true that our biggest regrets are based on inaction rather than action?

Today is a new, fresh opportunity to explore, dream, and discover—to take as many actions as possible, however small, to make our lives meaningful and fulfilling. As the Chinese proverb goes, "The best time to plant a tree was twenty years ago. The second-best time is now."

INVITATION

Imagine it's twenty years from now. On the following page, use the space provided to write down five regrets that you would *not* want to have.

continued on next page

INVITATION WORKSHEET

1.

2.

3.

4.

5.

Have a look at what you've written. What do you discover? Based on what you've written, what concrete actions could you take today that would help you build a fulfilling life?

JANUARY 18

You are always complete and in the process of becoming—a seed in full bloom. —REBECCA LOUICK

There is a tension between accepting ourselves as we are and being willing to grow. It can seem like a knife's edge and very easy to fall to one side or the other: being either accepting and complacent or judgmental and critical of ourselves for not being exactly where we want to be.

We can approach growth from a place of wholeness. If we decide we must grow because we're deficient, we may very well change, but perhaps not in a healthy way. It's nearly impossible to build well on a foundation of self-rejection.

Take the metaphor of an acorn: perfect just as it is, it won't *stay* an acorn—given the right conditions, it will develop into a perfect little seedling, and then a sapling, and eventually a tall oak tree. Even as a mature tree it will continue to develop, growing new branches, losing branches in storms, bearing the scars of lightning. And no matter how big and strong it is, at some point it will die.

The oak's body tells a story, just as our own bodies do. When we see a tiny baby, we don't think, "Hmm, not bad, but he could be better." We accept babies just as they are, even knowing that they have a lot to learn. The same is true with toddlers, teenagers, and even full-grown adults. We continue to grow, and we will always have a lot to learn. And we grow *because* we are whole, not to *become* whole.

INVITATION
Look for opportunities today to remind yourself, "I am whole," and, "I am growing"—and that both can be true simultaneously.

JANUARY 19

Don't compare your version of success with anyone else's. Everyone has their own unique path. There will almost always be someone richer, fitter, happier, or more successful than you. The real challenge is to learn to appreciate what you have while you pursue all that you want.

—RUBÉN CHAVEZ

I recently met up with a friend in Dubai. Parked outside was an astounding array of supercars: a McLaren, a Lamborghini, a Maserati, and a Bentley. Over a cup of masala tea, he shared that despite earning more in the last twelve months than any previous year, his dissatisfaction with his financial position was greater than ever, saying, "I can drive my Mercedes into the car park of a restaurant and feel like the poorest person there."

It would be tempting to judge this type of perspective, to see it as a folly fueled by greed or materialism. At the heart of that sobering statement, however, is the very human tendency to compare our own situation with that of others.

There will always be someone richer or poorer, fatter or slimmer, more or less intelligent than we are. Always. Our brains will automatically compare our situations with those of others. This is natural. The danger lies in basing our personal worth on these comparisons.

INVITATION

Today, notice when your mind makes snap judgments, evaluations, and comparisons with others. Allow any thoughts and feelings to be present and to pass. Reflect on what you are grateful for in your life and remember that you are worthy just as you are.

JANUARY 20

Embrace relational uncertainty. It's called **romance**. *Embrace spiritual uncertainty. It's called* **mystery**. *Embrace occupational uncertainty. It's called* **destiny**. *Embrace emotional uncertainty. It's called* **joy**. *Embrace intellectual uncertainty. It's called* **revelation**.

—MARK BATTERSON

There are a great many things to appreciate when we simply pay attention, which leads to a radically different experience from having vaguely uneasy preoccupations about how the day will go. We can spend much of our time worrying about whether things will turn out "our way." It's uncomfortable to acknowledge life's uncertainty. Nevertheless, we can make friends with the unknown, deliberately *embracing* uncertainty.

Indeed, most of life's enjoyment is based on uncertainty: winning in sports would mean nothing if we knew we couldn't lose, just as succeeding professionally would be empty if failure were not a possibility. At the heart of our experience is the ultimate uncertainty of when and how this life will end. Uncertainty is woven into the very fabric of our existence, so to embrace uncertainty is to embrace *life*.

In fact, even if we don't get the outcome we wanted, things may turn out better than we hoped. In my own life, for example, my unfunded grant proposals left me free to leave academia and pursue what I found most meaningful. Life's disappointments and beauty are often inseparable.

INVITATION

If you find yourself worrying about an uncertain outcome today, remember, life is uncertain. Open yourself to the continual unfolding of life as it is revealed moment by moment.

JANUARY 21

We are shaped by our thoughts. —BUDDHA

The effects of some thoughts are enhancing; the effects of others, diminishing. But when we look more closely, even seemingly negative thoughts can be of help.

For instance, this morning I felt a mix of pre–Dubai Marathon anxiety and excitement. I noticed my mind coming up with different future scenarios. In one, my dehydrated body was being peeled off the side of the street; in another, I crossed the finish line in personal-best time. A simple realization then struck me: I don't know what will happen right now, and I won't know until it does happen. As much as I might want life to speed up, the world goes at its own pace.

With this insight came a choice: I could buy into a certain thought about the future and swallow it whole, without doubting its truth, or I could inspect it and see what it's telling me. I could learn from the thought and use it to prepare myself for the journey ahead. Even the image of me lying dehydrated on the street could teach me: perhaps I need to drink water at every station and run in the shade wherever possible. In this way, thoughts can be our guides. Rather than ruling us, they can inform us. And once we've learned from a thought, we can let it go and bring our attention to the present moment.

INVITATION

Today, notice the connection between your thoughts and your feelings. Which thoughts leave you feeling empowered, and which feeling disheartened? When you have thoughts that are accompanied by anxiety or fear, in what way could your mind be helping you to prepare? What can you learn? Once you have taken what you need, bring your attention back to the present moment, smile, and breathe.

JANUARY 22

Sound can paint a picture, produce a mood, trigger the senses to remember another time and place. —LOUIS COLAIANNI

One of the ways we can reconnect with our present experience is to notice the sounds around us. Vibrations continually collide with our eardrums, which transmit them into the middle ear, where the smallest and most intricately designed bones in our bodies pass them along to the inner ear, where they are transformed into electrochemical signals. These signals then travel through bundles of nerve cells to the thalamus and then, finally, on to the hearing centers in our brains.

Even as you sit here reading, you might be aware of the ticking of the clock, each car that passes, a bird chirping outside. So many of our day-to-day actions are facilitated by hearing: enjoying music, talking on the phone, responding to a timer while making dinner—countless ways.

No matter where we are, we can choose to pay attention to what we hear. Some sounds are obvious: voices talking, a car honking, a slamming door, the floorboards creaking as you try not to wake your sleeping spouse. We can deepen our awareness of sounds by listening for the subtler ones: your footsteps when you're alone, your pen moving across a page, your hand sliding along a handrail, the peeling of an orange, the dotting of an *i*, each breath you take.

INVITATION

Today, deliberately tune in to the sounds around you, both big and small, that connect you to your experience.

JANUARY 23

Dance first. Think later. It's the natural order.

—SAMUEL BECKETT

During a marathon, there can be personal peaks—like the sun rising from the horizon, lifting the desert city of Dubai out of darkness, or running past a professional athlete. (To be fair, that last one may be less impressive than it sounds as the athlete in question was, unfortunately, injured at the time and hobbling along at the side of the course.) But as with life, there are troughs too—particularly after mile twenty, when one's legs grow tired and thirst really kicks in.

Moving our bodies is a powerful way to change our emotional state. A recent study tracked the activity and mood of over ten thousand participants. Running a marathon is obviously at one end of the spectrum; the researchers, however, were far more interested in "non-exercise" activity—for instance, when you walk from your desk to the restroom. The data demonstrated that people who are more physically active in their day-to-day lives are happier in general. Furthermore, analysis revealed that individuals are happier during those specific moments of physical movement. Activity linked to everyday functioning is easy to overlook and take for granted. It can, however, be another way to feel fulfilled during the day.

INVITATION

Find small opportunities for non-exercise activity during the day—like the following, for instance:

- Going for a short walk after lunch
- Taking the stairs whenever possible
- Parking farther away from building entrances
- Dancing in an elevator with music playing—whether you boogie on your own or with others is entirely up to you (and them), of course

When you do move, drop your attention into your body like a ship dropping an anchor. Allow your mind to rest, and enjoy this moment of happiness.

JANUARY 24

When you arise in the morning, think of what a precious privilege it is to be alive—to breathe, to think, to enjoy, to love.

—MARCUS AURELIUS

I know a young mother who had a freak medical crisis in her midthirties. She had to have an emergency procedure, and there was no guarantee she would see her husband and two little girls again. When she survived and got to stay in this world among her loved ones, she described how she no longer took anything for granted. She was grateful to have any experience at all, and each day felt like waking up into a reality that might not have been. Her gratitude extended even to painful follow-up procedures because feeling pain meant she was still here. The cliché we often hear felt to her as true as the ground we walk on: Each day is a gift—and today as much as any day.

Reconnecting has a lot to do with letting go of our obsessive focus on the 1 percent of life and remembering the other 99. Even when our health isn't perfect, for example, we can remember that it is good in many other ways. If you're lucky, you have a house to shelter you, clothes to cover you, a warm bed, and people you love as much as life itself who love you right back. This is your ordinary, extraordinary life.

INVITATION

Consider what makes your normal, ordinary life amazing beyond description. If you find yourself fixating on narrow for-me-or-against-me concerns, allow your grip to soften, if only a little, and your attention to encompass more of what you love.

JANUARY 25

It is impossible to live without failing at something, unless you live so cautiously that you might as well not have lived at all—in which case, you fail by default.
                                                                    —J. K. ROWLING

L ife doesn't always go the way we hope it will. Despite good intentions, careful preparation, and hard work, we still make errors. We misjudge, misinterpret, and miscalculate. We've all made mistakes—at work, in our relationships, as a parent, when you offer your train seat to someone you think is pregnant but isn't, or grow your hair out to form a microphone dome, thinking it'll be a good look. (Well, these last two may apply only to me.)

To err is fundamentally human. We can easily forget this and create an expectation that we'll glide through life without blundering. When we mess up, we can be so hard on ourselves that we learn to stay quiet, to avoid speaking up in meetings, to sidestep new opportunities, to evade responsibilities, and to stay within our comfort zones.

The wonder of the human mind is that we can reframe situations. Rather than seeing failure, we can experience growth. The most creative minds in history recognized this. Albert Einstein once pointed out that "a person who never made a mistake never tried anything new." Apparently, when ten thousand experiments with a storage battery failed, Thomas Edison said, "I have not failed. I have just found ten thousand ways that don't work." As Henry Ford remarked, "Failure is simply the opportunity to begin again, this time more intelligently."

INVITATION

Today, when you notice you're criticizing yourself, remind yourself that we are all imperfect. Remember that even failure can provide useful information. Try asking yourself these two questions:

1. What has gone *well* here?
2. How can I learn from this situation?

JANUARY 26

The most terrifying thing is to accept oneself completely.
—CARL JUNG

A big part of loving someone involves seeing the person—really paying attention. If you bring to mind someone who cares deeply about you, I'll bet they know you really well—your likes, your dislikes, your strengths, your limitations. They see you, and they meet you where you are, accepting and loving you unconditionally.

And just as important, good friends help us grow by being honest with us. If we mess up, they don't tell us that we're perfect. Part of the love they show us is their willingness to see even our shortcomings.

Befriending ourselves requires this kind of seeing too—recognizing our emotions, our needs, and our victories as well as our faults. It's often hardest to befriend ourselves when we haven't been the person we want to be. Maybe we've angrily overreacted toward someone or been impatient. Or perhaps we've struggled with self-discipline, like not sticking to a diet or neglecting to exercise, and when we feel the consequences, we fall into self-loathing.

However we may have fallen short, we have the opportunity to be friendly to ourselves. That friendliness begins with an honest acknowledgment of our faults because honesty allows us to improve. If we were impatient, maybe we can give ourselves more time in the future so we don't feel as pressed. Or perhaps we can identify thoughts that did not serve us well and look for ways to change our perspective. We can be a true friend to ourselves in the best and worst of times.

INVITATION

Today is as good a day as any to practice active, interested, attentive friendliness toward yourself. Look for opportunities to practice seeing yourself and being good to yourself, especially if you fall down.

JANUARY 27

Be wise. Treat yourself, your mind, sympathetically, with loving kindness.　　　—LAMA THUBTEN YESHE

L ast night I was cleaning a baking dish that my wife, Emma, and I were given as a wedding present. A small piece of foil was stuck to the middle of it and just wouldn't shift. It was getting late and I was feeling tired. I took out a knife and scratched the little guy away—job done. Unfortunately, in doing so, I scratched the dish. "No big deal," you might think. But to my mind, what was once flawless was now marred. I was so frustrated with myself. "Why on earth did you do that?" my mind scolded, "Now it's ruined." Sharing my thoughts with my wife, she started laughing and sympathetically reassured me, "Honey, it's okay. It's just a dish!" She then said something that has stayed with me: "What would you say if this happened to me?"

As though by a trick of the mind, it often seems much easier to give others sound advice and to treat them with care. The ancient Stoics knew this. The philosopher Epictetus wrote that if our neighbor's servant breaks a wine cup, we're quite ready to say, "These things happen." But when we ourselves break a cup, we react with anger and condemnation. Epictetus urges us in such circumstances to "behave in the same way as when your neighbor's was broken" and, further, to "apply the same principle to higher matters." Rather than acting from a place of judgment, we can learn to respond more compassionately.

INVITATION

If you're feeling frustrated with yourself today, imagine how you'd feel and respond to a loved one or close friend if they were in the same situation. Picture it in your mind. What would you say? What would you do? Apply that wisdom and kindness to yourself.

JANUARY 28

*Look at the sky. We so rarely look at the sky. We so rarely note how
different it is from moment to moment.*
—BROTHER DAVID STEINDL-RAST

I often find myself half hiding as I walk outside—head down, eyes
focused on the ground, thinking about various things, often with a
vaguely negative tone of worry or rumination. When I lift my head, I'm
almost always amazed at what I see: *Was that house always there? Look how
the trees shift in relation to each other as I walk. The morning sky is glorious.
All the trees except the Norway maples have dropped their leaves.*

Some mornings I've seen a vee of geese, so high they're almost out of
sight, flapping silently together as they migrate south. Some days the sky is
a deep, brilliant blue, like it is in Maine, and dotted with high fair-weather
clouds. Other times the clouds hang low and heavy, rolling along like fog.
Even an overcast sky, seemingly dull and uniform, is always different—its
particular shades of gray, its texture, its height.

While the sky is never exactly the same, it's also a constant—always
there, rain or shine, day or night, everywhere we go. No matter what kind
of day we've had or anticipate having, we can count on the sky being
there. And no matter the quality of the sky, my spirits lift when I raise my
eyes. There's something about looking up that feels hopeful.

INVITATION

As often as you get outside today, take a moment to look up and notice
what's above you. What's the sky up to right now? As I gaze upward today,
I'll take comfort knowing that you and I are joined by the unbroken sky.

JANUARY 29

The first duty of love is to listen. —PAUL TILLICH

The ease with which we can overlook the loveliness of the people around us is startling. Just listening—truly listening—with curiosity and openness to the person in front of us is a wonderful way to connect to the vibrancy and richness of the present moment.

You may have heard of an organization called StoryCorps, which collects, preserves, and shares people's stories. It began as a "StoryBooth" in Grand Central Terminal in New York City. There, members of the public sat down and interviewed one another: A wife interviewed her husband about the notes he always left for her around the house. A son with Asperger's syndrome asked his mother if he was the child she had expected. Moments of truth, love, and courage shared with one another.

If you had one last opportunity to ask questions of someone you love, what would they be? If your next conversation was one of your last together, how would you listen? Questions can provide portholes into the minds, hearts, and souls of the people in our lives—if asked with genuine interest by one who's willing to hear something unexpected. Here are a few questions that resonated with me:

- What have been the happiest and saddest moments in your life?
- What have you learned about yourself or the world so far?
- What are your best and worst memories of childhood?

INVITATION

Today, spend some quality time with a loved one, whether over the telephone or in person. Ask that person something you're intrigued to hear his or her thoughts on. And listen. That's it. Just listen.

JANUARY 30

I don't want to be at the mercy of my emotions. —OSCAR WILDE

Like the sky, all kinds of "weather" visit our minds too—sometimes sunny and optimistic, other times brooding and stormy. The sky is always there, a constant, untouched by the elements below. We can connect with that sense of sky, allowing our challenging emotions to play across it without being overly attached to them.

Being patient with our kids is my biggest emotional challenge these days. Yesterday I felt pressed for time and had gotten a later start on grocery shopping with our two girls than I'd planned. Just as we started to shop, six-year-old Ada said, "I'm thirsty." I gritted my teeth and said, "Okay, no problem." We found a drinking fountain near the restrooms all the way at the front of the store.

Finally, I thought, as we returned to our shopping cart. But just as we started to head down the aisle, Ada said, "I have to go to the bathroom." I regretted my exasperated response: "Seriously, Ada? We were just there! Why didn't you go then?" Her predictable reply: "I didn't have to go." I sighed dramatically and took both girls back to the restrooms.

And then I realized, in a surprising moment of clarity, that nothing was the matter; I was just irritable. In that pause, I remembered that we don't have to take our negative moods so seriously. We can maintain a little distance from our moods rather than lose ourselves in them, which gives us more choice about how we react.

INVITATION

Today, when you feel challenged emotionally, acknowledge the feeling. Then see if you can take a step—or even half a step—back from it, as though watching it sit in your open hand until it moves on.

JANUARY 31

We must be willing to let go of the life we've planned, so as to have the life that is waiting for us. —JOSEPH CAMPBELL

Our experiences are bound by our expectations. For instance, we might have expectations about how the day will unfold. When a few curveballs change our plans, we might feel frustrated, as though we are behind schedule. We build internal mental models about the day's proceedings; this is a natural human tendency that guides us. Expectations are necessary and helpful in our work and personal lives. But when we cling rigidly to our expectations, we create a condition in which we can only relax and be happy if they are fulfilled and set ourselves up for tension, irritation, and resentment when they aren't. If we can find a way to ease our grip on our expectations, peace will be uncovered.

One way to live mindfully in the present rather than in our expectations is by connecting to the breath. Like life, the breath flows effortlessly. We can influence the breath momentarily by holding it or breathing more quickly, but sooner or later it returns to its own natural rhythm. Life has its own natural rhythm too. Rather than fight against it, we can choose to breathe with it.

INVITATION

See your expectations as guides rather than edicts. Hold onto them a little more lightly. If you sense a tug of restlessness or distress when your expectations clash with reality, place your hand on your stomach and feel your abdomen rise and fall, rise and fall. As you let go of the breath with each exhalation, also let go of the idea that your expectations must become reality. Breathe and rest in the flow of life.

FEBRUARY 1

Heaven is under our feet as well as over our heads.
—HENRY DAVID THOREAU

The uncertainty of the future can be terrifying. Will we be healthy? Will we find happiness? Will we be successful? Since we can't know what the future will bring, fears like these are based on fantasy. In contrast, the ground beneath our feet provides the opposite: a solid and immediate reality. We can bring our attention to the ground anytime we're feeling afraid or disconnected. We can notice the firm support of the earth as we stand, walk, or run.

I particularly enjoy noticing the feeling of my feet on dirt or grass, with no floor or pavement separating me from the earth. I like to remember that I'm standing directly on a planet—one of eight (or nine) that surround our sun, one that supports all of life as we know it, thank God, including my own. Like so much else, it's an easy thing to forget what a miracle it is to be here at all, to have a planet we can inhabit, to simply stand here.

As we stand, aware of our connection to the earth, the sky is above us. The air and our breath move in that space between ground and sky. Thus, as we stand, we have at least three simple ways of reconnecting: ground, breath, and sky—three free gifts, three invitations to the present.

INVITATION

The next time you stand up, simply notice the sensations in your feet. When you walk outside, remember that you're standing on a planet. Feel its support. If you feel afraid or lost or uncertain today, remember that you can always return to an awareness of ground.

FEBRUARY 2

There are only two ways to live your life. One is as though nothing is a miracle. The other is as though everything is a miracle.

—ATTRIBUTED TO ALBERT EINSTEIN

Here we are. Living on a 4.54-billion-year-old planet at a point in time when 99 percent of all the species that ever lived on it are now extinct.

We are part of a perfect, uninterrupted ancestral sequence that spans billions of years. The probability of you being born has been estimated as being one in four hundred trillion. Your existence rests on the likelihood of your parents meeting (maybe even talking) and dancing the Paphian jig—not to forget the probability of those specific reproductive cells fusing together, amid all the other possible combinations, to form the very unique you. This had to happen for every one of your ancestors going all the way back to the start of history, and further. If one of your ancestors had run a little too slowly from that dinosaur, eaten that poisonous berry, or mated with a different cavewoman, you would not exist.

To have this life is astonishing. We will forget this; but that's okay, for the wondrous part is that we can wake up again. We can pause and see that this moment we are experiencing right now, at this very second, truly is a precious gift.

INVITATION

Take a little time to consider all the tiny permutations that could have meant that you wouldn't have been born. See the lines of your ancestors standing behind you—from your mother and father, your grandparents and great-grandparents—going back thousands of generations. Realize that you are a marvel and that this is another miraculous day.

FEBRUARY 3

There is no peace of the sort you imagine. Oh, there is peace of course,
but not anything that lives within us constantly and never leaves us.
There is only the peace that must be won again and again, each new
day of our lives. —HERMAN HESSE

I find that I forget many things: that worrying is a waste of mental energy,
that gratitude is the surest path to well-being, that serving others sat-
isfies me in a way that focusing on my own narrow and petty concerns
cannot.

After realizing with complete clarity that I can lay them down, I will,
within a matter of minutes, inevitably return to my worries and fears.
Earlier this week, I had a very emotional yoga session, during which I felt
unalloyed gratefulness for life as it is and however it would be. And yet,
later in the day, I was so attached to my expectations for the future that it
was almost as though the experience had never happened.

It's easy to feel disappointed with myself: *Haven't I learned this yet?*
How could I have forgotten something so important? But that's how it seems
to be for all of us. Each day is a new beginning, a resetting. Nothing says
that an insight from today will stay with us tomorrow—or even that it
should. We need regular reminders of what is true and important and
worth paying attention to.

INVITATION

Each day is an opportunity to remember what you know so well. Celebrate each time today that you reconnect with what matters to you.

FEBRUARY 4

*Technology can be our best friend, and technology can also be the
biggest party pooper of our lives.* —STEVEN SPIELBERG

The digital pull is alluring. Surveys have found that 44 percent of
cell phone owners sleep with their phone next to their bed, that the
average office worker checks their email around thirty times every hour,
and that roughly a third of adults report using their phone while on a
dinner date. But does giving in to this pull serve us well?

A colleague recently mentioned to me that he checks his work email
at home to stay on top of work. A side effect of this is that work is often
on his mind for the rest of the evening. Rather than enjoying bathing the
kids, he's distracted and worrying about something he can't address until
tomorrow anyway.

This week my wife realized that the first thing she does upon waking
is pull out her phone to read the news. With alarming media predictions
at a time of political and economic uncertainty, she found herself feeling
unsettled before her feet even touched the bedroom floor.

Naturally, there's a balance to be struck between focusing on work
and focusing on family, between being informed by the news and being
emotionally affected by it. My colleague decided to turn off his work
phone until his children are sleeping. And my wife now leaves the news
for later in the day, when she feels more prepared. The first steps toward
striking the right balance are becoming aware of when we're connected to
technology and checking to see if this is in line with our preferences for
that moment—asking ourselves if now the time to be in the digital world
or the real world.

INVITATION

Notice when your phone or computer pulls your attention away at inopportune times. If you're feeling tension, stress, or anxiety, disconnect from
your devices and reconnect to the present moment.

FEBRUARY 5

To keep the body in good health is a duty. Otherwise we shall not be able to keep our mind strong and clear. —BUDDHA

Our perspective can hinge dramatically on our physical state. For instance, last night while trying to get our three kids ready for bed, I ended up on the floor of our two-year-old's room, sobbing hard while she asked me what I was doing. Everything seemed pointless and hopeless. I felt bewildered.

After the storm had passed, I was curious about the surprisingly deep hole I'd sunk into with seemingly little provocation and wondered about the possible emotional effects of the diet I'm on for a health issue. A quick search revealed numerous reports showing that for some people this diet leads to irritability, apathy, fatigue, and mood swings—sounded a lot like my night.

What had seemed like a meaningful reaction to my circumstances might have been primarily an effect of nutrition on my hormones and neurons in the mood and thought centers of my brain. The mind is very dependent on the machine that houses it. We can affect the state of our minds through how we treat our bodies. We know all too well the effects of too little sleep, poor nutrition, and lack of movement. Without being heavy-handed about it, we have a responsibility to care for ourselves, both for our own well-being and for the well-being of those around us.

INVITATION

Look for any excuse to be good to your body and, thereby, your mind and spirit. If you notice yourself feeling "off" at some point, consider whether there might be something your body needs.

FEBRUARY 6

Hug Machine is always open for business. —SCOTT CAMPBELL

When we're in the throes of despair, a comforting embrace from someone who loves us can go a long way. Research supports this: hugs are associated with drops in stress hormones, heart rate, and blood pressure. A hug may also trigger the release of the hormone oxytocin, which contributes to feelings of calmness, a reduction in anxiety, and improved immune function and pain tolerance.

Recently I ran a mindfulness group for individuals with chronic pain. Some participants had been feeling overwhelmed by pain for the past forty or fifty years. At the end of the course, they reflected on their experiences. Through mindfulness practices, participants had begun to change how they related to their bodies and their experiences of pain. One exercise that participants initially doubted the effectiveness of but which ended up proving beneficial was a mindful movement called Hugging Arms. This basically involved participants crossing both of their arms over their chests and giving themselves a hug. To an outsider, it would look like they simply had their arms folded. Individuals then focused on the breath, feeling how the chest and back expanded with each in-breath and contracted with each out-breath. When painful thoughts arose, they directed their attention back to their breath as they held themselves with love.

Even when no one else is around, we can always be a source of compassion and comfort for ourselves.

INVITATION

Today, give someone you love a hug. As strange as it may sound, I'd also like to invite you to hug yourself. Guide your attention to your breath as you settle into the present, smile a little, and rest in the warmth of a hug.

FEBRUARY 7

To wait is often harder than to work. —PETER MARSHALL

It's hard to wait, whether for the train, the bus, a stop light, a meeting to start—for anything, really. We don't like having "empty" time and will fill it with *doing* if possible.

We might even prefer unpleasant activities over idle time. In fact, one study found that many people given the option chose to give themselves painful electric shocks over doing nothing. Are a few seconds or minutes spent alone with our thoughts so aversive that we'd prefer physical pain?

Instead of seeing downtime as something to avoid at all costs, we might welcome it as an opportunity to reconnect. In our often hectic and overscheduled lives, how refreshing it is to have a small space in the day to just breathe, to check in with ourselves, to notice the people around us, and to simply *be*.

We also open ourselves to experiences we might otherwise never have. Someone I know described stopping for a bite to eat and being alarmed to discover that her phone was dead. Since she couldn't be on her phone, she ended up having an uplifting conversation with the café owner. When we're habitually on our phones, the scenery never changes. When we override the automatic reach into our pocket and instead stay in the world around us, we never know what might happen.

INVITATION

When you find yourself with "time to kill" today, consider treating it instead as "time to live." See what it's like to be in the experience instead of escaping into technology. If you're around other people, you might look at them with curiosity and openness. If you're alone, see if you can rest in the moment. And breathe.

FEBRUARY 8

To see a World in a Grain of Sand
And a Heaven in a Wild Flower
—WILLIAM BLAKE

Today I decided to leave my phone behind when I was out for part of the day. Rather than spend my waiting moments glued to email or social media, I grounded myself in the moment. I felt my feet on the surface below and took in my surroundings. I noticed so much more than I usually do—a single bird soaring through the sky, two friends chatting and laughing together, the subtle tones and silky texture of my hot coffee. An intricately designed and vibrantly colored scarf caught my eye. The time, thought, creativity, and effort involved in designing, producing, transporting, and selling just one item like this seemed impressive.

One experience particularly struck me: the beauty of an old woman's face. In my mind, each wrinkle told a story—stories of joy, pain, laughter, heartache, hope, regret, wisdom, and folly. Hers was not a classical beauty, but the beauty of something simply being the way that it is. It made me wonder if we can willingly remove the culturally prescribed filters through which we see. Is it possible to suspend our expectations, rules, preferences, dislikes, and judgments and simply savor the charm and magnificence of the world before us? Do we dare to see intrinsic value and beauty wherever we look?

INVITATION

To borrow words from the writer and theologian Thomas Merton, today I invite you to come alive to the splendor that is all around you and see the beauty in ordinary things.

FEBRUARY 9

The moment he stopped being busy, he felt his heart quake. He had to cry. Life was suddenly too sad. And yet it was beautiful. The beauty was dimmed when the sadness welled up. And the beauty would be there again when the sadness went. So the beauty and the sadness belonged together somehow, though they were not the same at all.

—WILLIAM STEIG

The joy and sadness we feel when we really see things seem like two sides of a coin. In the beauty there is also an awareness of transience—that everything is fading away. Looking deeper and recognizing beauty seems to open our hearts in a way that feels very tender.

Chögyam Trungpa described the "genuine heart of sadness" we discover when we're present and open. Two years ago I was standing in our driveway with my wife, Marcia, taking in one of those mind-blowing sunsets that stop you in your tracks. It was backlighting the home of a friend of ours who had recently lost her father rather suddenly. As we looked at the sky and the lights on in their house, Marcia said, "There's so much beauty in life, and so much sadness." She was right. A couple of weeks ago, this same friend lost her mother too.

When we're willing to be present and see life as it is, we risk feeling the full suite of human emotions. We may be wounded in the process, even as we're enriched.

INVITATION

See if it's possible today to open yourself to a deeper awareness of your world. In the process, notice the emotions you experience. Don't worry about *trying* to feel any particular emotion. Whether it's elation, grief, boredom, or your heart melting, simply be with that experience.

FEBRUARY 10

The light shines in the darkness, and the darkness has not overcome it.
—JOHN 1:5

Last night, I had a dream. My brother was six or seven years old and started to run toward me. As he came closer, my heart began to shake. He looked so ill. His face was pale, his eyes bloodshot, and his body bloated. It looked as though the cells in his body were breaking down. Yet he had this glorious, uplifting smile. I tried to mask my shock as he gave me a full, loving hug. I woke up to find myself crying. Instinctively I put my arms around myself as though I were still hugging him and sobbed.

The dream could have been a consequence of working with children with terminal cancer. As I got ready for work, I felt a wave of sadness. My instant reaction was to reach for the remote control, as though I'd be able to drown out my emotion with the sound of the news. I paused and saw this as a covert act of avoidance. On my walk to the hospital, I decided to be gentle with myself for the rest of the day. I still felt an ache of sadness, but also a deep gratitude for this experience and for my brother's health. My heart felt open. This openness was accompanied by a feeling of strength. In vulnerability lived courage.

INVITATION

Today, connect fully to your heart, your body, and the world. Notice if you try to avoid an experience by turning on the television, reading the newspaper, playing with your phone, or just distracting yourself with thoughts of something else. See if you can cultivate a gentle willingness to accept the uplifting and challenging aspects of your experience and courageously face the world.

FEBRUARY 11

Our moods do not believe in each other.

—RALPH WALDO EMERSON

It's almost unbelievable how different our moods and our thoughts can be from moment to moment. When I'm feeling down and resentful, it's as though I've never found reason to hope—other than to have my hopes dashed. When I feel well, calm, and open, my gripping worries from even earlier that day may be scarcely remembered.

How challenging it is to maintain our equanimity—to recall that all experiences will pass. When we experience "good" circumstances, emotions, or mind-sets, it's easy to see our experience as something solid, and metaphorically close our hands around it. And we might feel robbed as our hands are pried away, feeling pain, loss, sickness, shame, or any other condition we try to avoid. When we're having "bad" experiences, we may get lost in our pain, believing implicitly that it will be permanent, and forgetting painless times.

As aware as I might be of the transience of our moment-to-moment experiences, I struggle to hold these experiences lightly, allowing them to come and go as they do. Often I'm riding the waves of my fortunes, at the mercy of their ups and downs. I feel regretful when the wave pulls me up again and I see how reactive I was to the low, how I allowed it once again to determine my mood and mind-set. When I do find grace, no matter the circumstances, it's as though my hands were open both to receive and to surrender, and I'm as free as I've ever felt.

INVITATION

When the opportunity next presents itself, see if it's possible to hold lightly to your current experience, recognizing that for better or worse—whether loss or gain, pleasure or pain—it is temporary. Notice what it feels like to acknowledge the inevitable ebbs and flows of your life.

FEBRUARY 12

Life is not a problem to be solved, but a reality to be experienced.
—SARVEPALLI RADHAKRISHNAN

I sat in the grand hall of an 1830s Georgian townhouse with marble floors, stained-glass windows, and bronze chandeliers. In front of me were my beautiful wife Emma and a plate of waffles. I felt happy. A father holding his recently born infant sat down at the table opposite us. The baby's wrinkly little face was adorable. I felt a surge of sadness. The father and baby reminded me of a client whose newborn girl only had a few weeks to live.

As humans we are meaning-making machines. We create stories about what our experiences mean and link them to other stories. On this occasion seeing the father and child linked in my mind to a story about parents burying their own child and the suffering that this brings. This was an instant reaction. It popped up on its own. The choice then became whether to hold onto the story or to simply observe it.

Recognizing the thoughts and stories that arise in our minds gives us the opportunity to observe them rather than being swept away by them. We can allow the accompanying emotions to come and go of their own accord. When we continually run with these stories, we become trapped in them. These stories then pull us away from our current, concrete reality, and we find ourselves living in our heads rather than in the fullness, richness, and diversity of the present moment.

INVITATION

Notice when your mind adds anything to your current experience. Observe the thoughts, images, associations, memories, emotions, meanings, and stories that your mind layers on top of the present moment. Pause and allow your current experience to stand freely on its own. Let reality just be.

FEBRUARY 13

To care about other people who are fearful, angry, jealous, overpowered
by addictions of all kinds, arrogant, proud, miserly, selfish, mean…
means not to run from the pain of finding these things in ourselves…
Instead of fending it off and hiding from it, one could open one's heart
and allow oneself to feel that pain, feel it as something that will soften
and purify us and make us far more loving and kind.

—PEMA CHÖDRÖN

Sometimes another's pain can be overwhelming. My wife was having a rather tough weekend recently, as our two-year-old had been sick and miserable and demanding for several days. It's hard to be present for others while dealing with our own struggles. We might want to escape from their pain, especially when we can't take it away.

I forget how meaningful it is simply to *be* with one who is hurting, to open yourself to what the person is feeling and to breathe with it. We're accustomed to seeking comfort and avoiding discomfort, but we can counter that tendency and stay present. When faced with another person's suffering, we might ask ourselves, "Can I be right here? Am I willing to stay present?" We can even breathe in their suffering and breathe out compassion and peace, as in the Tibetan practice of Tonglen.

INVITATION
Today, if you find yourself faced with another person's pain, whether at work or in your personal life, see what it's like to use the breath as a vehicle for your compassionate presence. Inhale their pain and suffering. Exhale goodness and light.

FEBRUARY 14

When we feel love and kindness towards others, it not only makes others feel loved and cared for, but it helps us also to develop inner happiness and peace. —DALAI LAMA

Given that it's Valentine's today, I thought that a loving-kindness practice would be fitting. Take a moment to sit in a comfortable position with a relatively upright posture. Allow your shoulders to relax. Take some slow breaths to connect to your body.

Bring to mind someone who makes you smile, whether it's a family member, friend, or even a pet. Hold that being in your mind and feel what it's like to be in their presence. Recognize that, just like you, this person has hopes and fears, has known happiness and loneliness, and simply wishes to be happy. Look into this person's eyes and say to them with gentleness, "May you be happy. May you be healthy. May you be safe. May you have peace in your heart."

Allow loving kindness to flow from your heart and surround them. Now imagine this person smiling at you, looking into your eyes, and saying back to you, "May you be happy, healthy, and safe and have peace in your heart."

Breathe. Notice any feelings of tension or resistance you may have. Observe them with openness and curiosity. See if you can allow the other person's loving kindness fill your body. If it feels comfortable, place your hand over your heart. Say to yourself, "May I be happy, healthy, and safe and have peace in my heart."

Sit for a few minutes, breathe, smile, and rest in the present moment.

INVITATION
Take a few moments throughout the day to offer love and kindness to yourself and to others in whatever ways you wish.

FEBRUARY 15

My expectations were reduced to zero when I was twenty-one. Everything since then has been a bonus. —STEPHEN HAWKING

In any area of our lives, we can let our ideas of what *could* happen turn into rules about what *should* happen. When I played high school tennis, these kinds of expectations were a tremendous hindrance. If I was doing well in a game, I'd start to imagine that I'd win the set. Then I'd quickly lose a series of points and suddenly my opponent was on track to capture the set. Later I would find myself ruminating about what "should" have happened in the match and berating myself for messing up.

Thankfully, I had a coach who understood my mental game. He taught me that my nervousness reflected a lack of concentration as I mentally played out points and games and sets. His instruction: Focus on *this* shot. The one before is done. The ones to come are unknown and irrelevant. It was one of my earliest lessons in mindfulness.

In a world without unwelcome rain, we could have had a perfect vacation. In a world where wide receivers don't drop easy passes, we could have won the Super Bowl. In a world where illness doesn't prevent us from working, we could have made more money. But none of those worlds exist. This is our unpredictable world—real, raw, and wild.

INVITATION

See if you notice today any sense of *should* that comes with your expectation for how the day will go. Is it possible to embrace a reality that's much wider than what you hope for? Notice what it feels like as you open yourself to your world.

FEBRUARY 16

Three things in human life are important. The first is to be kind. The second is to be kind. And the third is to be kind. —HENRY JAMES

I am very excited to let you know that this is Random Acts of Kindness Week! The idea behind this global movement is to spread kindness and joy to others through simple, random acts of kindness.

The science behind kindness is striking. There are clear, scientifically based benefits to being kind. Here are some of the kickbacks found in research studies:

1. Doing good feels good. Giving lights up the brain's reward centers.

2. Kindness makes us happier. A global study found that people who were financially generous were happiest overall.

3. Kindness makes us healthier. Acts of kindness can produce oxytocin, which is linked to lowering blood pressure, improving heart health, and boosting self-esteem.

4. After helping others, participants often report feeling stronger and more energetic.

5. Acts of kindness stimulate the production of serotonin and reduce pain, stress, anxiety, and low mood. People who volunteer tend to experience fewer aches and pains.

Kindness is the gift that blesses the giver and the receiver.

INVITATION

Here are a few ideas to inspire others to believe in the goodness of people:

1. Write a nice note for someone and leave it for them to find.
2. Let someone else go ahead of you—for example, in the car lane or supermarket line.
3. Pay for a stranger's coffee—or even their meal at a restaurant!
4. Give a sincere compliment.
5. Smile at the next person you see.

The Random Acts of Kindness Foundation even has a random generator on the web that provides suggestions and makes it even easier to be involved.

FEBRUARY 17

Lay your hand over your heart and feel. Feel my light inside of you.
You hold my light and make it live. You are living sunlight.
—MOLLY BANG AND PENNY CHISHOLM

We think of the heart as the center of our emotions and passions: We fold our hands at our hearts in prayer and in yoga. We place a hand over our hearts to show respect for our country. Even before its function was understood, the heart was a metaphor for all that was dearest to us: "Above all else, guard your heart, for everything you do flows from it" (Proverbs 4:23).

At times it's easy to feel the sun's energy coursing through our heart. Other times we feel a chill in our heart and wonder whether we'll ever feel warmth again. We can't completely control the state of our heart; indeed, making the way we feel a problem to be solved can make us feel worse. Rather than fighting it, we can allow ourselves to feel what we feel—to experience instead of escape.

There will come a time when the right conditions nurture the glowing ember in your heart into a flame. Consider what these conditions are for yourself—perhaps the physical elements of nutrition, exercise, and sleep; a regular schedule with balanced time for family and work; being of service to others; or religious or spiritual practices you find meaningful.

INVITATION

Whatever condition your heart is in today, lay your hand over your beating heart as you recite the following brief meditation from Thich Nhat Hanh's *Living Buddha, Living Christ*:

- Breathing in, I am aware of my heart.
- Breathing out, I smile to my heart.
- I vow to eat, drink, and work in ways that preserve my health and well-being.

FEBRUARY 18

Love yourself, accept yourself, forgive yourself, and be good to yourself.
—LEO BUSCAGLIA

Sometimes it's difficult to feel the sunlight. We can see the sun shining, but the rays don't seem to touch us. We know intellectually that we have much to be grateful for in life, but we can't feel it.

This week I've been feeling a little run down. In typical British fashion, by "a little" I mean "very." I think it's a combination of later hours at the hospital, disturbed sleep in an uncomfortable single bed, fewer runs outside, and eating less healthy meals on the go.

As we've discussed, life is to be experienced rather than solved. There is no one way we *should* be feeling. Our moods ebb and flow, sometimes quickly, other times more slowly. All things change.

We can still act, just without expecting our behavior to change how we feel. We can still take steps, but without tying our happiness to a "successful outcome." The basic pillars of well-being are important: wholesome food, quality sleep, meditation, checking in with the present moment, and connecting to the people we love. We can nourish ourselves and let go of any expectations. What will be will be. It's okay not to feel okay.

INVITATION

When you notice that you're feeling off, low, dissatisfied, or disheartened, remind yourself that it's okay not to feel okay. You can still act without expecting grand results. Plan and do something nice for yourself and others. Take a stroll outdoors or even walk your neighbor's dog, cook your favorite meal, run a bath, pray, take a friend out for coffee. Nourish your heart and be gentle with yourself. Love yourself and look after yourself today.

FEBRUARY 19

The appearance of things changes according to the emotions and thus we see magic and beauty in them, while the magic and beauty are really in ourselves. —KAHLIL GIBRAN

It's easy to get locked into our routines and lose any sense of adventure. I often think back to times in my life that are easy to romanticize, like living in Maine right after college. I think about the cheap apartments we lived in, the hikes we took in the nearby national park, the cool summers, the feeling of truly being on our own for the first time.

It's much easier to see the charm of my life at previous stages than in my present one. I have to wonder, What will I idealize about my current life a few years from now? Sometimes that question helps me find the romance in my life as it is now.

I often wonder about others' lives—how it feels to be them, to live where they live, to do what they do. I wonder, in your own life, how often you're able to really feel what it is to be you right now—with your physical qualities, your living situation, your work life—at this age. Can you feel for yourself what it is to be the person you are? The contours and textures of your life, your schedule, your responsibilities, your relationships?

INVITATION

As you look back years from now, what will you be nostalgic for about this time in your life? Today, allow yourself to feel what it's like to be you, right now—both your self as a person and your life situation.

FEBRUARY 20

Nothing in life is quite as important as you think it is while you are thinking about it.
 —DAVID SCHKADE AND DANIEL KAHNEMAN

Some things in life seem so important: how much money we have, the car we're driving, the size of our house. Not to undermine the significance of being financially secure, but I wonder if at times we unhelpfully inflate the weight of specific aspects of our lives.

Nobel Prize–winner Daniel Kahneman and David Schkade conducted a study in which midwesterners and Southern Californians rated overall life satisfaction for themselves or for someone similar living in the other location. The participants expected that people living in California would be happier since the weather there is better. But there was no difference in overall life satisfaction in those two areas. Focusing on one aspect of living (for example, climate) appears to lead to an exaggeration of its impact.

By directing our attention to only one factor, we overlook others. This partly explains why we overestimate the impact money will have on our happiness. We might imagine lying on a yacht, but we neglect the fact that as income increases, people tend to spend more time at work.

Our attention is like a magnifying glass, expanding the importance of whatever we're thinking about. What will you focus on today?

INVITATION

If you find yourself concentrating on one area of your life, pause for a moment and consider whether this restricted attention is beneficial or unhelpful. Is it helping you meet a work deadline, for example, or is it merely a symptom of overestimating the impact this will have on your life and making you feel worse as a result? Try to take a step back and see a bigger picture, with multiple elements, like different brushstrokes making up a painting.

FEBRUARY 21

Morality binds and blinds. It binds us into teams…but thereby makes us go blind to objective reality. —JONATHAN HAIDT

In recent years there has been an incredible amount of political division here in the US. It's easy to demonize those on the other side of political arguments and to assume they disagree with us because of willful ignorance, arrogant elitism, or narrow self-interest. It's much harder to seek to understand another's point of view and to assume motives as noble as our own.

I find few things more moving than seeing people find shared humanity that transcends apparent differences. Years ago, when my wife and I were working at a bed and breakfast in Bar Harbor, Maine, I couldn't stand a particularly obnoxious breakfast guest—he was loud, bossy, complaining. Later that night, I saw him enjoying a meal with his family in the Opera House Restaurant, where we bussed tables. There was something terribly humanizing about seeing this person I had so disliked putting food into his mouth. Even many years later, I can still feel how my heart softened when I saw him as not all that different from me.

When we focus on our disagreements, it's easy to forget that we are united at a higher level. We might think of the disagreements as clouds: if we can get high enough, there's always blue sky.

INVITATION

Look for areas of shared humanity with a person or a group you disagree with. It might mean reaching out to someone you don't get along with or reading a news source you usually avoid and trying to understand a very different perspective. Look for blue sky.

FEBRUARY 22

What you see and what you hear depends a good deal on where you are standing.
                                                                —C. S. LEWIS

No matter what year we're living in, political conflict appears to continue across the globe, whether between Democrats and Republicans or Israelis and Palestinians. Humans have a basic tendency to demonize the other side. Studies have shown that during times of conflict, people attribute their own actions to love and the actions of the other group to hate.

In everyday life, we often give ourselves the benefit of the doubt by taking the context into consideration yet cast judgment on others in similar situations. So, if I'm late for a work meeting, I'll know that there was an accident on the highway, that my child was sick this morning, and that there were no parking spaces when I arrived. When my colleague is late, however, I'm more likely to think that they're disorganized, lazy, and disrespectful. I'm aware of the external social situations that may influence my own life but struggle to see this for others.

When we make sweeping judgments about others, we stop seeing them. We overlook the subtleties, nuances, and intricacies that make each individual and each situation unique. We lose sight of that person and the rich context in which they are acting.

INVITATION

Today, truly see or hear the person in front of you, whether they're physically present or on the other end of the telephone or email thread. Consider what may be happening in their lives. Engage with reality. What you find might surprise you!

FEBRUARY 23

We drink and eat all the time, but we usually ingest only our ideas, projects, worries, and anxiety. We do not really eat our bread or drink our beverage. If we allow ourselves to touch our bread deeply, we become reborn, because our bread is life itself.

—THICH NHAT HANH

Many of us struggle to be present as we eat. Countless times I've found myself shoveling food into my mouth in a greedy rush, even if I'm not all that hungry. I've often asked myself, "Why am I taking such big bites that I don't chew thoroughly? And why am I hunched over my food with my face so close to the table?"

When we're able to experience it, food can provide connection. Years ago a good friend of mine had a freak heart attack at age thirty-six (she recovered completely). Her sudden life-or-death crisis called into question the assumptions we make about life's stability. That evening, I found such comfort in the familiar ritual of guiding my knife through vegetables as I prepared dinner.

We have at least three opportunities a day to deliberately experience our food. We can appreciate the colors and textures of the food, the aromas that trigger salivation, the feel of the food in our mouths, the sounds of our utensils, and of course the tastes—all five senses. We can also notice our emotional responses to food: the craving if we're famished, the satisfaction of the first bite, our gratefulness for another nourishing meal.

INVITATION

At each meal today, experience eating with as much presence as possible. Savor your food with awareness. Notice how this approach affects your relationship with the act of eating. I will be eating in spirit with you. Bon appétit!

FEBRUARY 24

There is more to life than simply increasing its speed.
                                        —MAHATMA GANDHI

Yesterday's quote brought to mind fond memories of my time with Zen Master Thich Nhat Hanh and the Buddhist monks and nuns at their Plum Village monastery in France. This is where I first experienced what it means to *live* mindfully. Everyone staying there is encouraged to participate in the daily community activities as a way of learning to weave mindfulness into each moment. Meditation is practiced throughout the day, whether sitting, walking, cleaning the bathrooms, washing dishes, sweeping the hall floor, or eating.

While I was at Plum Village, I found that I naturally slowed down. My breathing slowed down, my mind slowed down, my movements slowed down, and even the speed with which I chewed slowed down.

We often find ourselves rushing from one place to the next, during the day and in our lives in general. Even so, studies have found that slowing down has numerous benefits, including reducing the likelihood of being in a traffic accident, eating fewer calories during a meal, lowering the risk of high blood pressure, greater strength gains when resistance training, and (seemingly paradoxically) higher productivity at work. Slowing down can also be a way of being present, a way of engaging with each activity rather than viewing it as a means to an end, a way of connecting to the joy and fulfillment that lives in each moment.

INVITATION

Today, play with the idea of slowing down during your day. This could be when breathing, eating, drinking, walking, talking, driving, working out in the gym, or spending time with others. What other creative ways can you find to slow down?

FEBRUARY 25

The height of sophistication is simplicity.

—CLARE BOOTHE LUCE

As challenging as it can be, there's something very centering about simplifying our lives and streamlining our efforts. The essentials in life can be complicated enough, and yet we seem to add unneeded complexity. We work more than we have to so we can spend more than we need to. Or we work hard to be famous even though fame doesn't bring happiness.

My fantasized life has always been simpler than the one I live. I think of my grandfather, my mother's father, who worked as a physician in rural Kentucky for over fifty years. His life seemed to consist of serving his patients, taking care of his hundred acres of land, and enjoying time with his family. It's hard to understand why we create lives that are so complicated when our spirits are drawn to simplicity.

We can deliberately simplify our lives, in big ways and small. We might choose a lifestyle that allows us more time with family rather than having to work overtime to pay for everything. We can forgo certain purchases that will add clutter but not joy to our lives. We might cut something out of our schedule because it's going to complicate our day and stress us out unnecessarily. We can *do* less so we can *experience* more.

INVITATION

For a few moments right now, envision your life as you want it to be. Are there ways it would be simpler than it is now? Are there aspects of your current life that might be unnecessary, even if they're hard to give up? And are there ways you can begin to simplify your life, focusing on essentials, even right now?

FEBRUARY 26

The secret of happiness is to count your blessings while others are adding up their troubles. —WILLIAM PENN

It's easy to fall into the trap of craving. We want more money, a nicer car, a bigger house, and more holidays. Gratitude, though, is the antidote to this dissatisfaction.

When we start with gratitude, we appreciate what we have in this moment. We find joy in our lives right now. We can then act from a place of peace. We can still move toward our goals, without tying our happiness to them. The journey becomes even more enjoyable.

Each night in bed, Emma and I tell each other three things for which we're grateful. It's a lovely way to connect with one another. Researchers at the University of Pennsylvania studied a similar exercise called Three Good Things. Here are the basics:

- Each day for at least seven days, write down three things that went well that day, whether small (like someone holding the door for you) or big (like your partner proposing).
- Write out what happened in as much detail as possible.
- Add how you felt then and how you feel now.
- Provide your explanation for why this event was possible or what caused it.

The researchers found that this exercise was associated with increased happiness immediately afterward as well as one month, three months, and remarkably, half a year later! By tapping into the good things in our lives and the sources of happiness, we can transform feelings of dissatisfaction into feelings of gratefulness and joy. What more could we want?

INVITATION

Look out for things that go well in your day. This can be as small as the smile of a stranger. Recognize the sources of beauty and goodness in your life. You could even try the Three Good Things practice this week.

FEBRUARY 27

We all have those things that even in the midst of stress and disarray,
they energize us and give us renewed strength and purpose. These are
our passions. —ADAM BRAUN

What is the deep call that draws us out of ourselves, out of small-mindedness and petty resentments? What fuels this work of living, lifting our hearts and bringing us to our knees? In short, what are our passions?

Twenty years ago in a small church in Bar Harbor, Maine, Pastor Frank asked his congregation this question. He was a tall, thoughtful man with large glasses that magnified his kind eyes. His question hit me right in the gut, and I felt I could cry.

After the service, Marcia and I drove to Jordan Pond in Acadia National Park where we often spent our time off. As we walked among the birch trees along the water's edge, we talked about the challenging message that had stirred us both—a message we still discuss from time to time.

I have no idea what happened to Pastor Frank; he was an interim minister who moved on a few Sundays after we arrived. Given his age at that time—now twenty years ago—I wouldn't be surprised if he is no longer in this world. But the passion behind his words lives on.

INVITATION

Consider today these three questions: What sets your heart on fire? What inspires your body and your being? What excites you? As often as you remember today, breathe with an awareness of what matters to you more than anything.

FEBRUARY 28

Vision is not enough; it must be combined with venture. It is not enough to stare up the steps, we must step up the stairs.

—VÁCLAV HAVEL

This time of year, around Lent, seems as appropriate a time as any to reflect on what matters to us more than anything. The practice of examining our hearts and being guided by our values is one that transcends religious boundaries.

The act of fasting for forty days has become increasingly popular. Some of my family, friends, and work colleagues this year are giving up chocolate, sweets, alcohol, and meat. Fasting doesn't have to be restricted to the edible, of course. We may choose to fast from indifference and become involved with a cause that resonates with us. We can choose to give up grudges that we've been holding onto and allow forgiveness to flow. Motivated by the joys of a simpler life, we might decide to give away some of our wardrobe and remember to wear clothes of love and appreciation every day. As we give up, we can also take up.

Today is a new day. Today is a fresh opportunity to connect to your values and to act with love. Today we can make a difference, no matter how small, to our own lives and to those of others.

INVITATION

Carve out some time today to consider what changes, small or big, you're motivated to make in your own life. Think about what you could give up, or take up, today. Once you've decided, act! Even if it's just for twenty-four hours, be bold and take that first step.

MARCH 1

No matter what the practice or teaching, ego loves to wait in ambush
to appropriate spirituality for its own survival and gain.

—CHÖGYAM TRUNGPA

I t's fascinating how our minds can insert unhelpful patterns into practices that could be liberating. I once had an unexpected ecstatic experience during Shavasana (the "Corpse Pose") at the end of a yoga class. At the end of the next class, I couldn't wait to have that feeling again—which of course did not happen. By focusing on the outcome that I wanted rather than enjoying the relaxing conclusion of the class, I ended up feeling a bit let down, like I'd missed out on something.

It's only natural for our minds to want an enjoyable experience, yet seeking that experience as an outcome can get in the way of having it. We might seek the *feeling* of being connected rather than the connection, or the *feeling* of being inspired rather than what led to the inspiration.

If we practice meditation, we might chase a sense of calm rather than simply being with our experience regardless of whether we're feeling at peace. And perhaps even more destructively, we might criticize ourselves for not having an experience we think we "should" have.

It makes good sense to structure our lives in ways that allow for those enjoyable experiences. But at the same time, we can be mindful of the sometimes-subtle ways in which we may try to separate the outcome from the process.

INVITATION

If you notice the mind craving a certain feeling, state, or outcome, ground your presence in the present. Open yourself to the surprising.

MARCH 2

Are you feeling a bit shaken, maybe stirred, maybe fearful and doubtful, or completely, utterly, wildly terrified? Good. Keep going.
—VICTORIA ERICKSON

I'm starting to prepare for my first ultramarathon (thirty-four miles) in South Africa in April. On a recent run, I noticed my mind's tendency to comment on my current experience with different opinions and recommendations, including "You're tired" and "You should probably stop for a break, Aria." This was during mile one!

When I heard this, I laughed out loud. I could see that, in a strange way, my mind was trying to protect me—to conserve my energy, prevent unnecessary labor, and keep me away from a tough physical challenge. All of this is, well, thoughtful of the mind but also rather unhelpful when I'm trying to achieve something I've never done before. At other times, the voice in our heads sounds colder and harsher. Behind disparaging remarks is often fear, including fears of failing, being judged, and making a situation worse.

At that moment, I thanked my mind for bringing this to my attention. I acknowledged that it was just trying to help. I told it, "Don't worry, I've got this under control. I can keep on running and see how it goes." I then directed my attention back to the moment. I felt the sensation as each foot touched the ground; I followed my breath as the fresh air moved in and out of my lungs; I listened to the chorus of birds singing. I connected to my body and enjoyed the experience of running outdoors.

INVITATION

Notice when your mind comments on your experience. Decide if these opinions are helpful to you right now. If it feels appropriate, try genuinely thanking your mind for its advice. Then ground yourself in the present—and keep going.

MARCH 3

If the only prayer you said was thank you, that would be enough.
—MEISTER ECKHART

Every day we rely on others' skills: the driver of my train, the cashier at the supermarket, the long-haul truckers who deliver our food, the insurance specialist who processes my medical claims, the doctors who treat our kids, and on and on. And, of course, others rely on our own expertise too.

When we practice gratitude for the service of those around us, we deepen our interconnections with them. Around fifteen years ago, I made a point to thank our local fishmonger in Philadelphia for the care he always took in getting us our fish. A couple of years ago, he was transferred to our local store here in the suburbs, and all these years later I have a very warm relationship with him. I see him most Saturday mornings as we're grocery shopping, and he knows our kids by name. He still provides us with the best seafood.

By expressing appreciation for another's service, we honor their efforts, perhaps reminding them in the process that their work can have profound human implications.

INVITATION

As you move through your activities today, notice the efforts of everyone around you who contributes to your life in some way. How does it feel to locate yourself within a web of interdependence? If possible, make a special effort to express your gratitude to someone who's not expecting it for their expertise and how it makes your life better.

MARCH 4

When people talk, listen completely. Most people never listen.
—ERNEST HEMINGWAY

We all have moments when we're more focused on our own voice than the other person in the conversation. We're not fully listening to the individual in front of us. We're presuming that we know what they're going to say. We're already formulating our reply, particularly when arguing. Our mind drifts to other ideas, like what we might have for supper.

We may think that the other person doesn't notice, but we've all experienced the difference between talking to someone who's absorbed in the conversation and someone whose mind is elsewhere. Listening can be profoundly powerful. When we listen to others, we're offering them respect. We're saying that their voices are important and should be heard. We're valuing them. Very few things are more validating, comforting, or empowering than feeling listened to. To listen, truly, is to love.

We all want to be heard. The wonderful part is we can give this gift to someone today.

INVITATION

Today, listen to the person in front of you, whether your partner, work colleague, friend, or the cashier at the supermarket. We can listen to a person's words, as well as to their tone of voice, facial expressions, postures, and actions. Listen and learn. Listen and be inspired. Listen and love.

MARCH 5

There is something infinitely healing in the repeated refrains of nature—the assurance that dawn comes after night, and spring after winter.
                                        —RACHEL CARSON

There is so much to experience if we can get out of our heads and listen to our world with all our senses. Around this time of year in southeastern Pennsylvania, the bulbs are coming up, the woods are lined with green, and the buds are elongating on the bushes. Trees are in full bright-pink blossom.

In college I took a course called Vascular Plants. In it, we learned how to identify several species of plants and trees. It opened my eyes to the design and variety around me—variety that before had merged into more generic categories. I often sense a deep connection with trees, which now feel like old friends. I see the deeply grooved bark of the tulip poplars, the rough bark of the sugar maples, the rugged-looking Scots pines, and my heart says, "Hello again."

We can always look, listen, feel, and smell our world to see what's around us and what we're a part of. We can notice (in any season) what's happening with the plants and trees, what the animals are up to, the angle of the sunlight, the feel of the air in our noses. Every day brings an invitation to participate in our ever-changing world. As we connect with our physical world, we can be reminded of the tilt of the planet, the gift of the sun, our place in this universe.

INVITATION

If you'd been asleep for years and awoke just now, would you know what time of year it was just from clues in nature? Feel what it's like to connect with the natural world in your specific place and time. Enjoy!

MARCH 6

Nature's first green is gold,
Her hardest hue to hold.
Her early leaf's a flower;
But only so an hour.
Then leaf subsides to leaf.
So Eden sank to grief,
So dawn goes down to day.
Nothing gold can stay.
—ROBERT FROST

This weekend, I had an exhilarating trail run with my father-in-law. Over muddy hills, across streams, and through forests, we looked for clues of spring as we ran. A lovely sign was the sight of baby lambs! We saw two, huddled close to their mother.

Being in the countryside reminded me of the transience of life. The seasons roll into one another. Everything passes. Everything changes. This is a law of nature.

We often forget about the transitory nature of life.

We all know how easy it is to take our health and family for granted. Once something or someone is taken away from us, we're jolted back into reality and truly appreciate what we had.

We forget that the pain and suffering we experience will pass too. We overlook that all feelings are transitory.

We fight against life's impermanence. We clutch onto people, riches, positions, and power, craving for everything to stay the same.

There is of course another way: We can accept the impermanence of life. We can remind ourselves that everything changes. We can be thankful for this fleeting moment as though appreciating the beauty of an ice sculpture. At times when we're feeling low, upset, anxious, or lost, we can remember that these feelings, too, will pass like a sandcastle on a beach—here today but gone tomorrow.

continued on next page

INVITATION

See the world with fresh eyes. Notice the transitory nature of life. Hold your current experience a little more lightly, whether pleasurable or unsettling, and see what unfolds.

MARCH 7

There is no water in oxygen, no water in hydrogen: it comes bubbling fresh from the imagination of the living God... The very thought of it makes one gasp with an elemental joy no metaphysician can analyze. The water itself, that dances, and sings, and slakes the wonderful thirst... this lovely thing itself, whose very wetness is a delight to every inch of the human body in its embrace... this water is its own self its own truth, and is therein a truth of God.

—GEORGE MACDONALD

Where would we be without water? As I type, my humidifier is pumping steam into the air and has raised the humidity in my office 8 percentage points since I arrived this morning. On my desk are mugs of tea and water. In the restroom downstairs, water flushes away our waste products and cleans our hands. Earlier today, I used hot water to shower and shave. Tonight, I will do a load of laundry. We will wash our vegetables in water, cook with it, and rinse and wash our dishes with it.

Water is versatile in all its forms. Cubes of frozen water cool our beverages. Mist soothes a child's croup. Frozen water falls from the sky and makes a beautiful scene. Without water, there would be no sound of rain as we fall asleep, no majestic waterfalls, no rainbows.

And yet, like so many things, water is easy to take for granted because it's always there, like the air we breathe. And just like our air, water sustains life as we know it.

INVITATION
Notice water today in all its manifestations. See it, feel it, taste it, hear it (hopefully, don't smell it). Enjoy this gift.

MARCH 8

In today's rush we all think too much, seek too much, want too much, and forget about the joy of just being. —ECKHART TOLLE

A wonderful practice taught in Mindfulness-Based Cognitive Therapy is the "three-minute breathing space." This exercise grounds you in the present moment and can be done throughout the day, wherever you are. These are the three basic steps:

1. Attending to your current experience
2. Focusing on the breath
3. Attending to the body

We start by broadly checking in with our current experience: notice what thoughts, emotions, and bodily feelings you're currently experiencing. Rather than judging or trying to change these aspects, simply observe them. The second step involves focusing your attention onto a single point: your breath in the body. Stay with the full cycle of the in-breath and out-breath, whether feeling the air as it effortlessly enters and leaves your nostrils or the natural rise and fall of your abdomen. Finally, expand your awareness again to take in your whole body and any sensations that are present. Each stage can be about one minute, or shorter or longer depending on your circumstances.

Sometimes we need a little sanctuary during the day to just *be*. The three-minute breathing space is another tool we can have in our kit—a tool for sinking into the present moment and resting our minds and bodies.

INVITATION

We often stop for a few minutes during the day to chat with someone, go on social media, or surf the web. Today, take a few minutes to practice the three-minute breathing space. Create your own little sanctuary wherever you are and see what benefits you find.

MARCH 9

Life is what happens to us while we are making other plans.
                                        —ALLEN SAUNDERS

There is so much to enjoy in just being, yet it's easy to live most of our minutes focused on how much we're accomplishing. I often feel pressure at night once the kids are in bed. How many activities can I squeeze in before my own bedtime? It can feel like I've missed out or done something wrong if I don't do all I had planned.

So many things in this life can get in the way of our plans. Our habitual response is to assume that something is going wrong, that the life we ought to have is somewhere else, or maybe to feel like we're getting a raw deal. Even if we don't put it into words, the underlying mind-set may be "This is not what's supposed to be happening." We're not "supposed" to be inconvenienced, get sick, suffer, or experience anything else that interferes with the smooth and successful life we envision.

Yet we do. Being in this life to the fullest entails embracing what Jon Kabat-Zinn calls "full catastrophe living"—life in all its unpredictability, for better and worse. While none of us want bad things to happen, we can practice fighting less and opening more to what is. Even when we don't like the unexpected things that happen, we can let ourselves be in our reality, whatever that may be.

INVITATION
If you do find yourself being thwarted in any way today, let go of your resistance to reality—if only a little bit—and deliberately acknowledge that whatever is happening in that moment *is* your life. Feel the softening of resistance.

MARCH 10

The most common way people give up their power is by thinking they don't have any.
                                                    —ALICE WALKER

When life takes an unexpected turn, it's easy to feel as though we don't have any control. We can feel powerless, like a boat battered by the wind and rain, at the mercy of bigger, stronger elements. Naturally, there will be forces that are beyond the scope of our governance. However, we do have control over our own actions.

We often fall into the trap of thinking that we *have to* do certain things. We believe that we *have to* go to work, that we *have to* make our children breakfast, that we *have to* be faithful to our partners, and so on and so forth. It might sound strange, but we don't *have to* do any of these things.

There are always options, even if we don't think there are. These different options simply have different consequences. Now, we may not *like* the consequences—we may not want to lose our jobs, have hungry children, or create tremendous pain for the people we love—so we choose to do certain things. The reality is that we're still actively *choosing* to take this action. We're in control of what we're doing in that moment. Acknowledging this can be remarkably liberating.

By taking ownership of our actions, we're taking responsibility for them. We can start to see that responsibilities are simply made up of our *ability* to *respond*. We always have choices. We always have options. We always have power.

INVITATION

Today, I'd like to invite you to see that in this moment you have a choice. You have freedom and control. You can choose to act or not act in certain ways, now and throughout the day.

MARCH 11

Smell is a potent wizard that transports you across thousands of miles and all the years you have lived. —HELEN KELLER

Our sense of smell is different from our other senses. The pathways in our nervous system for sight, hearing, taste, and touch all pass through the thalamus, the brain's "relay station." In contrast, smell bypasses the thalamus and travels directly to the olfactory part of the brain as well as to memory and emotion centers—explaining why it can trigger such visceral memories. We might be *reminded* by vision and hearing, but we *reexperience* through smell.

For example, on a recent walk, I passed through an area where arborists had recently done some work. When I smelled the freshly cut wood, I was immediately back in eastern Kentucky hiking along the creek in my grandparents' hundred acres of woods—living memories that are over thirty years old. I recalled images of my father and grandfather cutting fallen trees into firewood all those years ago.

Our very lives may depend on our sense of smell, like when we detect smoke before any other signs of a fire. And an industry has been built around the sense of smell, in colognes and perfumes designed to attract others. So we may have our sense of smell to thank for our existence, not only through helping us and our ancestors survive, but perhaps also through attracting them to one another to produce offspring!

INVITATION

Pay attention today to the smells around you: your coffee or tea before the first sip, flowers, your food, the air outside, the pages of a book, a friend or loved one. Breathe with these smells and let them ground you in your experience—present or possibly past.

MARCH 12

Dwell on the beauty of life. —MARCUS AURELIUS

A few summers ago, I fell at work in the hospital grounds. I hit my head and damaged the brain cells involved in forming the sense of smell. For the next twelve months, I couldn't smell anything!

Having no sense of smell was fascinating. I had no idea how much our perception of flavor is dominated by our ability to smell. Initially, I noticed a huge difference. If the typical meal is like watching a film with 3-D glasses at an IMAX cinema, eating without smell was like watching a small black and white television with poor reception—and no sound.

During those months a new normal developed. Textures became more important. The visual aspect of food was more pleasing. I found that I appreciated my other senses much more. The ability to see, hear, and touch seemed simply glorious.

It's easy to take parts of our lives for granted. I hadn't fully appreciated the joys of smelling, whether it was freshly brewed coffee, baked bread, my wife's skin, or a baby's head. We all have blessings in our lives. There is beauty all around us. All we have to do is wake up and smell the roses—or not, as the case may be.

INVITATION

Think about something positive in your life, whether a sense, a person, something health-related, where you live, or anything else that comes to mind. Consider what your day would be like without it. What other areas of your life would it affect? In what ways? Throughout the day, see if you can tap back into a sense of appreciation for that valued aspect of your life.

MARCH 13

The real voyage of discovery consists not in seeking new landscapes, but in having new eyes. —MARCEL PROUST

I t's amazing the things we miss that are right in front of us. For instance, yesterday I was in the bathroom at my in-laws' and just happened to look up. I realized I'd never noticed the crown molding where the mirrors meet the ceiling. I've been visiting their house and using that bathroom for over twenty years, and never once had I looked up to see the molding. It made me wonder what else I had missed at their house that had been in plain sight all these years. What's more, it made me wonder what I was missing in the people right in front of me.

As I ate breakfast with our six-year-old, Ada, this morning, I took a moment to really see and listen to her and felt my eyes fill with tears as the awareness of her filled my heart. Ada is full of life, energy, and spunk and can be quite challenging at times. She is also absolutely delightful.

I've had other experiences of seeing as though for the first time, like walking home and seeing a house or a tree I'd passed hundreds of times but never noticed. Whether taking the time to look or looking more deeply into what we already see, we can connect with what's in front of us, hidden in plain sight.

INVITATION

Pick at least one occasion today to deliberately notice your surroundings. It could be a room at work, a part of your commute, a familiar lunch setting, or even something in your home. Really see what's in front of you with new eyes.

MARCH 14

Life is about not knowing, having to change, taking the moment, and
making the best of it, without knowing what's going to happen next.
　　　　　　　　　　　　　　　　　　　　　　—GILDA RADNER

L ife's voyage of discovery continues regardless of what happens. Two
days ago, I wrote about falling and losing my ability to smell. A brain
specialist informed me afterward that whether my sense of smell would
return was unknown. I just had to wait and see.

Faced with uncertainty, the mind imagines different future scenarios,
and these "predictions" often tend to be negative. The father of cognitive-
behavioral therapy, Professor Aaron Beck, called this "catastrophizing." My
mind would come up with different smells that I might not smell again,
such as the unique smell of my wife and any children we may have.

When there's uncertainty in your life—whether with work, relationships, health, or finance—if your mind is drawn toward imagining negative outcomes, then a more useful strategy can be to ask,

1. What is the worst-case outcome?
2. What is the best-case outcome?
3. What is the most likely outcome?

By asking these questions, we can see that there are multiple possibilities.
From my clinical practice, I've found that the vast majority of people's
fears don't materialize. Once we've prepared for the future in whatever
ways we can, sometimes we just have to wait and see. Rather than hold
onto future scenarios, we can still enjoy the present moment.

INVITATION

When your mind jumps into the future, notice how this affects your emotions, motivation, and body. Ask yourself the three questions above. Learn
what you can, and then return your attention to the present moment.
Take in the world, and continue your voyage of discovery with fresh senses
and a new perspective.

MARCH 15

In life, there isn't always a second chance for many things. If there is then make the most of it.   —RAJA SHAKEEL MUSHTAQUE

Almost losing something can make us very thankful for what we have. When I was diagnosed with glaucoma four years ago, my doctor said, "It's not a guarantee you'll lose your vision." I didn't realize we were having the you-could-lose-your-vision conversation and felt blindsided (no pun intended) by the diagnosis. What brought tears to my overpressurized eyes was the thought of not being able to see my kids' faces.

On a larger scale, I've found that some people who survive a suicide attempt develop a deep resolve to live differently. As one survivor told me, "I didn't come back to keep living the life that drove me there in the first place." This young woman was determined to align her actions with her passions because, previously, she had done only what she thought others expected of her. Not surprisingly, she'd found herself living a life she hated. In a way, she *did* die in that she put to death her willingness to continue living a life that wasn't truly hers. Mercifully, she survived, so she could start truly living.

Thankfully, we often do get second chances in this life. We grab a child's hand before she runs into the street. We learn that the prognosis is excellent for closely monitored glaucoma. We decide—or life decides for us—that there's more living to do.

INVITATION

Take advantage of any second chances that present themselves to you today. You might even see each day as a second chance to live the life you want, to focus your attention in ways that serve you, to give thanks.

MARCH 16

The clock ticks for every one of us. It is your own choice how you spend your remaining days.
　　　　　　　　　　　　　　　　　　　—BRONNIE WARE

Each day is a second chance. Each moment is a second chance—a chance to take another breath, see the sky, feel gratitude, and make someone else's day brighter. The wonderful part is that as long as we're alive and conscious, we have a second chance in some way.

Life itself is often taken for granted until the possibility of it being taken away confronts us. But we don't have to wait for something drastic. Life's clock is always ticking. This realization can spur us to live our life courageously and honestly rather than the way we think others expect.

INVITATION

Imagine that your life suddenly ends. It happens right now, without warning or time to say your goodbyes. Allow this idea to sink in. Then consider these three questions:

1. What aspects of your life did you love?
2. What regrets do you have now that your life has ended?
3. If you had one more chance to live your life, what would you do?

You probably know what's going to happen next: you're about to have that second chance to live your life! What will you do with this opportunity? Spend some time reflecting on what you love about your life, what regrets you could have, and what you might do differently. Take those thoughts and act on them. How will you spend today's second chance?

MARCH 17

*I look back over the events of my life and see the hands that carried
Moses to his grave lifting me out of mine.* —RICH MULLINS

When I look back from beyond the grave and consider what my life will have been about, what I will have loved most of all are my connections with family. A common human experience joins us all—not just the living, but those who have passed on as well as the yet-to-be-born.

I find comfort in knowing that struggles are part of our shared experience. Our parents faced challenges, as will our children. While we may occupy different contexts, at a deeper level a commonality makes our struggles timeless—a continuous thread through the chain of human existence.

We see this thread when Jesus sought the strength to face the cross in the Garden of Gethsemane, in the self-doubt of Arjuna on the battlefield in the *Bhagavad Gita*, and in Siddhartha Gautama's quest for freedom from suffering. It is very much the same story in each case. And each of us gets to tell that story through our own lives.

INVITATION

Take a moment right now to breathe three times, with awareness.

- On the first breath, notice that you are drawing into your body the same air as anyone who's ever lived.
- With the second breath, bring to awareness any challenges you've been having, and recognize that you are part of a universal body of being that faces daily struggles, including all your biological and spiritual ancestors.
- With your third breath, bring to mind what you love. Know that joy and the ability for deep connection dwell in all of us—the same passion that inspires spiritual awakening in every place and time.

MARCH 18

Inhale, and God approaches you. Hold the inhalation, and God remains with you. Exhale, and you approach God. Hold the exhalation, and surrender to God.

—TIRUMALAI KRISHNAMACHARYA

Jesus, Cleopatra, Shakespeare, Joan of Arc, Aristotle, Martin Luther King Jr., Beethoven, Rosa Parks, you—what do they all have in common?

One answer is that they've all breathed in the same molecules. Statisticians and theoretical physicists have forwarded the proposition that the same air molecules that we breathe have passed through the lungs of every historical figure to date.

The breath is a symbol of life. It connects us to every living thing that has ever roamed the earth. The breath can also connect us to our own bodies. We can easily wander through our day living in our minds, caught in a cloud of thoughts; the breath is always there, though, like a trusted friend. By connecting to the breath, we can connect to a soft, safe, peaceful place within us. We can rest without having to think about or do anything.

INVITATION

Today, connect to your breath throughout the day. Become aware of the sensations of breathing as you follow an in-breath and out-breath. If you wish, take a few breaths with a longer, slower exhalation. Deep, rhythmic, diaphragmatic breathing with longer exhalations has been found to activate the body's relaxation system, reducing the heart rate and blood pressure.

Try a few slow, full breaths. Then allow your breathing to fall into its own rhythmic pace. Notice how your body feels. You can use this exercise when you're feeling stressed, anxious, angry, or worried or simply as a way to sink into the present moment.

MARCH 19

To be yourself in a world that is constantly trying to make you something else is the greatest accomplishment.

—RALPH WALDO EMERSON

In many areas of my life, I've given priority to what others might think of me. For example, when designing the first website for my clinical practice, I took pains to present as little of myself as possible for fear of others' criticism—"Why did he say that? Who does he think he is?" It's been a challenge to let down my guard enough to allow others to see me.

The best motivation is intrinsic, which means we find enjoyment and satisfaction in the activity itself. In contrast, extrinsic motivation comes from something outside the activity, like money, status, or the approval of others.

In a study I find both instructive and chilling, older adults who reported having met more of their extrinsic goals were less accepting of their own eventual death. In contrast, those who reached more of their intrinsic goals reported greater acceptance of death, less anxiety about death, and greater psychological well-being.

INVITATION

Take three slow, mindful breaths. Now, consider areas where you're holding yourself back from the full expression of your "self" by focusing on the expectations of others. Pause a moment and breathe again with any such areas that come to mind. Could this be the day to begin stepping more fully onto your own chosen path?

MARCH 20

Don't take life too seriously. You'll never get out of it alive.
—ELBERT HUBBARD

Finding a way to bring our true selves to each moment takes courage. We all have different versions of ourselves. We vary how we speak, joke, and behave depending on whom we're with and where we are, whether at home or work, with our in-laws or colleagues or partners or best friends. For example, there's the Aria who dances around in his boxers to '90s hip-hop music at home to make his wife laugh, but bringing him to work might not be the best idea. Despite changing social contexts, if we're honest with ourselves, we all intuitively know if we're living authentically and truthfully.

Just as there may be areas of our lives where we're holding ourselves back from the full expression of ourselves, sometimes we keep ourselves from truly enjoying life by taking it too seriously. We take work, traffic queues, restaurant service, the comments of others, our Wi-Fi speeds, and ourselves all too seriously. We become tight and tense, trying to control how others perceive us. Instead, we could be at ease and relaxed, responding to the gifts of life in the moment. This is a way of being that flows. This is a way of being we can cultivate.

INVITATION

Today, I invite you to laugh. Yes, laugh! Allow yourself to fully revel in the present moment as you take yourself less seriously. Look and listen for opportunities to shake that belly like a bowlful of jelly. Seek nonhurtful humor, rather than laughing or making jokes at the expense of someone else. Find the funny and connect with others.

MARCH 21

Anybody who is imitating somebody else, no matter who it is, is heading in the wrong direction. —JON KABAT-ZINN

It takes a leap of faith to be ourselves truly and fully. To be oneself is to blaze a new trail—no wonder it can be scary. Thankfully, there are guides we can look to, and we learn from the paths they've walked. But if we focus too much attention on what they're doing, we're liable to wander off our own path and into the woods.

I used to want to emulate my grandfather, Dr. Alec Spencer, a family doctor in the hills of eastern Kentucky for over fifty years. Everyone admired—even revered—Dr. Spencer, who was kind and generous with his countless patients. At age eleven, I decided that I wanted to follow his example and be a doctor when I grew up.

As I got older, I saw the irony in wanting to be like a man who wasn't trying to be like anyone else. In fact, he pretty much did what he wanted and seemed to care very little what others thought of him. Dr. Spencer was an original, so to imitate him would be as *un*like him as possible. In a way, I still do want to be like by my grandfather, only now I take that to mean being more fully who *I* am.

Ultimately, each of us must walk the path that's before us—with openness, a light touch, a willingness to laugh at our inevitable mistakes, and a sense of integrity that binds us to our own truth.

INVITATION

Take a few moments right now to think about the combination of talents, quirks, desires, and foibles that make you who you are. Make space today to rest in being the only *you* there is.

MARCH 22

Life's under no obligation to give us what we expect.
—MARGARET MITCHELL

Yesterday on my way to London, my brother messaged me, saying I could no longer stay at his flat, as the spare bedroom was now being used. I looked out the train window as we sped past sprawling green hills. I felt disappointed, frustrated, and annoyed. I then noticed a deeper, creeping sense of entitlement underlying these feelings. I realized that I was assuming that I had the *right* to stay with my brother that evening. And because reality wasn't conforming to my expectations, I was retaliating with judgment and hurting myself with painful feelings.

I asked myself a few questions: Did life owe me this? Was it reasonable of *me* to expect my brother to always follow through with what he says? Do *I* always do what I say I will? Taking this perspective created some wiggle room between my emotions and myself. This headspace allowed me to adjust and approach this challenge with a sense of adventure. Through an unexpected turn of events, I ended up in a large suite with a four-poster bed in a quaint hotel overlooking Hyde Park.

Not all problems are this small or easily overcome. However, we often assume that the world owes us something, whether an absence of traffic jams, continuous—and fast!—Wi-Fi, happy bosses, perfect restaurant service, or continual good health. We can react without contemplating whether there's another way to think, act, and be.

INVITATION

Notice any feelings of frustration, anger, or low mood throughout your day. Check if there's an underlying sense of entitlement. Ask yourself, Does life owe me this? Stop for a moment, connect to your breath, and slowly recalibrate. Is there a way to move forward with a sense of excited anticipation?

MARCH 23

The more you fail to experience your life fully, the more you will fear death. —IRVIN D. YALOM

Neither our hopes nor our fears determine what will be. I'm having an opportunity to practice embracing this fact. I had blood work done earlier this week, and two days ago got a call: "The doctor wants you to come in so she can discuss the blood work results with you." My stomach tightened. "I can come in tomorrow morning," I said hopefully. I wanted to know immediately what the bad news was but couldn't get an appointment until three days later.

I hung up the phone and experienced about two minutes of dread: *Was it cancer? an autoimmune disease? Would my kids grow up without a father?* And then, miraculously, I chose to smile, the grip of dread loosened, and I knew everything would be okay—even if it wasn't. I'd been terrified by the thought that I had no idea what it might be. As I smiled and embraced an uncertain future, the same words appeared lighter, tinged with excitement—and even a little funny: *I have no idea what it might be! Ha!*

If I had continued to focus on my fears of illness and loss and leaving my kids, I would have felt less alive. Instead, I was immersed in life with my family that evening. I have no idea what I'll hear tomorrow, and yet, as the line from the song goes, "It is well with my soul." And that feels like life everlasting.

INVITATION

If your attention starts to close in around a feared outcome, use the approaches you've found useful to reengage with the real world: smile, let go of the story, embrace uncertainty, and breathe. Come back to life.

MARCH 24

Every morning when I wake up I can choose joy, happiness, negativity, pain … —KEVYN AUCOIN

In London we're in the aftermath of a suspected terror attack. The harsh reality is that, while uncommon, horrific acts of violence do happen. Every country has deep wounds.

Where does this leave us? Should we let our minds be dominated by fear? Should we lose hope in humanity and despair for the future?

The words of Antoine Leiris, a husband who lost his wife Hélène in a French terror attack, can light the way for us. This excerpt is from an open letter that he published to those responsible:

> "On Friday night you stole the life of an exceptional being, the love of my life, the mother of my son, but you won't have my hatred…You want me to be afraid, to view my fellow country-men with mistrust, to sacrifice my freedom for security. You have lost…We are two, my son and I, but we are stronger than all the armies of the world. I don't have any more time to devote to you… For his whole life, this little boy will threaten you by being happy and free."

The way we respond—even to the unimaginable—is not set in stone. We don't have to fall into fear and hatred. We can be devastated with grief but find a way forward. We can be in great pain and draw close to our loved ones. We can still live with happiness and freedom.

INVITATION

I invite you to see the blessings in your life. The disasters that occur across the globe can be reminders to wake up right now and live our lives to the fullest. See if you can feel rich gratitude for simply being alive.

MARCH 25

When my body won't hold me anymore
And it finally lets me free
Will I be ready?

—THE AVETT BROTHERS

We all know that one day we'll die, yet it's easy to live as though we won't. It's almost impossible for me to accept that one day my lifeless body will lie in a coffin or a cremation chamber; I don't find it horrifying so much as implausible. Maybe it's hard to imagine life without us because we experience every scene from our first-person perspective. And as in franchise movies, you can't kill the protagonist! Little do we know that we're actually playing a small role in this drama, not the lead.

Most of us live with a basic sense of dread about death, which can lead us to avoid truly living. Or we might seek immortality in harmful ways, like working to amass a fortune at the expense of our connections to others.

Maybe we can make friends with death. Why should we fear something that's as natural as breathing or sleeping? We could anticipate a sweet rest, a laying down of our burden, whether that means cold black sleep, everlasting life, joining everything we've ever loved, or being reborn anew as something else entirely. As the great wizard Albus Dumbledore said, "To the well-organized mind, death is but the next great adventure."

If we no longer fear death, what else is there to fear? Perhaps we can approach the notion of our death with openness, curiosity, acceptance—maybe even gratitude—for only the living can die.

INVITATION

Today, sit with death. Look at your body, at your face in the mirror, and know that one day your spirit will leave this vessel. As you walk around, consider that everyone you see will die. And enjoy being in this life!

MARCH 26

Love is our true destiny. We do not find the meaning of life by ourselves alone—we find it with another. —THOMAS MERTON

When I think back to the happiest moments in my life, they've invariably involved others: my wedding day, holidays, laughing and joking with my brothers, eating a falafel wrap and chatting with Seth on a park bench, making peanut butter cupcakes with a group of friends. Sharing experiences amplifies enjoyment and meaning. This collective social aspect is one of the reasons why going to sports matches and concerts can be so powerful.

At the same time, it's easy to neglect our relationships. We take them for granted. We don't invest the time in them that they deserve. We forget to show our appreciation.

The other day, I was speaking to someone approaching his retirement. He said that while he'd had the privilege of living and working in different cities and countries in his lifetime, the downside was that he'd lost contact with good friends along the way. He wished that he'd maintained these friendships rather than allowing them to fade.

INVITATION

Reconnect with someone you care about. It could be going out of your way to show love for someone you see every day. It could be reaching out to a family member or friend through a call, text, letter, or email. It could be taking a colleague out for coffee. It could be imagining having a conversation with someone close to you who is no longer alive. It could even be drawing closer to a spiritual figure, such as Jesus, Buddha, Moses, or Mohammad, through prayer or meditation. Present or past, alive or passed, reach out, reconnect, and show your love.

MARCH 27

In everyone's life, at some time, our inner fire goes out. It is then burst
into flame by an encounter with another human being. We should all
be thankful for those people who rekindle the inner spirit.
                                            —ALBERT SCHWEITZER

People bring us to life, whether through a poem, a movie, a book, a spoken word, or the touch of their hand. Many years ago, when we lived in Maine, I'd had a disheartening day and just wanted to withdraw from life. I resisted Marcia's invitation to go hiking in nearby Acadia National Park as I lay on our bed and wallowed in my low mood. Eventually, she literally pulled me up off the bed by the hand.

A short drive later, we were at the trailhead of Dorr Mountain in the lengthening afternoon light of an early summer day, when all my senses came alive. I smelled the richness of the rotting leaves on the forest floor, the freshness of the air along the stream; I heard the silence all around us, broken at times by the call of a wood thrush; I felt the solid earth beneath my feet, layers of dirt resting on granite; I witnessed heartbreakingly beautiful scenes from vistas.

As we walked, I felt my heart come alive as I shed the sadness of the day. I was alongside the person who had promised to walk through this life with me—and who had kept her word that day by not allowing me to wallow in my misery. She had brought me back to life.

INVITATION

Let yourself be enlivened by others today, whether through listening to a favorite song, reading a meaningful passage, calling a friend or family member, or anything else outside yourself.

MARCH 28

If you want others to be happy, practice compassion. If you want to be happy, practice compassion. —DALAI LAMA

R ecently I had a client whose infant son was in intensive care. Despite numerous tubes and wires connected to his little body, this beautiful baby boy looked serene. The prognosis was uncertain. For his mother, it was literally one day at a time. Even starting to think about what the next day might bring was overwhelming. When we were identifying her ways of coping at this unimaginably difficult time, the first word she uttered was the name of her other child. Her little girl meant that she had to get out of bed in the morning, make breakfast, leave the house, and focus on her. Looking after her daughter gave routine to an unpredictable stage in her life and helped her to stay grounded despite the surrounding chaos. Almost ironically, the person who depended on her most was her greatest source of strength.

The idea that we need love from others to be happy doesn't reflect the full picture. If we truly want to be fulfilled, we need to give love too. When we give generously, we feel better about ourselves and implicitly invite others to respond to us with kindness.

We can start wherever we are, however small or insignificant we think the act of love will be. As Mother Theresa once said, "Do small things with great love."

INVITATION

Today, show love. If you're feeling tired, anxious, low, or withdrawn, then this is the perfect time to act generously. If you have an abundance of joy in your heart, then share it with others. Love others and notice how it feels. I hope that you have a wonderful day.

MARCH 29

We're here to study ourselves and to get to know ourselves now, not later...So come as you are. The magic is being willing to open to that, being willing to be fully awake to that. —PEMA CHÖDRÖN

In big ways or small, our reality is not always pleasant. Just this morning I found myself reacting to minor frustrations with irritation and annoyance. As I walked to work, I recognized the beauty all around me yet felt like I couldn't really experience it. It was as though I needed to make my bad mood stop before I would be allowed to come into the moment.

We might think of mindfulness practice as pure or proper—even virtuous. If I'm feeling angry or disgusted, impatient or fearful, I'll often think I need to "fix" myself before I can come into the present. It can feel like the sacred is somewhere else, while I'm stuck in the profane.

But we can find the sacred exactly where we are. Being in our experience can be a raw business—not always proper or nicely varnished. Our presence is every bit as real as we are, in all our confusion and complexity. And we don't have to wait to be any particular way before coming into the moment.

We extend a profound kindness to ourselves when we're willing to experience life just as we are. A deep sense of peace is available when we let our experience be what it is.

INVITATION

If you find yourself struggling in any way today, consider turning toward your experience and holding it in your awareness with compassion. Even if you don't feel like "holding your experience with compassion," let yourself be with *that* experience. Take it all in today.

MARCH 30

The time will come
when, with elation,
you will greet yourself arriving
at your own door, in your own mirror,
and each will smile at the other's welcome,

and say, sit here. Eat.
You will love again the stranger who was your self.
                                                    —DEREK WALCOTT

Sometimes we wake up feeling more tired than usual. We're not in peak condition. We don't feel like we're firing on all cylinders and bringing our A game. We may have slept poorly, be recovering from an illness, or simply have a lot on our mind. At times like these, we can greet the present moment with open acceptance.

When we take each moment just as it comes, we can feel off and still explore the day with a sense of peace. We can learn to suspend our expectations and be gentle with ourselves. We can nurture a warm inner voice to support ourselves throughout the day.

INVITATION

Today, develop a specific inner voice—one of kindness, compassion, forgiveness, love, and support. This voice is going to accompany you throughout the day and look out for your best interests. The voice may sound like you or like someone who loves you. You might want to imagine what your warm, wise granny would say to you—no, the *other* granny, who wasn't as tough as a battle-axe.

At times you may notice a harsher, more critical voice speaking in your head. That's okay. You can say hello to it and then allow your number one fan to say a few words as well. Allow this compassionate voice to look after you as your day unfolds. Who knows what you two will get up to together?

MARCH 31

If you want to conquer the anxiety of life, live in the moment, live in the breath. —AMIT RAY

As long as we're alive, the breath is available as a means of reconnection. We often think that breath meditation takes a long time, but even brief periods of focusing on the breath can release tension, fear, regret, or any thought process that's not serving us.

I first learned of this practice from a friend whose young son was going to have major surgery. She said she used it many times a day and found it invaluable in facing the fear and uncertainty around her son's health. Chances are we'll need to return to the breath many times as the mind pulls us away from the moment.

We can also use the breath to ground ourselves in other aspects of our experience. As I return to my breath right now, I become more aware of the keys under my fingers, my posture, my elbows and where they rest. Tonight, it may be the blue of my toddler's eyes, the smell of sautéing onions, the pillow supporting my head as I drift toward sleep. Returning to the breath is returning to life.

INVITATION

Set a timer for one minute. Breathe slowly for the full minute, focusing on and counting each in-out breath cycle. Remember your number when the minute is up. Today, when you find yourself needing to let go of worries or come back to the present for any reason, you can practice "seven breaths" (or whatever your one-minute breath number is). Come home to the breath.

APRIL 1

Man muss die Dinge nehmen, wie sie kommen.
(You have to take things as they come.)
　　　　　　　　　　　　　　　　—GERMAN PROVERB

As I sat up on the side of the bed, my head was spinning. I was surprised to find that I wasn't in my bedroom! Two dachshund sausage dogs were sleeping by my feet. I stood up and felt unsteady, as though I had a hangover, but I haven't drunk alcohol in over five years. What was going on?

The last thing I could remember was being at a mindful cooking event in London. I was sitting next to this hilarious German couple. They'd brought bottles of this delicious German herbal drink that they said has health benefits. After our fourth bottle of something called Jägermeister, I vaguely recall sitting for a meditation.

I went to the window. Outside were snow-covered spruce trees and a sign that read Ochsenkopf. I quickly walked out of the bedroom and into a small living room. On the mantelpiece was a photograph of the German couple from the night before with three young children. What a relief!

I racked my brains for their names, in case I'd taken their telephone number and could call them. His was there on the tip of my tongue— Harry? No. Hegel? No. *Hans! Yes!* I grabbed my phone and scrolled through the contacts list. It was then that I remembered that my mobile was Hans-free!

Der erste April! Or as we say in England, April Fool's Day! That bizarre story is my attempt at an April Fool's joke. It seemed like a good idea when I started writing it, at least.

INVITATION

In the spirit of April Fool's Day, have some lighthearted fun! Take part in this national celebration with a prank or two. Involve a friend! Enjoy yourself! But maybe stay off the Jägermeister.

APRIL 2

Getting free from the tyranny of past mistakes can be hard work, but definitely worth the effort. —STEVE GOODIER

It's hard to acknowledge our faults without letting them define us. Yesterday, I took our two-year-old, Faye, to run some errands. Predictably, she insisted on getting into her car seat herself, so I said impatiently, "You have till three, or I'm going to help you." She tried to land in her seat with some kind of spin move that didn't work, and by then I had counted to three. So I picked her up and buckled her in. She started crying as I explained unconvincingly that she needs to do it when I ask her to.

Afterward I felt quite guilty, knowing I could have handled the slight delay more graciously. Then I considered that it may be more productive simply to acknowledge that I could have been a little more patient with her (okay, a lot more) and aim to do better next time.

After the bank, Faye once again wanted to get into her seat unassisted and tried the same spin move. When she didn't quite make it, she looked at me uncertainly, probably expecting me to lift her into her seat again. This time, I said, "Almost! Want to try again?" She smiled and nodded. On the next try, she nailed it.

We can fail without being a failure and disappoint without being a disappointment. When we trust that we're okay even when we're not perfect, it's much easier to be honest with ourselves about our shortcomings—and to be willing to try again.

INVITATION

If you fall short today, speak to yourself with a voice of compassion. Notice what a little kindness does for your willingness to keep trying.

APRIL 3

When Life speaks, all the winds become words...when she comes walking, the sightless behold her and are amazed and follow her in wonder and astonishment. —KHALIL GIBRAN

L ast night as I walked up to the house after work, I noticed the stunning sky. It was as if an artist had splashed pinks, reds, and blues onto a canvas. It stopped me in my tracks. I stayed for a few minutes and just looked. My awareness expanded, moving outside of my body and reaching up to the beautiful skies. I felt a sense of awe and humility as I noticed the glorious world around me.

Researchers at UC Berkeley have started to explore human experiences of awe: the feeling of being in the presence of something vast that seems to transcend our understanding of the world in some way. This could be during an iconic moment, like looking up at the Sistine Chapel for the first time or during everyday experiences, like seeing a child laugh or gazing at the scattered stars in the night sky.

Studies indicate that when we experience awe, we feel less self-important and less entitled. We experience greater feelings of wonder, curiosity, and well-being. We're more likely to help someone in need.

All we have to do is open our eyes and attend to this wonderful, miraculous world around us.

INVITATION

Pause, even if only for one minute, to look at the world around you. Take in life. Step outside yourself and allow your awareness to expand. Rest in the current moment and experience your place in the vast tapestry of this universe.

APRIL 4

Gratitude can transform common days into thanksgivings, turn routine jobs into joy, and change ordinary opportunities into blessings.
—WILLIAM ARTHUR WARD

Slowing down and paying attention gives us a chance to appreciate what we have. I recently met an otherwise healthy person whose life had changed profoundly because of a metabolic condition that prevented him from walking more than a very short distance. He could no longer go with his family on hikes or even on leisurely walks through botanical gardens. Stairs were out of the question, and even careful planning couldn't prevent unpleasant surprises like an out-of-service elevator. Social encounters had to be carefully orchestrated with the hope that others would be understanding of his limitations.

What a gift it is to be able to walk anywhere we need to, if we're able-bodied. Need something from upstairs? No problem, just walk up and get it. Escalator out of service? Just use it as a staircase. Going somewhere new? Just hop in the car or, if it's close enough, walk—no planning necessary!

Even if we can't walk, we have other abilities we can take for granted. It's easy to feel self-critical when we recognize this lack of gratitude in ourselves. We can practice a more compassionate response, acknowledging that sometimes we're ungrateful. This doesn't mean we're bad; it just means we have an opportunity to say "thank you."

INVITATION

If you're able to walk, practice awareness today of all the things you're able to do as you move about on two legs. If you're unable to walk, choose another ability like seeing, having hands that work, etc. We might even experience something like awe when we bring our full awareness to what it means to have and use a body.

APRIL 5

You never really understand a person until you consider things from his point of view...until you climb into his skin and walk around in it.

—HARPER LEE

When someone we know is struggling, it can be tempting to offer our "words of wisdom" out of love. Sometimes this can be useful. At other times the person might feel misunderstood.

Often the most helpful thing we can do is listen. To be heard and held kindly in mind is incredibly powerful. When we feel heard, we feel valued, treasured, appreciated, and respected. Sometimes, even when someone starts a conversation with "Could I have your opinion on something?" what they really mean is "I'd really like it if you'd just listen to me for a couple of minutes without making any judgments." I've been with my partner for eight years now and I still forget this. There have been countless times when I've just listened to her speak, and afterward she has felt much better. It's as if the grip of the problem loosened of its own accord. All I had to do was take off my problem-solving hat and hear her.

INVITATION

Today, my friend, listen to others. Whether it's your loved one, your friend on the phone, the barista in the coffee shop, your colleague at work, or anyone else you meet today, give them your full attention and care. Put down your phone or any other distractions for a few moments and try to stand in their shoes. Climb into their skin. See with their eyes.

APRIL 6

Self-love is not the process of ignoring your flaws. Self-love is expanding your awareness to include your flaws and your strengths.

—VIRONIKA TUGALEVA

Most of us are good at focusing on the parts ourselves that we're unhappy with and want to change: *I want to lose ten pounds. I need to be more patient. I struggle to exercise consistently.* It would be easy for me to berate myself for all the times I'm not the best listener. Yesterday morning I had a rare opportunity to walk my loquacious six-year-old daughter to kindergarten. Because she talks so much, it's easy for me to only pretend to listen while thinking about other things instead. When I made an effort to listen to her stream of consciousness, I got to hear that she wishes the sunlight would make shadows rainbow-colored and that a forest is what you get when you "smoosh two woods together"—I suspect she could tell I was actually listening.

We don't have to be great at everything. Maybe you have a hard time self-motivating, but you're a great listener. Or maybe creativity isn't your strong suit, but you're deeply connected to those around you. Research in positive psychology has identified twenty-four character strengths:

- Appreciation of beauty and excellence
- Bravery
- Creativity
- Curiosity
- Fairness
- Forgiveness
- Gratitude

- Honesty
- Hope
- Humility
- Humor
- Judgment
- Kindness
- Leadership
- Love
- Love of learning

- Perspective
- Perseverance
- Prudence
- Self-regulation
- Social intelligence
- Spirituality
- Teamwork
- Zest

When we play to our strengths, we emphasize our wholeness, even with our imperfections.

continued on next page

INVITATION

Pick three to five strengths from the list above that seem to describe you. Write them down on a piece of paper and carry them with you today. Review your strengths several times and look for opportunities to exercise them. Enjoy expressing the best parts of yourself today.

APRIL 7

Many of us crucify ourselves between two thieves—regret for the past and fear of the future. —FULTON OURSLER

"If only" are two words that can stir immense emotional pain. We've all made relationship mistakes. We've all said and done things to our friends and family that we wish we hadn't. We've all let career opportunities fall by the wayside instead of courageously pouncing on them.

It's prudent to learn from our mistakes, of course, but if we're not careful, we can needlessly crucify ourselves. We can let shame steal the precious time that we have now. So how do we let go of regret?

We let go of regret when we forgive ourselves. Where judgment lives, forgiveness dies. Forgiveness can only flourish in the presence of understanding. We're all trying our best with the skills and resources we have in that moment. When we truly accept this, we can begin to accept ourselves. If we look back at relationships that ended, rather than judging our own characters as selfish, we might instead see a lack of emotional skill.

Acceptance does not mean abandoning responsibility. It is, however, easier to lift the mantle of accountability when we view our flaws as skills-based rather than as character deficiencies. For then, we can then ask ourselves what skills we need to develop in order to act differently in the future. We can find peace and grow, as we live firmly grounded in the present moment.

INVITATION

Be completely honest with yourself: Are there regrets from the past that you're still holding onto? Explore the possibility of forgiving yourself, letting go of the past, and living more freely now.

APRIL 8

Therefore encourage one another and build each other up.
—1 THESSALONIANS 5:11

Take a moment to consider someone you love deeply—perhaps a sibling, partner, or child. What are his or her best qualities? (Feel free to refer to the list from April 6 if needed.) You might bring to mind a recent time when this person enacted their strength. I'm remembering a recent walk with Ada to her kindergarten and her unshakable cheerfulness as we walked hand-in-hand on that wet, windy, chilly morning.

Just as our own strengths can carry risks, so too can those of our loved ones. It's easy to appreciate how strongly Ada feels her emotions when she's expressing love for her family members—less so when she's crying inconsolably at bedtime for a stuffed animal we no longer have. Whatever you admire in your loved one might also annoy you at times. Maybe we were drawn to a partner because we appreciated their stability but now tend to find them, frankly, a bit boring. Or perhaps we respected them for their discipline, which has now started to feel like rigidity. Maybe our highly creative child also has a tough time following rules. The traits we complain about in those we love are most likely also some of the things that make them wonderful—that make them who they are.

INVITATION

Notice a loved one's strengths in action today. You could even comment on them to the person, building them up by highlighting their best attributes. If there are things about this person that you find irritating, see if there's another side to the coin—does the annoying trait also have a positive aspect that you appreciate? Enjoy the full experience of knowing this human being.

APRIL 9

You will never reach your destination if you stop and throw stones at every dog that barks. —WINSTON CHURCHILL

Who will be sharing your bed tonight? We've known each other long enough for such a personal question, right?

The reason I ask is that last night I shared my bed with Emma (as usual) as well as the head of a cancer center, an operations manager, and a lead psychologist. I should probably explain. Those last three will be on the panel of an upcoming interview, and as I lay in bed last night, my mind projected ahead to it—I had brought the interviewers into bed with me.

At night, our mental reserve is usually low. After a long day, the mind often takes advantage of this and runs rampant. Our attention is pulled toward different thoughts.

The practice of mindfulness involves noticing these pulls, kindly acknowledging them, and then returning our attention to the present moment. We can do this formally during meditation or informally in the real world, whether we're trying to complete a work project or fall asleep. Mindfulness strengthens our ability to direct our attention. Like going to the gym or learning a new instrument, this takes time, but it does mean that you'll have more choice over who sleeps in your bed tonight.

INVITATION

Simply notice when thoughts vie for your attention. You can then decide if you'd like to follow these thoughts or choose to bring your attention back to the present moment. The breath can be used as an anchor to the present. Bring your awareness to your abdomen as it rises and falls or to the sound of the breath as it enters and leaves your body. Try a few things and see what works best for you.

APRIL 10

Come forth into the light of things,
Let Nature be your teacher.

—WILLIAM WORDSWORTH

Scientists estimate that around 85 percent of the sensory information we process comes through our visual system. I was keenly aware of my visual experience yesterday—colors, shapes, textures, movement—as I walked the hills of a nearby arboretum with my wife and kids. If it weren't for light, we would have no concept of vision.

Light affects our experiences beyond the basic ability see, such as influencing our moods—the most obvious example being the different feelings day and night bring. Overcast days tend to bring us down, while bright sunny days cheer us. Seeing the first rays of sunlight rake across the landscape, casting long shadows, evokes a particular feeling, as does the rosy light of sunset as the day fades.

The ambience of a room changes entirely with the lighting, as when we throw open the curtains to greet the day. Think of the different moods created by the glow of candles or cozy lamplight compared to bright over-head lighting or the harsh fluorescents of a department store. Without light, there would be no rainbows, no sunsets, no image of your loved one's face. Like air, it's easy to forget what a blessing it is to have light.

INVITATION

Attend to the light in different contexts today, from early in the day until you turn off your light at bedtime. What are you able to see and do today thanks to the many sources of light in your life, including the light of the sun? Enjoy the visual feast!

APRIL 11

I go to Nature to be soothed and healed, and to have my senses put in tune once more. —JOHN BURROUGHS

The peril of the flu knows no boundaries. Despite being separated by thousands of miles, Seth and I both awoke with a sore throat and a general bodily feeling of malaise yesterday. As I lay in bed, the sun shone into the back garden, hitting our cherry blossom tree.

This moment reminded me of a groundbreaking study published in the mid-1980s. In a suburban hospital in Pennsylvania, the rooms on two floors looked out onto either a small group of trees or a brown brick wall on the other side of the wing. The only essential difference between rooms was what you could see through the window: trees or a brick wall. Researcher Roger Ulrich obtained medical data over a nine-year period looking at patients that had either the "tree view" or "wall view." The results of the analyses were remarkable. Compared to those with the wall view, the group with the tree view had shorter hospital stays after their surgery and took fewer doses of strong pain-relief medication, taking drugs such as aspirin rather than powerful narcotics. The view of the trees appeared to have a real influence on patient recovery.

Ulrich proposed that the window view affected the patients' emotional states and thereby their recoveries. Recent research supports this, indicating that viewing and engaging with the natural environment has beneficial effects on our mental and physical health.

INVITATION

Take a few moments throughout your day to see the natural world around you, even if it's simply looking out of your window or at a potted plant. Go for a leisurely stroll or brisk walk on a break. Use your senses to soak in the present moment and notice how you feel.

APRIL 12

My body is broken, my mind is neurotic, and my soul is at peace.
—DANIEL GOTTLIEB

Whether we're fighting off an inopportune illness, battling allergies, or dealing with chronic health conditions, it's common to be frustrated when we're not well physically. We might feel like our body is betraying us or see illness as a personal failing. In my own case, I recall being very self-critical when I was struggling with a prolonged vocal issue that made it difficult to speak.

Whatever our strengths or ailments, we can foster a sense of kindness toward our bodies—these bodies that are entrusted to us for our whole lives. Literally everything you experience—even reading these words—happens through the vehicle of your body. We can see ourselves as our body's friend and caretaker, rather than seeing it as a bad host.

If we do at times grow frustrated or resentful toward our bodies, we don't have to feel bad. It only means we're human. We can turn toward our frustration—acknowledge it, breathe with it, respond with gentleness. It's not easy when we're struggling physically. Stay with your experience. When the storm has passed, you and your body will still be there, inextricably joined, until death do you part.

INVITATION

Practice friendliness toward your body and your physical health. If you're "firing on all cylinders," revel in your good health and acknowledge the ways your body serves you. If your body is struggling in any way, consider how you would respond to a dear friend who was having a tough time. Your kindness is an investment in a lifelong relationship.

APRIL 13

Vulnerability is about showing up and being seen. It's tough to do that when we're terrified about what people might see or think.

—BRENÉ BROWN

The unpredictability of life can catch us off guard. We don't expect a rainstorm on our wedding day, traffic jams when we're already late, or falling ill just before a big interview. At these times it's easy to feel stressed, anxious, or overwhelmed.

Yesterday I was unwell and had an important job interview. My goal was simple: show up and try my best. I drew on the past few invitations to help me.

First, I became aware of what my mind was saying, which largely consisted of pessimistic judgments about feeling awful and being unable to do the interview.

Second, I paused and directed my attention to my breathing for ten to fifteen seconds. Focusing on the breath gave me a moment to slow down and connect to the present moment rather than instantly identify with my thoughts.

Third, I responded with compassion. I spoke to myself with an encouraging voice and decided to apply the character strength of gratitude. I started to notice all the parts of my body that weren't aching and to appreciate that I wasn't feeling worse. Rather than focus on what was going wrong, I expanded my awareness to acknowledge all the little things that were going well.

INVITATION

If the day isn't going your way, try this three-step strategy to boost your resilience and help you to make the most of difficult circumstances:

1. Awareness: become aware of your thoughts
2. Breath: focus on your breath for ten to fifteen seconds
3. Compassion: choose how you'd like to respond; draw on your own strengths to support yourself in this situation

APRIL 14

Pause. Listen for the whispers of your Soul.

—NANCY LANKSTON

Most of us feel at least a little rushed most of the time and would like a break more often than we get one. When vacation finally does come, it can leave us feeling more stressed than we felt before. And no matter where we are, we may carry the stress of a harsh internal voice.

Thankfully, we don't have to wait for vacation to find a pause in life's stresses. A practice from the field of positive psychology encourages us to take a "daily vacation." It can be any activity we choose, like these:

- Taking a warm bath
- Watching the sunset
- Enjoying lunch without work or distractions
- Reading on a bench outside during your lunch break
- Listening to relaxing music during your commute
- Looking out the window for a few minutes

We can bring our full attention to whatever activity we choose, taking a break from our worries as much as possible. We can notice what's happening in our body, what sensations we're aware of, what thoughts and emotions might be present: Are we feeling calm? inspired? grateful? By marking positive emotions in the moment, we're more likely to remember them later. We can make a point, later on, to savor our positive experiences from our daily vacation, which is a powerful counter to our tendency to dwell on worries and disappointments.

INVITATION

Take a minivacation today: a yoga class, massage, a long walk, dinner out with a friend—anything you would look forward to. Remember to "clock out" from worries and other preoccupations during your vacation; it's your time to enjoy being off duty. This evening, you can think back to the vacation and experience it again.

APRIL 15

You are the light of the world. A town built on a hill cannot be hidden. Neither do people light a lamp and put it under a bowl. Instead they put it on its stand, and it gives light to everyone in the house. In the same way, let your light shine. —MATTHEW 5:14–16

In life, we can "show up" in different ways. We can physically show up—for work, meetings, appointments, and social commitments or to collect the kids from school. We can also show up as our authentic selves, bringing our attention and true personalities to the present moment, with all our quirks and idiosyncrasies.

There is often pressure in life to be a certain way and to fit into a particular mold. This pressure might be from society or from our families, partners, friends, or work colleagues. We may also create our own internal expectations about how we *should* be. We might hold back from truly, wildly, vibrantly, richly being present ourselves. This would be a tragedy; you'd be depriving the world, and yourself, of *you*. As my wife says, if we were all the same, the world would indeed be a very boring place.

INVITATION

Today, be you. Bring yourself to each and every moment. Be present and allow your light to shine.

APRIL 16

To pay attention, this is our endless and proper work.
—MARY OLIVER

The human attention span is limited, so it's hard to focus on a single task for more than a matter of minutes. When we work for long blocks of time, our attention will almost certainly start to drift. For example, if we're working on a computer, we may start to check email, social media, or online news and then will need to refocus to get back to work.

When we're trying to finish a task, we might be inclined to work for long stretches without stopping, telling ourselves we can't afford to take a break, because we have so much to do. But working for hours at a time with no end in sight can feel like a sentence.

An alternative is to plan minibreaks throughout our work sessions. This approach is not only gentler on our spirits, but more productive and profitable in the end. Knowing we have a limited amount of time in each work block will make us less likely to fritter away our time on extraneous things. We also get to look forward to the downtime and can fully enjoy it because we know it's time-limited and we'll soon return to our task.

When we take care of our responsibilities, we're more likely to feel good about the life we're living. This means that finding ways to complete our work with ease is an act of self-love.

INVITATION

If possible, break up today's work blocks into smaller segments with short breaks in between. You might try a free app or online tool like Tomato-Timer.com, which keeps track of the time for you. (I'm using it now as I write.) Happy working, and happy breaks!

APRIL 17

When you come to the end of your rope, tie a knot and hang on.
—FRANKLIN D. ROOSEVELT

The alarm went off at 4:45 a.m. I hit snooze, but it only took a few milliseconds for the nerves to kick in. Race day: the Two Oceans Ultra Marathon in South Africa. Time to get up.

About thirty kilometers into the run, there's a nine-kilometer stretch called Chapman's Peak with 114 curves etched into the mountainside. Needless to say, this section presents some unforgivingly long inclines. While making the ascent, I felt the effects of the virus I was recovering from. When I tried to breathe deeply, the passageways in my lungs would spasm and a coughing fit would start. A quote by Tim Noakes that my wife had read out loud the night before came to mind: "Your body will argue that there is no justifiable reason to continue. Your only recourse is to call on your spirit, which fortunately functions independently of logic."

As I ground out Chapman's Peak, I called on my spirit. As I saw runners collapse and helped others get to the nearest medical tents, I called on my spirit. Any time that I had to dig deep and carry on, I called on my spirit.

INVITATION

There are times when we struggle, when something seems too difficult, when we feel that we just can't go on. At these times, we can call on our spirit. This will mean different things for different people. Today, find out what this means for you. You don't have to be running an ultramarathon; during any moments that are testing or challenging, call on your spirit and see what happens.

APRIL 18

Don't be ashamed to weep; 'tis right to grieve. Tears are only water, and flowers, trees, and fruit cannot grow without water. But there must be sunlight also.
—BRIAN JACQUES

On a recent family outing to an arboretum on a spectacular spring day, I was struck by the awareness that life is filled with beauty and pain—at times, inseparably intertwined. There was a warm breeze, and bursts of color were everywhere: white magnolias, sunny daffodils, pink cherry trees. We followed the enchanting sound of a cappella singing into a courtyard where our kids played together in the sunlight.

Earlier that same day, I was saddened to learn that a recent acquaintance had died. I kept wondering what this spring day was like for his family.

Of course, both sad and magical moments are fleeting. Eventually the singing ends. The gloriously flowering trees lose their leaves in fall and stand naked in the winter snow. When the ice thaws and buds burst open again, kids will laugh and run in the warm sunshine. If they're fortunate, they'll experience many trips around the sun. The earth will be their constant, feeling these feet dance on her for a while, before each pair takes its inevitable leave.

What are we to make of these endings? Perhaps the best we can do is to dance when it is day. Following the earth's example, we can find stillness in our depths—a stillness unmoved by what's happening on the surface, whether we call it good or bad, beauty or sadness. We can allow all of it to be experience.

INVITATION

Observe your experience today. Notice beauty, as well as pain. Feel your feet grounded on the earth when you walk. Notice what's happening within and around you. Be witness to this life.

APRIL 19

The greatest glory in living lies not in never falling, but in rising every time we fall.   —NELSON MANDELA

Today, I walked through the former District 6 in Cape Town. In the 1970s the government declared District 6 a "whites only" area. Over sixty thousand of its inhabitants were forcibly removed by the apartheid regime. Thousands of homes were destroyed, and families were displaced to the outskirts of the city. It is difficult to comprehend injustice and inequality of this magnitude.

The vicissitudes of life are inevitable, whether sickness, injury, accidents, natural disasters, job loss, relationship breakdowns, or death. While some people's lives contain more than others, we're all tested at certain points in our lives.

In the midst of painful experiences and uninvited events, it's natural and understandable to respond with sadness, grief, anger, and regret. While no rationalization can explain away this suffering, there is solace in knowing that the pain will pass. Even in places of great tragedy, there is hope. As the English theologian and historian Thomas Fuller put forward, the darkest hour is just before the dawn. With hope, we can rise. We can rise above oppression, adversity, and even the most challenging of circumstances.

INVITATION

Invite hope into your day. If there's pain, suffering, anxiety, or worry in your life, try seeing if you can place this aside, and instead pick up some hope. What does this hope look like? How does it make you feel? Give this hope the conditions it needs to flourish today.

APRIL 20

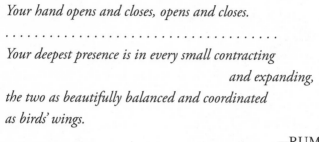

Your hand opens and closes, opens and closes.

. . . .

Your deepest presence is in every small contracting

and expanding,

the two as beautifully balanced and coordinated
as birds' wings.

—RUMI

We're all gripped at times by powerful thoughts and feelings—burning anger, icy fear, a choking sadness. We rarely make our best decisions when overwhelming emotion hijacks our attention. It can make us prone to respond in ways that aren't aligned with our values, like saying hurtful things in anger.

While we can't completely avoid being seized by states of heart and mind, we can work to loosen their grip:

1. First, acknowledge when we're gripped. For example, we might say, "I'm terrified about this medical procedure tomorrow." Labeling our experience shifts our relationship with our thoughts and feelings.

2. Second, feel where the gripping sensation may be present in your body. Is your stomach in a knot? Are your neck and shoulders tense? Explore any physical feelings of being gripped.

3. Now, breathe with awareness into those areas of your body. Imagine directing the breath into your stomach, shoulders, jaw, or wherever might be tense. Bring your full awareness to each breath.

4. Finally, find a welcome movement in the body. It could be flexing your hands, stretching your neck, rolling your shoulders, or anything else. Moving our bodies encourages our minds to "get moving" too, relaxing their grip.

This whole process can take as little as a few seconds. As the grip begins to loosen, we're in a better place to handle whatever the situation might be.

INVITATION

Today, if you find yourself struggling, practice this four-step process: *acknowledge*, *feel*, *breathe*, and *move*. Notice how you feel before and after this practice.

APRIL 21

There is freedom waiting for you,
On the breezes of the sky,
And you ask "What if I fall?"
Oh but my darling,
What if you fly?

—ERIN HANSON

On April 27, 1994, millions of South Africans lined up to exercise their right to vote. After all the ballots were tallied, Nelson Mandela was elected president—the country's first black chief executive. Mandela had the mammoth task of uniting a nation both scared of and scarred by each other. He could have easily been gripped by revenge and hatred. Instead, he chose compassion and freedom for all.

Today I read through South Africa's constitution while visiting Robben Island, the political prison on which Mandela served most of his imprisonment prior to being elected. The constitution sets out the rights of its citizens, among them the following:

- Everyone has the right to life
- Everyone has inherent dignity and the right to have their dignity respected and protected
- Everyone has the right to freedom and security
- Everyone has the right to privacy
- Everyone has the right to freedom of conscience, religion, thought, belief, and opinion
- Everyone has the right to freedom of expression
- Everyone has the right to freedom of movement
- Every citizen has the right to choose their trade, occupation, or profession freely
- Everyone has the right to have access to adequate housing
- Everyone has the right to a basic education
- Everyone has the right to use the language and to participate in the cultural life of their choice

Our rights can become such a basic part of the fabric of our society that we take them for granted without realizing how much we have to be grateful for.

INVITATION

Read the list of rights above. Are there ones that you particularly value and appreciate? Notice and acknowledge the freedoms that you enjoy as you go through your day.

APRIL 22

Open your heart to the incredible gifts that civilization gives to us. You flip a switch and there is electric light. You turn a faucet and there is warm water, and cold water—and drinkable water.
—BROTHER DAVID STEINDL-RAST

Earlier this week I got up in the middle of a stormy night to settle our toddler. As I was holding her, the power went out. The house gave that "powering down" sound—the fans stopped, the white-noise machines were silenced, and everything went black. Faye noticed right away and tried in her half-asleep state to articulate her question about what had happened. When I told her the power just went off, she said she didn't like it. I assured her it would come back on soon. A minute later the night-light glowed again, and the house hummed back to life.

Every day we rely on products and systems that people produce, with new inventions appearing every year. Often we forget how much we rely on them until we can't use them. We might also take for granted countless marvels of human ingenuity, including this computer I'm typing on and the cars that transport us hundreds or even thousands of miles, keeping us cool on the hottest days and warm on the coldest. By considering the people who make these things, we can sense a human connection through the inanimate objects that surround us.

INVITATION
Notice today a few human inventions you might tend to overlook simply because they're always there. Pay attention to seeing them, being aware of what it means to have these things in your life.

APRIL 23

Freedom is not worth having if it does not include the freedom to make mistakes. —MAHATMA GANDHI

Making mistakes is a necessary and inevitable part of the messy nature of progress. Through mistakes, we develop, improve, and advance. Through mistakes, we grow. Despite this, in our everyday lives we often fear mistakes. We try to avoid making mistakes. We attempt to hide our own mistakes from others.

When we make a mistake, we often view ourselves as failures. The irony is that we are inherently fallible creatures. By holding ourselves to perfectionist expectations, we set ourselves up to fail. Then, when we do, we beat ourselves up for not being better, stronger, wiser, or more.

What if we gave ourselves the freedom to make mistakes? What if we realized that mistakes are natural, necessary, and inevitable? Knowing that it's okay to make mistakes, how would you feel?

We can start to alter the way we view mistakes. Instead of seeing problems, we can begin to see opportunities; instead of dead-ends, openings. Rather than coldly condemning ourselves, we can compassionately accept our mistakes and ourselves. Mistakes are simply another part of our experience—a part we can learn to accept, turn toward, and explore. As the saying goes, "There is no failure, only feedback."

INVITATION

Give yourself the freedom to make mistakes. Be compassionate and forgiving toward yourself and toward others when they make mistakes. Ask yourself, What would I try today if I didn't fear making mistakes?

APRIL 24

To live is to fly
Low and high
So shake the dust off of your wings
And the sleep out of your eyes.
  —TOWNES VAN ZANDT

One of the best-tested ways to boost our mood is behavioral activation—a fancy term for doing things that provide enjoyment or a sense of accomplishment. While the practice is often used to treat depression, it's important no matter how we're feeling.

I've personally benefited from this approach many times. One time in particular stands out: I'd been struggling for weeks with low motivation, irritability, exhaustion, insomnia, and a tendency toward isolation. My world shrank. I didn't want to leave the house, and I'd stopped exercising. It pained me to realize how my mood was affecting my wife and kids. I finally admitted to myself that I was in a true depression.

That realization and acceptance led me to make a plan, with my wife's help, to return to life. We took stock of the major areas of my life—areas like relationships, work, and leisure—and looked for ways I could invest more time in enjoyable activities and take care of tasks I'd been putting off. Things didn't improve overnight. I had to start small and work up gradually. But over time, these changes came to be a crucial part of my return to life.

INVITATION

However you're feeling today, examine the domains of your life. Are there any in which you'd like to be more active? Maybe you want to spend more time with friends and family, take time to care for yourself, complete tasks you've been putting off, find moments of uplift and expansion, or anything else—you get to decide. Move toward the things you love.

APRIL 25

Let today be the day you stop living within the confines of how others define or judge you.
—STEVE MARABOLI

We will all experience times in our lives when we're weighed down by our mood. For about one in ten of us, at some point in our lives, the duration and severity of our experiences will meet the medical criteria for depression.

In terms of age, gender, background, education, ethnicity, and wealth, depression does not discriminate—it knows no boundaries. Even public figures who symbolize strength and power in our celebrity culture are not immune to mental health issues. For instance, one of these very symbols, wrestler and actor Dwayne "The Rock" Johnson, has talked about depression taking hold at different points in his career. Sadly, due to social stigma, many of us often hide what we're going through from others.

Whether we're currently experiencing a mental health condition or not, we can let go of the fronts we hide behind. Pretending to others (and ourselves) that everything is fine is tiring. We end up trying to avoid and suppress our feelings, often making our situation worse.

It takes courage to let go of a positive facade. There is freedom to be found in making peace with where we are and what we're experiencing. The great irony is that accepting our situation allows change to take place—it allows us to return to what matters most to us and take action in line with our values.

INVITATION
Take off the mask you might be wearing. Give yourself a break from micromanaging how you come across to others. Allow yourself the freedom to be you, with all your virtues and vices. Doing so will embolden and empower others to try the same.

APRIL 26

Behold, my friends, the spring is come; the earth has gladly received the embraces of the sun, and we shall soon see the results of their love!
—SITTING BULL

What would spring be without an obligatory gardening metaphor? As we tend our plots, some of the work will be immediately apparent and gratifying, like clearing away weeds from flower beds.

Other steps take more time, especially waiting for newly planted seeds to grow. But sooner or later, after preparing the soil and placing the seeds, bright green cotyledons or "seed leaves" appear, followed by the mature leaves. As the plants grow and you continue to nurture them, eventually you have flowers, then tiny fruits, and finally the harvest. Each in its due time.

The same principles apply to any of our efforts. Some of the small changes we make will pay off immediately; the effects of others, evident only in the long run. Just as in tending a garden, there's an element of faith involved in tending to our lives. But in both cases, without planting, a harvest is unlikely, so plant now.

INVITATION

Consider an area of your life that needs attention. Perhaps it's a valued relationship. Or it could be tending to your daily responsibilities. Maybe it's quite literally your garden. Whatever it is, spend some time thinking about what it will take to nourish it. Are there steps you could take that are likely to provide immediate results? Are there others that are more like planting seeds? Consider taking a small step or two today. Enjoy tending to your garden.

APRIL 27

Happiness is not a matter of intensity but of balance and order and rhythm and harmony. —THOMAS MERTON

When we have balance in our lives, there is a sense of harmony. We feel grounded, calm, and in control of different aspects of our lives. We all have our own equilibria. What works for one person may not fit for another. The elements that push us off-kilter also vary. In the many different areas of our lives, consider the balance between:

- **Work**: working hard and creating boundaries so you have time to relax and rejuvenate
- **Relationships**: giving to others and asking for help when you need it; spending time with others and taking some restorative time on your own
- **Focus:** paying attention to the details and seeing the bigger picture
- **Goals:** progressing toward important goals and enjoying the process

As you can see, both ends of the spectrum can have positive effects. But if we tip the scale too much either way, the results in each case can be unhelpful—or even harmful. With the right ingredients and proportions, we can all find some balance.

INVITATION

Are there areas of your life that may be taking up too much of your effort? Check in with yourself. See if you feel balanced and decide if you would like to redress any imbalances. What steps could you take today to bring more balance and harmony into your life?

APRIL 28

A solid anchor is indispensable to one who intends to live life fully. To have an anchor is to be centered and well grounded.

—STEVE GOODIER

When we think of mindful presence, we often use the word *centered*. This word evokes the idea of balance, like a top that spins cleanly on its point.

All of us have things that can throw us off center, including the following:

- Time crunches, like fighting traffic to get to work on time
- Powerful emotions, especially ones like anger, fear, and resentment
- Illnesses that leave us feeling spent, overwhelmed, and anxious about when (or if) we'll feel well again
- Worries that lead us to feared places—some that may not even exist
- Excesses like spending too much time working or not working

Some of these factors are obviously ones we control—our time spent watching television, for example. Others, like whether we get sick, are not.

Even so, there are times when we may give away our sense of balance unnecessarily—times we may have more control over than we realize. For example, if the news is compounding our irritation on the evening commute, we can turn on music that calms rather than inflames our nerves. I recently found that by setting an alarm for when I needed to start getting our kids ready for bed, I feel much more relaxed during the nighttime routine. Sometimes a simple change can help us stay centered.

INVITATION

Notice if there are predictable times in your day when you tend to feel uncentered. Is there anything you can change that would help you feel more balanced at those times? Consider taking one step today toward greater balance in that area.

APRIL 29

The best and safest thing is to keep a balance in your life, acknowledge the great powers around us and in us. —EURIPIDES

Time, responsibility, and expectations—of the many obstacles between ourselves and attaining harmony, these three are the most common. Here are a few ways to work with them wisely:

1. **Time.** Sometimes there are just not enough hours in the day. Since life won't create extra minutes for us, we need to carve out pockets for ourselves. What times could you "mine" for restorative activities, such as going for a run, prepping meals, or meditating? Taking the time to plan your day and week ahead will give you more time in the long run.

2. **Responsibility.** It's tempting to blame others and external circumstances for our frustrations. Commitments can add pressure to our lives, including looking after children, commuting, and working long hours in a demanding job. But we will move toward a more balanced lifestyle only when we accept that it's our responsibility to do so.

3. **Expectations.** Perfectionist tendencies can be a major barrier to feeling centered. We can adopt an all-or-nothing mind-set, putting workouts on hold and cutting back on sleep. We may intend to look after ourselves once the kids go to school or we've secured that promotion, but the next stage brings with it its own duties, and we can quickly run ourselves down. The principle of "good enough" can be lifesaving. You will never be a perfect mom, dad, or worker. Compassionately accepting your limitations is liberating. Good enough is good enough.

INVITATION

Dig a little deeper when finding ways to feel more centered in your life. Consider your time, responsibility, and expectations. See if you can enjoy the process of taking hold of the opportunity to create the life that you want.

APRIL 30

The fear of taking a shot at anything in life, lives in the fact that there are no guaranteed outcomes. —CHRIS HILL

Fear is essential for our survival. Without it, your ancestors would have been removed from the gene pool and you wouldn't be here. Moving away from situations we fear gives us a sense of relief: "Whew! Thank goodness I avoided that." That feeling of relief makes us even more likely to avoid bad things in the future, a crucial process that learning theorists call negative reinforcement.

The downside is that fear can also lead us to avoid things that would add value to our lives. We may pass up asking someone out because we're afraid they'll reject us. Or we might put off starting a business because we don't know if it will succeed. We may avoid having a difficult but important conversation with our partner because we fear conflict.

I recently found the benefit in facing my own streak of social anxiety as I introduced myself to a new neighbor. We ended up having a very enjoyable talk, which put me in a great mood afterward. I can easily imagine passing up the opportunity to speak with him, making it even harder in the future. When we recognize the limits of our fear, we have the choice of giving priority to something else.

INVITATION
Notice at least one time today when fear tries to hold you back from living fully. It could be something very minor—saying hi to someone instead of pretending you don't see them—or a more significant matter. What happens if you decide to face your fear?

MAY 1

The creation of a more peaceful and happier society has to begin from the level of the individual, and from there it can expand to one's family, to one's neighborhood, to one's community, and so on.

—DALAI LAMA

How many of your neighbors do you know? Research suggests that the more we talk to our neighbors, the happier we feel. The more names of people on our street that we know, the safer we feel. Higher levels of community participation and charitable giving are linked to greater levels of happiness. The countries that consistently top the list of the world's happiest countries (Norway, Denmark, Sweden, and Finland) have high levels of community trust. Trust grows out of strong social bonds.

We are all potential agents of social change. And not all change must be groundbreaking. Here are a few ways we can build stronger connections with those around us:

- Smile at your neighbors, ask how their day is, and even bake a cake for them!
- Organize shared school runs with other families.
- If you see a homeless person, say hello, introduce yourself, and buy them something to eat or drink. Even better, ask them what they need and do your best to help.
- Become involved in a cause or project you're passionate about.
- Join a community group aligned with your interests, such as a reading or sports group.

INVITATION

Step outside of your comfort zone and try to connect with someone in your area. If you can face initial fears of social awkwardness and act in line with what you value and care about, the future is likely to be more adventurous, exciting, satisfying, and meaningful. Who would say no to that?

MAY 2

If we learn to open our hearts, anyone, including the people who drive us crazy, can be our teacher. —PEMA CHÖDRÖN

We can learn a great deal through our difficult interactions with others. My favorite professor from graduate school noted that we all have certain types of people that irritate us, and that the more we focus on how much we can't stand such people, the more of them we're likely to encounter.

What my professor said next really stuck with me: By simply noting that we have a strong reaction to this type of person, we take at least a little bit of ownership for our reaction. We might notice how our body reacts, or what thoughts and emotions come up. Perhaps we have a habitual automatic response to such people, like criticizing them or swallowing what we'd really like to say. Noticing our reactions may not make the person easier to get along with or make us less irritated by them, but it just might give us an opportunity to grow from the challenge.

INVITATION

If you encounter anyone today that you find to be difficult, consider using the interaction to learn something about yourself. What triggers you? Think about what this person may teach you about yourself, including the way you would most want to respond the next time a similar situation arises.

MAY 3

Life is a series of natural and spontaneous changes. Don't resist them; that only creates sorrow. Let reality be reality. Let things flow naturally forward in whatever way they like. —LAO TZU

Life doesn't always go the way that we'd like it to. We interview for a job but are passed over for it. We imagine a lifetime with someone, but it doesn't work out. Facing situations at odds with our hopes, desires, ambitions, or expectations can be tricky. At difficult times, we can explore what's happening within us by asking,

- How is my body reacting?
- What emotions am I feeling?
- What thoughts do I notice?
- What does this situation tell me about myself?

The emotions, thoughts, and bodily feelings we experience may take time to sink in. They may also change naturally and spontaneously. Over time, you may come to recognize patterns. We can then prepare ourselves for certain thoughts, emotions, or ways of feeling whenever we face rejection, disappointment, and missed opportunities. We do not have to buy into our thoughts or cling to our emotions. Rather than ignoring them or trying to turn a blind eye, we can greet these old friends with kindness and compassion, acknowledging their presence and allowing them to leave of their own accord. We can be gentle with ourselves. We can go that extra mile to look after ourselves at a time when we might need a little loving care.

INVITATION
If any part of your day doesn't go your way, notice what is triggered within you. Greet these thoughts, emotions, and feelings with openness and curiosity. Open your heart and offer yourself a little compassion.

MAY 4

Any weapon is a good weapon as long as ye can use it with
honor and skill. —BRIAN JACQUES

We all need to feel like we're good at what we do and that we have
ample opportunity to exercise our abilities. Having a sense of
competence is one of the fundamental psychological needs. When we
have ways to use our talents on a regular basis, it strengthens our sense of
confidence, engagement, and self-efficacy.

Researchers have developed scales that measure competence, which
ask questions like:

- On a typical day, how much do you feel a sense of accomplishment from what you do?
- To what extent do you get a chance in your life to show how
  capable you are?
- How often do people you know tell you that you're good at
  what you do?

When our need for competence is unmet for long enough, we're likely to
experience self-doubt, hopelessness, and even depression. On the other
hand, a strong feeling of competence enhances our motivation; we're more
inclined to exert ourselves when we believe our efforts will be worthwhile.
Thus we can enter a positive feedback loop—one in which our feeling of
competence and our efforts mutually reinforce each other.

INVITATION

To what extent do you feel like you're good at what you do? How would
you answer the questions posed above? Whether you answer "a lot" or
"a little," think of ways today that you might flex your competence, in
any area of your life, be it at work, in the kitchen, at the gym or pool, as
a caregiver, or in any other areas of your life. Look for opportunities to
express what you're good at.

MAY 5

Faith gives you an inner strength and a sense of balance and perspective in life. —GREGORY PECK

We've all had our fair share of rejections in life. One way to survive—and even grow through—difficult times is with faith.

An old Scottish friend of mine used to say, "Whit's for ye'll no go by ye." The idea being that what's meant for you in this life, won't pass you by. For some, this belief is tied to God or religion; for others, the idea of fate or the universe or a general belief in something larger simply stands on its own. The underlying, connecting thread is a sense of trust in something—whether we have evidence of its existence or not.

Rather than ruminating on times of failure in our lives, we can learn to take a step back, see the broader landscape, and look for occasions when initial disappointment took us to unexpectedly meaningful places.

Through an initially disheartening chain of events when applying to universities, a certain girl and I both ended up at the University of St. Andrews. I thought that she was beautiful, and she thought I was an idiot. I'm delighted to say that she's now my wife. Our relationship stemmed from events that felt like knock-backs at the time. Often it takes time before we take a step back and connect the dots. The threads that start with suffering frequently form part of the beautiful and rich tapestry of our lives.

INVITATION

If you face disappointment today, explore what faith might look like to you. Consider times when difficult circumstances led to valued parts of your own life. See if you can foster the belief that there's an unknown path that's meant for you. Be held by trust and see where this takes you.

MAY 6

Nobody can tell what I suffer! But it is always so. Those who do not complain are never pitied. —JANE AUSTEN

When you recall your life story, it probably includes some hardships that very few people know about. Maybe it's a chronic psychological or medical condition, or a traumatic childhood that still haunts you. The people around us almost certainly have pains we know nothing about.

In my own life, very few people knew how hard it was for my wife and me to have kids. We had a tough time conceiving our first child and lost two pregnancies along the way. It was a heartbreakingly dark period in our marriage. Even as I write these words, I still feel a lot of emotion about that time. When the second miscarriage started one Sunday afternoon, we just lay down wordlessly on the couch and took a nap together, too sad to speak. Afterward, we walked to Ben and Jerry's and got ice cream cones.

Our son Lucas finally arrived on Christmas Day, four years after we started trying to conceive. Ada arrived three years and one more miscarriage later, followed by baby Faye. Without the particulars of our journey to parenthood, we would never know these three children. Nor would I have the same level of empathy for others going through such trials. That we wouldn't change our personal history—even the painful parts—is a powerful realization.

INVITATION

As you interact with people today, remember that they probably struggle with things you don't know about—just as they don't know your full story. Notice if this recognition of shared suffering influences your thoughts, feelings, and interactions.

MAY 7

I do not ask the wounded person how he feels, I myself become the
wounded person. —WALT WHITMAN

We've all experienced hardships and heartache. While circumstances may differ, the emotions we experience are likely the same. Recognizing our shared suffering can bind humanity.

Today I ran past some of London's most iconic buildings: the Houses of Parliament, Big Ben, and the majestic Buckingham Palace. The streets were busy with tourists photographing these world-famous landmarks. At first, I felt annoyed. I was running, after all, and they were in my way. Everyone seemed so slow and unaware.

Suddenly it struck me that I hadn't given any consideration to *their* way. I'd reduced these whole human beings to objects. I didn't know their story. When I recognized that these individuals had also experienced suffering in their lives, my feelings of frustration softened. I felt connected to these people even though I didn't know them. As I ran, I took delight in watching them marvel at their surroundings, take another photograph, and wander slowly with their ice creams. I even wished them a good day in my head as I passed by!

If we want to develop our compassion and empathy, one way is to ask, Have I ever felt this way?

INVITATION

Stand in another person's shoes today. It could be while a friend tells you about their day, as a work colleague shares a story, or during an argument with a loved one. Ask yourself if you've ever felt this way, connecting to your own emotional experience and the feelings of the whole human being in front of you.

MAY 8

You get people to help you by telling the truth. Being earnest.
—RANDY PAUSCH

There seems to be a shared assumption that to be earnest about the things we deeply care about is to invite ridicule. When few people around us are talking about their deepest passions, fears, pains, or sources of inspiration, we're likely to hide those parts of ourselves too rather than risk "over-sharing" or seeming weird. The result is a tragic shallowness in the ways we relate to others.

I used to assume that certain types of people wouldn't have deep emotional experiences or a sense of spirituality, which led me to relate to them in more superficial ways. I didn't want to embarrass myself by seeming "soft" or overly sentimental.

For example, once, when teaching on the topic of mindfulness, I was worried about the reaction of one audience member. He seemed very serious and skeptical, and I was afraid he would think the whole topic was silly. I found myself treading lightly, trying to emphasize the scientific support and downplay my own emotional connection to the material. To my surprise, he talked at length about how useful mindful awareness could be in his own life, particularly in dealing with his young daughter's behavioral issues. I realized then that I shouldn't have assumed that he and I were so different.

INVITATION

Consider whether there's a part of you that you might want to share with someone else. Maybe it's a life dream you've felt self-conscious about voicing. Perhaps it's a past or present hurt or your genuine feelings toward someone. Whatever you find, maybe today is the day you talk about it with someone else—and possibly connect with that person on a deeper level.

MAY 9

Each friend represents a world in us, a world possibly not born until they arrive, and it is only by this meeting that a new world is born.
—ANAÏS NIN

At the start of relationships, we generally spend time getting to know someone. We ask about different elements of the other person's life: family, childhood stories, aspirations, passions, hobbies, girlfriends or boyfriends. After a while, conversations often move toward everyday life: how the day went, plans for the weekend, bills to be paid, the latest news from the family. This is natural. Even after we've made the shift from getting to know someone to knowing them, it's still possible—even desirable—to explore the rich, abundant, and colorful layers of complexity and beauty of that person's history, experiences, values, and thoughts.

The key to unlocking this exciting world is to ask questions—such as these, for example:

- If you could visit any event at any point in history, what would it be?
- What was your favorite activity or place during the summer as a child?
- In your life so far, what has been the biggest blessing in disguise?
- If you could go back in time to visit a younger version of yourself at any point in your childhood, when would you go? And what would you say to yourself?
- Who has had the biggest influence in your life and in what ways?
- What would your perfect day look like?

INVITATION

Write down the names of three people in your life and the questions you'd like to ask them. Explore, strengthen, and deepen your relationships. Learn something new about the extraordinary people around you.

MAY 10

If you want to hear the dharma [the right way of living], you can hear it from many different places, but you are uncommitted until you actually encounter a particular way that rings true in your heart and you decide to follow it. —PEMA CHÖDRÖN

Many of us will experience a crisis of meaning as we wrestle with issues of religion and faith, especially if we feel compelled to leave the religion we were born into. I experienced this crisis as a young adult when I left the religion of my youth. Both of my parents were fervently Christian, and my dad was a Pentecostal minister. I fully subscribed to what I was taught while growing up, but eventually grew angry and bitter over feeling like I had been misled. I ended up abandoning my beliefs as a young adult.

And yet, over the past few years, I've been surprised to find myself drawn back to a different vision of Christianity. There are still few things that move me like sacred music or bring me as much comfort when I'm struggling as the scriptures and songs I learned in church.

You may find your own fulfillment through a different religion or spiritual practice, a commitment to scientific truth, an appreciation of love or beauty, or something else entirely. At some point, each of us must decide where we find the greatest sense of belonging and the greatest connection to something beyond ourselves.

INVITATION
What can you do today to nurture your deepest connection to meaning and purpose? Allow yourself to embrace what feels right, whether or not you think other people would approve, as you follow your path.

MAY 11

People take different roads seeking fulfillment and happiness. Just because they're not on your road doesn't mean they've gotten lost.
—H. JACKSON BROWN JR.

Where do our beliefs come from? What are the influences that shape what we hold to be true? Our parents, authority figures like teachers and religious leaders, our friends, our community, our culture, and our experiences at home, school, and myriad other contexts are just some of the forces that leave their fingerprints on what we know and believe.

The impact of factors outside of our control can be striking. Whether we're born into a Catholic or a Protestant family in Northern Ireland, a Jewish household in Israel or an Islamic one in Palestine, a Hindu family in India or a Buddhist community in Tibet has monumental consequences. In most cases, we grow up believing that we hold the "truth"—the precious, valuable, rare truth. As we grow, these beliefs can fuse with our own identity. They can become linked to who we think we are. Any challenges to these core beliefs can be deeply uncomfortable and upsetting.

Looking broadly at beliefs, do you ever question or doubt your own? Does it make you uncomfortable to consider adopting another way of seeing the world? Have you been holding onto someone else's beliefs all these years rather than finding your own?

INVITATION

Today, consider "another truth." Sneak a peek over the fence that guards your own belief systems. Open yourself up to the possibility of seeing the world in a fresh way and learning something new.

MAY 12

Hold your beliefs lightly, but while you hold them, treat them as though they were true and explore them as deeply as you can.

—JOHN BECKETT

We often build walls between ourselves and others based on our beliefs. I certainly alienated many of my floormates in college with a brand of Christianity I'd now consider to be a bit overzealous.

It's somewhat paradoxical that we can be so strongly attached to beliefs that will almost certainly evolve. A few years after college, I reconnected with one of my old floormates who was passing through town. He was an atheist when I knew him, and I had recently moved away from Christianity, so I was looking forward to finally being able to connect without the barrier of our opposing beliefs. Much to my surprise, he had converted to Catholicism in the years since I'd seen him!

In the grip of our present ego state, we can argue our positions with such force that we damage our relationships. And yet, our beliefs may change—as may those of our friends and loved ones. If our own beliefs can shift—and shift profoundly—perhaps it's a good idea to not get too hung up on apparent disagreements between ourselves and others. This is not to suggest that we should believe nothing; on the contrary, we can boldly follow our deepest convictions as we tackle our driving questions. And we can do so with a light touch.

INVITATION

Look out for the grip of ego when something threatens your beliefs, whether religious, political, philosophical, or otherwise. Can you feel the defensiveness rise? Explore that feeling, breathe with it, and maybe even smile. Notice how the body and mind react when your beliefs are contradicted. And maybe, just maybe, the grip will begin to loosen.

MAY 13

*There are truths on this side of the Pyrenees that are falsehoods
on the other.* —BLAISE PASCAL

Our beliefs adapt and change over the course of our lives. If we wish to
continue to grow in our understanding, one approach is the dialogic
method—in other words, growth through dialogue.

We don't have to wait until we meet someone with different views
to engage in dialogue. Researchers at Columbia University conducted a
study in which participants were asked to imagine a dialogue between two
experts representing different sides of an issue. Compared with a control
group, those participants who constructed a dialogue in their minds gained
a more nuanced understanding of the topic, identifying more problems
and linking more solutions to the issue. Participants in the control group
were more likely to make unsubstantiated claims. Creating a hypothetical
situation in the mind was an effective way to explore an issue more fully
and to more effectively solve problems.

INVITATION

Today, have a virtual interaction! Choose a topic that's important to you
right now. It could be a work project that you're currently involved with,
an issue that causes arguments with your partner, or an area of contention
between yourself and a family member or friend. Then, imagine a dialogue
between advocates of the two sides. Construct a dialogue, shifting back
and forth between the two perspectives, as the expert debaters put forward
credible arguments, listen, and rebut what the other has said. Take on
multiple roles and perspectives to develop a richer and more sophisticated
understanding.

MAY 14

Look again at that dot. That's here. That's home. That's us. On it everyone you love, everyone you know, everyone you ever heard of, every human being who ever was, lived out their lives.

—CARL SAGAN

I t's easy to feel distinctions from others based on race, profession, political leanings, religion, and other factors. It can be a moving experience to recognize the shared humanity that connects us despite our differences.

I experienced that sense of connection last week during the end-of-year concert at our son's elementary school. As we sat in the auditorium with hundreds of other parents, the high voices of fourth and fifth graders sang one of my favorite children's songs, "This Pretty Planet":

> *Golden sun going down,*
> *Gentle blue giant, spin us around.*
> *All through the night, safe 'til the morning light.*

As the students sang, I imagined that all of us were journeying together through space on a vessel we depend on for life—which is in truth the case. I felt our collective dependence on this singular planet, no matter what our background or beliefs may be. Our differences seemed to melt away because we call the same place home.

INVITATION

Notice any points of friction with another person today. Is it possible to see them as a fellow traveler on this starship, sharing the same resources, fears, limits, and mortality as you? Notice how this shift in perspective might affect your interactions with this person.

MAY 15

*I expect to pass through life but once. If therefore, there be any kindness
I can show, or any good thing I can do to any fellow being, let me do
it now, and not defer or neglect it, as I shall not pass this way again.*
—WILLIAM PENN

Our presence on this planet is ephemeral. Time flows like sand through
an hourglass. How long do we have? Most of us do not know. We'd
like to imagine years and decades, but the sobering reality is that each day
is a gift. We do not earn time or even deserve it. We cannot store or bank
it. No amount of power, wealth, or knowledge can buy time.

We pass through this world but once. After a day passes, it is gone,
never to be found again, except in our memories. Let us then live each day
with as much truth, authenticity, compassion, and love as we can.

INVITATION

Today, do whatever good you can. Show any kindness possible, to yourself
and to others. Whether holding the door open for someone or giving up
your seat on the train, find your own personal, simple, and creative ways
to be kind. There is only one place to start: on this planet. There is only
one time to begin: now.

MAY 16

The ache for home lives in all of us. —MAYA ANGELOU

When we want to know where a person is from, we often ask, Where's home for you? Personally, I never had a strong sense of home as a location, probably because I had at least nine addresses across three states before I turned eighteen and nine more in another three states over the next eighteen years. Home was wherever my family—the people I'd known all my life—was.

There's something honest about being at home. It's a place where we can "slip into something more comfortable," drop pretense and formality, and simply be ourselves. We can talk the way we want, eat how we want, and wear whatever we want (including nothing at all). What a relief it can be to drop the facade we wear for the outside world.

When we come back to center, we can find a similar home within ourselves. Even when we feel far from our mental and spiritual equilibrium, home may be as accessible as taking a few focused breaths.

The world is filled with endless opportunities to leave our home, our center. Most of them aren't "bad." For example, there's nothing wrong with checking email, using social media, watching movies, or reading the news. But we might decide to limit these and any other activities that don't lead to a balanced heart and mind—activities that don't lead us home.

INVITATION

Consider what it means to come home to yourself. What do you lay down, mentally and emotionally, when you "step inside the door"? What defines that sense of being-at-home for you? Does it include a way of thinking? certain actions? Is it connected to your faith? Take a few moments throughout the day to "come home," returning to your truest self.

MAY 17

Be content with what you have; rejoice in the way things are. When you realize there is nothing lacking, the whole world belongs to you.
—LAO TZU

Society has been set up to encourage consumption of new clothes, the latest technology, faster cars, more sparkly jewelry, bigger houses, and nicer holidays. While there's nothing inherently wrong with this, danger does lie in attaching our happiness to certain conditions—in thinking, *I will be happy when ...*

Millions of people have less than you—in terms of money, power, opportunity, and status—yet still live happy lives. Despite knowing this, there will be times when it seems as though our happiness is fixed to an event or experience—this promotion, this relationship, this dessert, etc. At these times, when missing out will make us feel discontent, it can be helpful to ask ourselves a question: Do I really need this in order to be happy?

Certain aspects of our lives are naturally connected to our well-being: meaningful work, close relationships, physical nourishment—the whole hierarchy of needs. The rest, however—this promotion, this person, or this slice of chocolate cake—we can scrutinize and determine whether we truly need them in order to experience happiness. Were you ever happy before this, whatever it may be, presented itself? Of course you were. So cheer up. You'll likely be happy again after it has left.

INVITATION

If you experience any missed opportunities throughout the day, whether it's a green light you missed when driving, an item of clothing that isn't available in your size, or something bigger in your life, ask yourself if you truly need this thing in order to be happy. Let go of this expectation, craving, or attachment, and happiness just might find a way to pop up and say hello.

MAY 18

When peace like a river attendeth my way,
When sorrows like sea billows roll;
Whatever my lot, Thou hast taught me to say,
"It is well, it is well with my soul."

—HORATIO SPAFFORD

How easy it is to predicate our peace of mind on external events. Countless times I have found myself setting these conditions, often related to time—"It will be good if I get in the shower by 7:40," "I'll feel on top of things if I'm at my desk by 8:20," "I'll be satisfied if I get this blog post done today." While there are obvious advantages to keeping a schedule, the downsides come when we make our well-being dependent on aligning with the clock.

We can quickly trade our happiness for something worth a lot less. Horatio Spafford, whose lyrics opened today's entry, seemed to understand in a profound way that well-being doesn't depend on circumstance. His wife and four daughters were traveling by ship across the Atlantic, when another vessel struck theirs. Each of his daughters perished. On his journey to England to rejoin his wife, who survived, he wrote the words to "It Is Well with My Soul." If we believe Spafford's words, in the face of unspeakable grief, we can be content whether peace is flowing around us or the waves are crashing over us.

INVITATION

Is there a situation in your life to which you've attached your well-being? It could be something small, like getting the evening leisure time you want, or something bigger, like finding a life partner. Whatever it may be, reclaim your wholeness from that uncertain outcome. Perhaps all can be well even when all doesn't go according to our plan. Allow your happiness to come home.

MAY 19

Time flies like an arrow; fruit flies like a banana.
—ANTHONY OETTINGER

Our experience of time is relative. As Einstein reported, time is an illusion. Technically, time passes faster at our face than our feet when we're standing: according to his theory of relativity, the closer we are to the center of the Earth, the slower time passes.

In physics, space and time are fluid, affected by gravity and speed. In our everyday life, though, we treat time as rigid. We create fixed ideas of how long something should take and what we should accomplish within a set period of time. When we fall short, we berate ourselves. Our ideas about time can become heavy, cumbersome structures, more like weights around our necks than helpful guidelines to organize our day.

Are you at peace with time? If not, what could you do to be guided by your schedule rather than ruled by it?

INVITATION

Explore your relationship with time. Reflect on the ways in which your expectations about time currently serve or sabotage you. See what changes you can make—perhaps to how you plan your day or to your expectations about how much you can achieve—to enjoy a happy and productive day.

MAY 20

Time you enjoy wasting is not wasted time.
—MARTHE TROLY-CURTIN

Sometimes we can forget that happiness isn't made of what we achieve or acquire—that our experience matters. We step away from our center. It happened to me recently on a Friday afternoon as I was battling thick traffic. Horns blared and tempers flared as drivers shouted out their windows at each other. I just wanted to start my weekend. And there was the irony: we all just wanted to get home and relax as soon as possible, yet the rush and impatience were making an unpleasant situation truly miserable.

Our push for maximal productivity and adequate leisure time often leaves out our happiness. When we manage to make peace with what's happening, even if it feels like a waste of our precious time, we might realize that all is well. Sitting in the car that Friday, for example, wasn't really a bad place to be. I was in an air-conditioned car listening to interesting stories on the news.

Whether we achieve a lot or a little, at some point none of it will matter. We will be gone from this earth, and eventually forgotten. Perhaps our experience of the time we're allotted matters more than what we accomplish in it.

INVITATION

Make friends with time for one hour today. During that hour, intentionally let go of any pressure you might feel about getting on to the next thing. Be in that hour. Maybe that hour is not just about what you do. Feel what it's like to remember that your experience counts.

MAY 21

The living are soft and yielding;
the dead are rigid and stiff…

The rigid and stiff will be broken.
The soft and yielding will prevail.

—LAO TZU

What does it mean to be friends?

Bring to mind someone who's a good friend of yours.

How do you feel about them?

I imagine you're fond of them, that they occupy a soft spot in your heart.

What do you know about them?

You'll likely be familiar with them and their past. You'll have shared some history together.

What experiences have you had with your friend?

You'll have had lots of fun, meaningful, and memorable times together. You've probably had ups and downs, arguments and misunderstandings. Through these times you may have grown stronger in your friendship.

How do you treat your friend?

With a healthy and strong relationship, I would predict that you treat your friend with love, respect, compassion, and understanding. You accept your friend for who they are, without trying to constantly change or control them. You love them for the way they are, with their virtues and vices. If they happen to hurt you, you'll probably forgive them.

INVITATION

Now that we've considered what it means to be a friend, today, make friends with reality. Whatever happens today, see if you can extend compassion and affection to the day as it unfolds. Recognize your familiarity and shared history with reality. Reminisce on your good times together. Treat each moment with love and respect, without trying to control it. If the day doesn't go your way, see if you can find forgiveness in your heart. Be soft and yielding, moving with the constant flow of reality.

MAY 22

You are imperfect, permanently and inevitably flawed. And
you are beautiful.   —AMY BLOOM

We often criticize ourselves when we're not the person we want to be, especially if our shortcoming is an issue that's plagued us for a long while. One of the kindest things we can do for ourselves is to recognize and accept those shortcomings—even embrace them—understanding that while they are part of us, they're not the whole story.

Honestly, when I look back on all the issues I've worked through in my life, I'm amazed I still have so many! There are the old favorites that show up daily, like bouts of impatience and wrestling with time. There are also new ones that arise, like the struggles that can accompany health issues. There are fears, jealousies, occasional paranoid episodes, and a tendency to feel taken for granted.

I used to long to drop these struggles, like taking off a heavy backpack, and indeed I can at times lay them down. I like to think that my overall trajectory is one of growth. I don't know if that's true or if I've simply exchanged the issues I've transcended for new ones. But as one of my insightful young students suggested years ago, perhaps we're perfect even as we aim to improve.

INVITATION

As part of the ongoing process of making friends with reality, today I invite you to befriend your own unresolved issues. If you notice you're struggling with something, try to welcome the struggle as you would a friend. Enfold yourself, with all your strengths and your challenges, inside your embrace of reality.

MAY 23

We habitually erect a barrier called blame that keeps us from communicating genuinely with others, and we fortify it with our concepts of who's right and who's wrong. We do that with the people who are closest to us, and we do it with political systems, with all kinds of things that we don't like about our associates or our society. It is a very common, ancient, well-perfected device for trying to feel better. Blame others. Blaming is a way to protect our hearts, to try to protect what is soft and open and tender in ourselves. Rather than own that pain, we scramble to find some comfortable ground.

—PEMA CHÖDRÖN

We often hold onto blame. We blame external circumstances to protect our hearts. We may temporarily feel better for pushing responsibility onto others. But there's often buried guilt within—as if we know, deep down, that we too are part of the picture. Accepting this can be painful, so we try to hide from it.

Pain arises from seeing ourselves as complete failures rather than recognizing that our weaknesses are only single strands in the much bigger tapestry of who we are. At times, we may grind our spirits further into the ground with judgment, criticism, and shame. These habits are as old as the hills themselves.

Today is a new day, though—a new day to let go of blame, a new day to live with compassion and with understanding.

INVITATION

Notice times during the day when you blame yourself or others. See if you can let go of the blame and instead seek to understand yourself, others, and the circumstances a little better.

MAY 24

Reason, Observation, and Experience—the Holy Trinity of Science—
have taught us that happiness is the only good; that the time to be
happy is now, and the way to be happy is to make others so.

—ROBERT G. INGERSOLL

Sometimes, when we're experiencing challenges, this world catches us off guard with sacred moments. For instance, last night, some health issues returned—as did the accompanying low mood. I felt the familiar grip around my mind and heart—a sudden irritability that led to my being unnecessarily short with both daughters as I got them ready for bed. I was sorry I'd let myself get there again. I wanted to do better. I felt stuck and unable to fix myself.

Later, when my son asked me to brush his teeth, I took a knee in front of him so I could see more easily. In that act of genuflection, I felt like I was honoring him, and I suddenly felt my heart release and tears fill my eyes. When I finished brushing, I embraced him. He hugged me back, saying, "I love you, Daddy"—a rare treat from a kid who doesn't exactly wear his emotions on his sleeve.

Having people to care for every day doesn't allow for a retreat from life. And while being bound in this way presents challenges, it also provides countless opportunities to stay engaged.

INVITATION

Today, choose someone to bow or kneel to—someone present or someone you hold in your heart. It may be someone easy to bow to or, if you're up for a challenge, someone harder to like. Allow the sacred in you to recognize the sacred in this person.

MAY 25

Seasons after seasons, we are unknowingly approaching our twilight years.

From the first cry on coming to earth till the hair turns gray, the baggage of our journey through life is filled with bitterness and sweetness as well as ups and downs.

How far we walk on the path of our twilight years will depend on our physical, mental and spiritual condition...

...We have to maintain peace, expect less, be more inclusive and forgiving, do not over react when receiving attention or when we are ignored. To stay or to go does not matter anymore. Keep smiling while moving ahead each day and be kind to ourselves.

Being honest and sincere will make friendships last.

Do not expect a return on what you have given to others. After all, making others happy is life's greatest achievement.

—YANG JIANG

Last night, I had supper with my mother. She was in London for medical appointments and considering the best plan following her breast cancer treatment. We sat in a Middle Eastern restaurant, ate with our hands, shared food, and spoke. I held her hand and listened. I looked into her kind eyes. She told me that she had aged since the chemotherapy. I told her that she looked beautiful. She shared with me the passage above—a passage that was written by its author at the age of 103. We reflected on how lucky we were to have this moment together.

INVITATION

Reach out to someone approaching their twilight years. It could be a family member, friend, neighbor, or stranger. Ask them about their lives, their experiences, and what they've learned from different phases of their lives. Look into their eyes. Listen intently. Be present.

MAY 26

The ideal state of tranquility comes from experiencing body and mind being synchronized. —CHÖGYAM TRUNGPA

It's especially hard to stay connected to our true self when we're overwhelmed by emotion. Powerful feelings can hijack our minds and hearts, leading us to act in ways we regret. But with awareness, we can navigate these challenging times with grace.

These days my own challenges often revolve around being patient as a parent. Earlier this week I was about to put the kids to bed, when I had a realization: "You're feeling humorless and irritable. Focus on kindness no matter how you're feeling. You want to be kind to your kids."

It felt like someone had handed me a gift. Frankly, it was not a reaction I've had very often, and I was grateful for it. It did end up being a much nicer time with my kids as they got ready for bed, and I avoided the painful regret I often feel when I've been unfairly cranky toward them.

I suspect life offers us such reprieves more often than we realize, but the clutter in our minds gets in the way of us seeing them. We'll never be perfect at being the person we want to be—thank God—but we can give ourselves a better chance of recognizing when life offers us a cup of cool water and taking a drink.

INVITATION
Think about a situation where you know from experience you tend to struggle, and decide on how you want to handle it. Focus your attention on the body and the breath as you move through the situation, firmly grounded in reality and with a sense of your proper place in it.

MAY 27

The present moment is filled with joy and happiness. If you are attentive, you will see it. —THICH NHAT HANH

There are those moments when we fully relax. We might be on vacation, sitting in the warmth of the sun in our swim shorts or bikini, and we just let go. We take a slow, deep breath and look out at the blue ocean as the birds chirp around us. We sink into our towel and the present moment. The only commitments we have are to choose which ice cream to have next and roll over when we feel too hot.

Remember that we don't have to wait until we're on vacation to relax. We don't have to save all our bliss for that trip abroad. Happiness exists right now. All we have to do is take a moment to be present. To put down our thoughts, worries, expectations, and plans. To simply be here right now.

INVITATION

Today, take what I call a "micro moment" to experience peace and relaxation. There are 43,200 seconds in 12 hours. Each one has the potential to be a micro moment—a present moment we can sink into and let go. Whether it's for a few seconds, five minutes, half an hour, or longer, on at least one occasion today, create an opportunity to unwind. Whatever you're doing, take a few slow, deep breaths to connect to the present moment. Exhale any stress or tension in your body. Smile. And enjoy.

MAY 28

To me…the really interesting question is why…we recoil from the dull. Maybe it's because dullness is intrinsically painful; maybe that's where phrases like "deadly dull" or "excruciatingly dull" come from. But there might be more to it. Maybe dullness is associated with psychic pain because something that's dull or opaque fails to provide enough stimulation to distract people from some other, deeper type of pain that is always there, if only in an ambient, low-level way, and which most of us spend nearly all our time and energy trying to distract ourselves from feeling, or at least from feeling directly or with our full attention.　　　　—DAVID FOSTER WALLACE

We seem to be driven to distract ourselves, to avoid whatever feeling we fear when we enter a place of stillness. Yet I suspect we'll often be surprised when we allow ourselves to settle into the present and risk being bored.

Yesterday I went for an early morning walk just before the sun rose. The thought of simply walking with no other entertainment felt like a sentence. I considered listening to a podcast, but I'm glad I didn't. If I had, I would have missed the loudest birdsong I've ever heard. The singing drew me into the rest of my senses. I noticed the lovely spring flowers everywhere, the smell of honeysuckle in the air, the feeling of my feet on the ground, and the cool morning air on my scalp. It felt like a vacation from my cares.

INVITATION

Take a "sensory walk" outside today, even if for just five minutes. Take in all that your senses are bringing you: sights, sounds, smells, touch sensations. Notice what your body, mind, and spirit experience in this deliberately attentive place.

MAY 29

Live with intention.
Walk to the edge.
Listen Hard.
Practice wellness.
Play with abandon.
Laugh.
Choose with no regret.
Appreciate your friends.
Continue to learn.
Do what you love.
Live as if this is all there is.
　　　　—MARY ANNE RADMACHER

"Why questions" can be immensely powerful. They take us beneath the surface, to the underlying passions, desires, intentions, reasons, roles, goals, and ambitions that drive our actions.

So why do you do what you do? Why do you work in your profession, have the friends or partner you do, spend your weekends as you do, or become defensive when someone says x, y, or z?

The *why* that starts a course of action may differ from the *why* that maintains it. We may have applied for a job for one reason, such as a pay raise, but then stayed there for another, say, the people. We might initially have felt inspired by our occupation but now feel trapped in it in order to maintain a certain lifestyle. We may have lost touch with why we're doing something altogether.

When we're disconnected from the *why*, we can become frustrated and disillusioned, feeling a sense of dissatisfaction and emptiness. The *whys* that fuel our actions may have become outdated, and no longer fit with our values or aspirations.

continued on next page

INVITATION

Discover the *whys* that drive your actions. It could be asking yourself a why question when doing an everyday task such as washing the dishes, when speaking to an old friend, listening to your partner, offering help to someone, choosing from a restaurant menu, or working on a project. Pay special attention to any hidden values or passions. Continue to learn about yourself and live each moment with intention.

MAY 30

I don't want a never-ending life
I just want to be alive while I'm here.
—THE STRUMBELLAS

Life is filled with things that can get in the way of our most meaningful connections. Some of these forces are outside our control, while others come from choices we make. For example, we might overschedule ourselves in a way that allows no time for reflection and decompression or that crowds out time with the people closest to us. Perhaps we drink more alcohol than we know is good for us, find ourselves glued to our phones more than is healthy, or put on emotional armor that prevents intimacy with others.

In my own life, I often choose "productivity" at the expense of my spiritual life and self-care, even when I can feel that it's happening. Just this week, I found myself abbreviating my morning exercise and meditation so I could get to work sooner. I quickly felt the effects on my body and spirit.

I often wonder why we ever leave that which nourishes us. If connection feels so good, why do we knowingly walk away from our center? I suspect it's forgetfulness as much as anything. Drawn by the allure of an immediate reward, we forget what the ultimate effects will be. With increased awareness and willingness to see our reality, we can better recognize where our actions will lead us and choose accordingly.

INVITATION

What pulls you away from where you want to be? Notice any justifications you give yourself for behavior that would lead you away from your center. Even if it doesn't change your actions today, you'll be building greater awareness and, ultimately, the freedom to choose.

MAY 31

Instruction does much, but encouragement everything.
—JOHANN WOLFGANG VON GOETHE

We never know when our actions are going to touch someone in the way that they need at that moment. Recently I received a heartfelt message from an old friend saying what a difference our relationship made in his life. I was feeling heavy and tired before I opened the email; minutes later, that heaviness was gone, the tiredness replaced by a sense of gratitude and connection.

Encouragement comes in different forms—the words we speak, the trust we show, the support we give. Encouragement lights up our lives. It warms our hearts and lifts our spirits.

We all know what a difference it makes to have a boss that acknowledges our efforts and gives genuine praise. We've all been children seeking recognition and validation from the parent figures in our lives. Hopefully, we've all known the grounding, life-affirming feeling when someone else shows that they believe in us.

INVITATION

Give words of encouragement to someone in your life. Maybe it's your significant other or another family member or someone at work or in a class you attend. It could be your train conductor or the cashier at the grocery store. You might do it by phone, text, email, or in person. It's likely to brighten that person's day—and might just come at exactly the right moment.

JUNE 1

Millions long for immortality who don't know what to do with themselves on a rainy Sunday afternoon. —SUSAN ERTZ

Most of us find boredom to be an uncomfortable experience. We avoid it if we can. I used to find relief from boredom in alcohol, more recently in food. A couple of years ago, I was in the habit of eating a massive dessert every night to calm some vague sense of unrest after dinner. I had a fully present but half-sensed feeling that to deny my dessert craving would be bad—not just temporarily uncomfortable, but *terrible*.

Then one night something moved me to stay with the cravings instead of following them to the refrigerator. It wasn't long before they calmed down. And then something surprising happened: I felt a deep sadness. I unexpectedly remembered a friend who had been going through a difficult time. I contacted my friend to let her know I was thinking of her.

It struck me that I never would have known what was on the other side of that acquisitive craving for dessert if I had simply succumbed to it. By settling into it and moving through it, I learned something I would have otherwise missed.

INVITATION

Notice times today when you experience boredom or the dread of boredom. Maybe your boredom triggers are predictable: waiting at a stoplight, walking somewhere, having lunch at your desk. See what your first inclination is—is it to prevent or relieve the dullness? Is it possible to welcome the boredom with curiosity, feeling and examining it? Is there any fear that comes with it? Allow yourself a chance to see what's on the other side of boredom.

JUNE 2

Character cannot be developed in ease and quiet. Only through experience of trial and suffering can the soul be strengthened, ambition inspired, and success achieved. —HELEN KELLER

We never know how disappointments may transform with time. My biggest disappointments came when my wife and I were trying to have a baby. Our first pregnancy ended in miscarriage just before the second trimester and was followed by another just a few months later. After eighteen months of struggling to conceive, Marcia woke me on an Easter Monday with the words "Seth, I'm pregnant!" Excitement and terror washed over me. Would this pregnancy bring a child into our lives or still more heartache?

Welcoming our first child into this world was the most stressful and joyful day of my life. I felt that a portal to the stars had been opened as I held tiny Lucas, "Bringer of Light," and looked into his strangely blue eyes. That portal opened for us twice more, bringing two precious girls, Ada and Faye.

The pain we went through changed me in ways I couldn't have foreseen. Even as it broke my heart many times, it also softened it. I seem to have a deeper awareness of others' suffering, not only that related to trouble having a baby, but suffering of all sorts. I'm not a big fan of easy truisms like "Everything happens for a reason," yet I can see how the losses in my life have made me who I am.

INVITATION

Think back to what you were you doing ten years ago. What were your hopes and plans at that time? Did everything go according to plan? What didn't go the way you wanted it to? Throughout the day, consider the twists and turns of the journey that have brought you this far.

JUNE 3

Some beautiful paths can't be discovered without getting lost.

—EROL OZAN

All of us have had surprising twists in our lives that brought us to where we are. Maybe our chosen path led to disappointment, or perhaps a rejection led to a better opportunity. Maybe our winding path led us to some of our dearest friends.

As I look back on my life after graduate school, everything fits together "on paper," telling a story that makes sense. Yet, while it was happening, it often felt messy and unpredictable. Ten years ago I was planning to go into clinical practice. At the last minute, I decided to take an academic position at a medical school, where I met Aria Campbell-Danesh.

Around the same time, I realized with utter clarity that I could not stay in my faculty position. I decided to transition to full-time teaching at a liberal arts college and opened a part-time private practice nearby. After three years, I left the college and entered full-time clinical practice. It was scary to let go of the familiar with each new step as I couldn't know where my choices would lead me.

When we look back at this time ten years from now, we may well remember not knowing how things were going to work out. With this perspective in mind, perhaps we can hold our future a bit more lightly.

INVITATION

Think back on your life history to things that involved the pain of loss or the fear of uncertainty. Are there situations that worked out even though you weren't sure they would? See if you can apply this experience to uncertain situations in your life right now. Welcome the adventure to come.

JUNE 4

The test of our progress is not whether we add more to the abundance of those who have much; it is whether we provide enough for those who have too little. —FRANKLIN D. ROOSEVELT

I recently read an article that described the lives of the poorest in the US. Where they live, running water is considered a luxury, heat is not guaranteed in the winter, and a refrigerator full of food is implausible. A three-bedroom house might be home to twenty people, with six children sharing one bed. Several days each month, there's too little food for everyone, and many are undersized from inadequate nutrition.

As I was reading this in my living room, I looked around at our "modest" house. The room I sat in seemed luxuriously large. It can be made warmer with the push of a button, and the electricity never goes out. The biggest issue we have with food is eating it all before it spoils.

INVITATION

Whether you live in a modest home or a grand home, take note of what you have—the essentials of your life that probably fade into the background. Try this exercise: Set a one-minute timer on your phone. For that minute, close your eyes. Each time you breathe out, bring to mind one thing you have in your life every day—for example, *inhale … exhale …* a dry place to sleep *… inhale … exhale …* a washer and a dryer, right in my home. When the timer goes off, you can stop—or keep going, if you wish.

JUNE 5

I have laughed, in bitterness and agony of heart, at the contrast between what I seem and what I am!

—NATHANIEL HAWTHORNE

Our perception of photos can be very different from the reality behind the scenes. A photo may depict the perfect couple to an outsider yet be one taken just before a break-up. This incongruence applies to social media and may be one reason that quitting Facebook has been linked to increases in happiness: We see carefully curated photos from the lives of others and imagine them to be as happy as they look there all the time.

This dynamic seems to be at work not only in photos but also in the face we show the world in general. When we're out in the world, we try to put on the best version of ourselves. Usually, only our families get to see the unfiltered version. When we see people who seem to be well put together, it's easy to imagine they're always that way. But we all struggle. We all have moments of generosity and pettiness, kindness and selfishness. We all have the full human experience.

INVITATION

Think of someone you admire or consider to be a role model. Is it hard to see them as a full human being—someone who loses their temper and picks their nose? Spend a few moments imagining them being fully human, flaws and all. As you go through your day, remember that even those we look up to struggle with the same things we do.

JUNE 6

We are frail, we are "fearfully and wonderfully made."
—RICH MULLINS

I t's easy to imagine people we admire as superhuman beings existing on a higher plane than the rest of us mere mortals. But anytime we elevate someone above the rest of humanity, we create an illusion. Inevitably, our view of the idolized person will turn out to be false.

Shortly after I was introduced to the idea of mindfulness, I came across a tiny volume on our bookshelf called *Shambhala: The Sacred Path of the Warrior* by Chögyam Trungpa. I'd never noticed the book before, and I couldn't believe how nearly every page described my own experiences so clearly. Never before had I been so deeply affected by an author's words—words that shaped my own practice of mindfulness.

Months later, I discovered that Trungpa died at age forty-eight, allegedly from chronic alcoholism. I felt shocked and disillusioned. What did this mean for all I'd taken from his writings? As I thought about the apparent contradiction between his transcendent words and the messy life he may have lived, I had to wonder if the insights he captured were possible only because of his struggles.

Part of what's uniquely hard about being human is that we have our feet on the earth and our heads in the heavens, as Trungpa suggested. We're pulled between gratifying our flesh and aspiring toward our highest spiritual selves. Perhaps the seeming contradiction between his life and his writing was another illusion.

INVITATION

I've adapted today's invitation from Trungpa's book *Shambhala*. Take a seat on the ground or floor if possible. With each inhale, foster a feeling of uplift in your posture; with each exhale, feel the sensations of the out-breath—*inhale*: posture; *exhale*: breath. Allow this practice to embody your dual nature: heaven and earth, spirit and flesh.

JUNE 7

Working with obstacles is life's journey. The warrior is always coming up against dragons. Of course the warrior gets scared, particularly before the battle. It's frightening. But with a shaky, tender heart the warrior realizes that he or she is just about to step into the unknown, and then goes forth to meet the dragon. —PEMA CHÖDRÖN

We all have our own struggles. All we have to do is open our eyes and ears to look and listen. Yesterday I saw a landscaper in what appeared to be a good deal of pain—and there he was, working the best he could. I also noticed that one of the people who cleaned an office I visited had some sort of physical condition that severely affected his gait, yet that didn't stop him from collecting the trash and giving me a hearty hello.

So much of being an adult seems to be about accepting that we are truly and ultimately responsible for ourselves. While others can help us in many ways, there are limits to what they can do for us.

Living—truly living—means that we're willing to try things despite the difficulties and fears we have.

INVITATION

Take a big or small step you've been contemplating for a while. It could be looking for a new job, trying a new recipe, starting to exercise, asking out someone you've grown fond of, starting to write your book, or anything else. You get to decide! Can you find the willingness to try, even without knowing what the outcome will be?

JUNE 8

There is no fear in love. But perfect love drives out fear.

—1 JOHN 4:18

Fear shows up in many places in our lives. We can easily find ourselves focusing on what might go wrong and what we stand to lose. We can go through each day trying to prevent bad things from happening—being late, messing up at work, somehow disappointing someone. When we're trying to avoid loss, fear is in control. The best we can do when fear is in charge is to get a zero for the day, to break even.

On the flip side, imagine dwelling on what might go really well today and thinking about what you might gain. What do you have to look forward to? What good might you accomplish? How can you be of service to those you care for?

As we emphasize the possibility of good things, we move from fear to love. A shift from fear to love can dissolve our anxiety. Love and fear exist in opposition: as one increases, the other decreases.

INVITATION

Today, think about what might go well. How would you fill in the blanks for these three statements?

1. One thing I'm looking forward to today is _____.

2. A really positive step I can take today will be to _____.

3. Today I will do something to brighten _____'s day.

Enjoy moving toward love as the antidote to worry and fear.

JUNE 9

If you are not willing to risk the unusual, you will have to settle for the ordinary.
                                                                    —JIM ROHN

We're often careful not to stand out in some way, lest people think we're weird—even if their opinions would have no real effect on us. Personally, I've kept walking with a painful rock in my shoe because I was self-conscious about taking my shoe off in public. In reality, people in the passing cars probably wouldn't have thought anything of it.

I have to wonder what we sacrifice in the push to be ordinary. When I think about many of the people I admire most, a lot of them have quirks that draw me to them rather than push me away. Indeed, some of the best moments in my own life have happened when I wasn't being "normal."

One evening years ago, I made it home from work just before the skies dumped torrential rain. As I looked out at the storm with our kids, I had an urge to dash outside. But then I thought, *The neighbors will think you're crazy.*

And then I thought, *Do what you want—it's* your *life.* So I took off my shoes and socks and ran out the front door, around the tree in our front yard, and back inside. I was soaking wet. Our kids were taken aback and then decided they wanted to do it too. So I ran around the tree again with each of them. It was exhilarating, not only because of the extreme elements, but also because it defied the tendency to be "normal."

INVITATION
Today, be willing to act in a way that's consistent with who you are and what you want to do, which won't necessarily be comfortable. Risk being weird.

JUNE 10

Daring ideas are like chessmen moved forward. They may be beaten, but they may start a winning game.
—JOHANN WOLFGANG VON GOETHE

In baseball there are two ways to strike out: swinging and missing, or not swinging at pitches the umpire calls as strikes. Nobody likes to strike out swinging, but everyone *hates* striking out *looking*. Players, coaches, and fans alike feel bitter disappointment when the batter doesn't even try to hit the ball.

So why do we hesitate to take chances? A client once shared her thoughts with me: "Because if I never try, I can always tell myself I could've done it. If I try and fail, I've lost the potential I thought I had." It's like scratching off a lottery ticket to see if we've won: until we scratch it off, we could be holding a $10 million ticket. As long as we delay revealing the numbers, we can hold out hope that we'll win.

We all face this dilemma in life: play it safe and risk nothing or do our best and risk failing. Would you rather strike out looking or swinging? And I should hasten to add a third option: not striking out at all, but hitting the ball out of the park.

INVITATION

Chances are there's something in your life you've wanted to pursue but haven't allowed yourself to. Today, I invite you to think about what that might be. What's held you back? Perhaps today is the day you see your opportunity. Keep your eye on the ball, and swing.

JUNE 11

We don't rise to the level of our expectations, we fall to the level of our training. —ARCHILOCHUS

When people bump into us in life, whether literally or figuratively, we can learn what we're full of based on what spills out. Do we respond with bitterness? With grace? With generosity?

Recently, I was rear-ended in the grocery store as I leaned over to fill my container at the olive bar. I felt a jolting thump, and when I turned around, I saw that a woman backing up her cart had plowed her butt squarely into mine. I felt immediately annoyed because I saw she was on her cell phone. She apologized. "That's okay," I mumbled as I turned back to my olives, hoping I sounded insincere. "She shouldn't have been on her phone," I told myself, to justify my irritation.

Hours later, I wished I'd given a more gracious response. I had assumed, based on scant evidence, that she was self-absorbed and inconsiderate. For all I know, she didn't want to be on her phone but had to talk with an ailing family member. Maybe the last thing she needed was to bump into a grumpy guy in the grocery store. A smile and a sincere "No problem!" would have been kinder.

I had to wonder if I might have given a different response had I been more practiced in cutting people a break. And why not give people some slack? We can add real value to our world when we resolve to treat each other graciously.

INVITATION

Decide in advance how you'd like to respond to any bumps from those around you. Can you prepare yourself so you're pleased with what spills out?

JUNE 12

We spent all our time outside
'Cause people say small things when they stay too long in little rooms.
—GREG BROWN

Summertime seems to lift everyone's spirits. The warmth of the sun entices us outside. It's often struck me that being outdoors feels healing, yet I can tell you from my own clinical experience that we're least likely to go outside precisely when we need it most.

In our heads, indoor life might feel like the "real thing," while going outside seems potentially unnecessary. We can all find pleasure in the easy comforts of our modern age, like central air, a fully stocked fridge, and endless entertainment at our fingertips. Why would we want to go *out there* when we have everything we need right here?

And then we step outside, and right away we remember: the sky, the trees, the sound of birds calling to each other, the clouds, the breeze on our faces, the warm sun on our skin. We step outside and we breathe slowly and deeply. We step outside and we feel alive.

INVITATION

Today, find an excuse to spend a little more time outside. You might eat one of your meals alfresco or take a slightly longer walk from the car to your office. Or maybe just step outside for a minute to look at the sky and listen to the wind. When you're outdoors, consider keeping your phone out of sight. Let yourself feel what it is to be you, to be alive, right here, right now.

JUNE 13

Love is that condition in which the happiness of another person is essential to your own. —ROBERT A. HEINLEIN

It helps to be reminded of what our dearest relationships mean to us. When my wife and I were newlyweds, we heard a pastor say that at some point in any relationship, people take each other for granted. We looked at each other and shook our heads—not us! But of course, we have, and do. I love my kids more than anything on earth, and I can take them for granted too.

I recently had a dream in which my wife and I were traveling to France for a year. I realized, at the airport, that I wouldn't see our kids the whole time. I had an intense craving to see them and couldn't imagine getting through an entire year without wrapping my arms around them and seeing their smiles.

I would have given anything to see them again, and we hadn't even boarded our plane. I was sobbing, not caring who heard me cry. When I woke up, I still had a visceral longing to see Lucas, Ada, and Faye, feeling the tenderness and depth of my connection with these three.

I often forget that this time with our kids at home is finite. Our oldest will head off to college in less than ten years, and our daughters won't be far behind. My dream reminded me to savor the moments I have with them.

INVITATION

Think of someone you care about deeply. What would you give to see them if you were separated for a long time? Would you interact any differently knowing your time together is limited? Consider showing your love for this person today, even in a small way.

JUNE 14

Resolve to be tender with the young, compassionate with the aged, sympathetic with the striving, and tolerant of the weak and the wrong. Sometime in life you will have been all of these.

—LLOYD SHEARER

All of us will go through trials at some point in our lives. Some people will be there for us, and others will not. We remember the ones who extend themselves to us at those times.

I still feel deep gratitude for the family who was there for me when I experienced a depression in my late teens. My dad let me know that he was always there if I needed his support. My mom would come and visit me at university, bringing homemade meals and encouraging me to take walks outside. My older brother listened to my disjointed thoughts. My youngest brother, who was only eight or nine years old at the time, showered me with hugs every time I saw him. Even though he didn't know exactly what was happening, he sensed that I wasn't my typical self.

None of us has had exactly the same difficulties as another, yet we can strive to understand what one another is going through. It can take some imagination, like asking ourselves how we might feel in their shoes. We can also ask others directly: What's this been like for you? We strengthen our relationships when we're willing to connect with another person's suffering.

INVITATION

Is there someone close to you who is suffering, in big ways or small? Consider contacting that person today to let them know you're thinking about them. It might be through a quick text message or a phone call or even getting together in person. What could you do today to extend compassion to them?

JUNE 15

A number of times I have suggested to a patient (in my work as a psychotherapist) that bringing order into the household might be helpful for all concerned. The result has sometimes been surprisingly profound, particularly in the long run. —BERNIE WEITZMAN

Completing small everyday tasks in our homes can provide a powerful sense of accomplishment. For example, lately I've found that simply emptying the dehumidifier promptly is doubly satisfying: I'm glad it's done, and I don't have the continual awareness that I haven't done it. I still don't *feel* like emptying it when I see the "Bucket Full" light flashing, but I know from experience that I'll feel satisfied after doing it.

Many of us tend to put off tasks, deferring them to the future, when we imagine we'll have more time. For instance, it took me months to get our garage door fixed, and I can think of many other needed repairs around the house too. I have to remind myself that each one is an opportunity to feel good about taking care of our home.

A professional organizer I know confirmed my impressions about the importance of order in our lives. Taking care of our living space tells us that we're worth the effort, that we deserve to enjoy spending time in a functional and tidy home. We can also find a greater sense of internal ease when our external world is well-ordered.

INVITATION

Think of a home project you've been meaning to do—one that would improve your living situation and communicate care for yourself. It could be something as simple as changing a light bulb, or a bigger task like cleaning out the garage. Make a plan to start the task even if you don't feel like it, and pay attention to how you feel when the job is done.

JUNE 16

The best possible way to prepare for tomorrow is to concentrate with all your intelligence, all your enthusiasm, on doing today's work superbly today. That is the only possible way you can prepare for the future.
—DALE CARNEGIE

What is it that leads us to procrastinate? Research suggests it's generally one of two things: Either we think the task is going to be a drag or we're not sure how to do it. Obviously, it can be a combination of the two. When we finally decide it's time to take care of the task, we often find that it isn't as bad as we feared.

It's easy to wait to do a task, telling ourselves that we'll get started as soon as we feel motivated or when we know how we're going to do it. In truth, the reverse is more accurate: We feel more motivated once we begin, and we figure out how we're going to do it once we immerse ourselves in the task. We may never begin if we wait until we're brimming with zest or know exactly what we need to do. But once we commit to doing it, the "how" can emerge. Once we begin, our enthusiasm can follow.

INVITATION

Consider a project you've put off starting because you didn't feel like doing it or weren't sure how to complete it. Can you decide to start today? Act, and the rest will fall into place.

JUNE 17

Look at a day when you are supremely satisfied at the end. It's not a day when you lounge around doing nothing; it's a day you've had everything to do and you've done it. —MARGARET THATCHER

Completing tasks is inherently rewarding, but unfortunately, so is putting them off. Each time we avoid doing something we think will be difficult or annoying, our brains feel a sense of relief that makes us likely to keep avoiding the task. We also miss out on strengthening the link between taking care of things and the satisfaction that follows.

One of the ways we can increase our likelihood of crossing a task off our list is to, well, make a list, to begin with! Obvious, I know. But there's something about writing things down that greatly increases our chances of doing them, and it certainly makes them easier to remember and prioritize.

There's also some accountability, if only to ourselves, that comes with making a list. The satisfaction we get from crossing things off no doubt helps too. Sometimes it can help to break tasks into smaller chunks, since crossing off more items can buoy your sense of accomplishment. Keep a hard copy with you so you can choose projects from it and cross them off as you finish them.

INVITATION

What goes on your to-do list? Make a list and keep it where you can find it. What's one activity you can start today? If you have any difficulty getting started, remember that committing to the task helps us figure out how to do it.

JUNE 18

Posture is important, not just in sitting practice but in whatever you do. Whether you are talking to a client or talking to your mate, whether you're talking to your pets or talking to yourself—which does sometimes happen—having a good posture of head and shoulders is an expression that you've stepped out of your cocoon.

—CHÖGYAM TRUNGPA

As psychologists, some of our clients are diagnosed with post-traumatic stress disorder, or PTSD. One of the most powerful parts of the treatment is asking individuals to retell their traumatic event. This gives them the opportunity to process the emotions surrounding the memory. Many people start telling their story sunk low in their chair, a hand covering their face. Understandably, many people have shame attached to their trauma memory, and their way of sitting embodies that shame.

Over time we might ask them what it would be like to sit up straight and remove their hands from their face. This invitation is often an important part of people's recovery: it sends a powerful message to our brains when we allow ourselves to face the world with our hearts open and our bodies unashamed.

We can foster a sense of respect for ourselves by embodying dignity in the way we carry ourselves. When we sit and stand, we can allow our heads to be upright, shoulders down, a feeling of uplift in our spine. We can find a posture that's dignified yet relaxed.

INVITATION

Today, practice having "a good posture of head and shoulders" whether you're driving, sitting at your desk, watching television, or engaging in any other activity. Remind yourself somehow to do this, maybe by posting a sticky note on your dashboard or putting a sign above your television. Notice any effects on the mind when you embody dignity.

JUNE 19

Having a soft heart in a cruel world is courage, not weakness.
—KATHERINE HENSON

There are countless things in this life, both within us and outside us, that will harden our hearts. Life is hard, and being treated unfairly or being disappointed by others can lead us to form a shell around our hearts to protect it. But these layers also make it harder to feel.

It can be a welcome relief when our hearts soften. There was a time in my life when I was quite bitter toward a family member and couldn't seem to get over it. I happened to start practicing yoga around that time, and in my first class the instructor led us through a loving-kindness meditation. As I followed her instructions, I felt resentment's grip loosen. Finally, I could let go of the anger I'd been holding onto.

Sometimes our hearts melt when we're not expecting it. Two years ago on Father's Day, I was working in our kitchen before dinner and could hear our kids playing together in the basement. Suddenly my eyes filled with tears, and then I was sobbing. I remembered telling Marcia a year earlier that I needed more beauty in my life. It struck me, there in the kitchen, that these kids had absolutely filled my life with beauty.

INVITATION
Sit comfortably on the floor or a chair, and place one hand on your belly and the other over your heart. Close your eyes and feel the breath move in your belly. What is the state of your heart? Is it soft, open, vulnerable? hard, closed, protected? Or is it hard to tell? Breathe with whatever you discover, noting that this is how things are right now, and making room for your experience.

JUNE 20

All he ever knew of her was who he saw every day. All I am is who I am every day. All anyone is to anyone is a series of days.

—CHARLES YU

I recently came across a study about a new treatment for couples when one partner is dealing with chronic pain. Mindfulness formed the core of the program: couples began with individual exercises, like meditation on the breath, before moving on to joint mindfulness practices. The first of these was mindful hand-holding, which I found quite touching (no pun intended). Couples also practiced listening fully to their partner, taking a breath with awareness before speaking to increase their ability to respond with compassion.

The other half of the treatment involved identifying deeply held values. In one of the exercises, participants considered what they would want their spouse to say about them on their wedding anniversary ten years in the future. They also looked for areas where their actions might not align with those values. For instance, we might want to be a caring partner but often find ourselves acting out of impatience. Additional work then focused on ways to increase the match between values and behavior. These mindful practices could be useful for any relationship.

INVITATION
Think about a relationship you value, whether it's one with a partner, child, parent, friend, colleague, or someone else. Choose one of the following to enact today:

- Mindful touch: for example, hugging your spouse with intentional awareness of the experience.
- Full listening: focusing as closely as possible on what the person is saying, their body language, and your mutual connection.
- Values clarification: ask yourself what you would want someone to say about you ten years from now. Does your answer suggest any changes you'd like to make in how you're living?

JUNE 21

The rose shadows said that they loved the sun, but that they also loved the dark, where their roots grew through the lightless mystery of the earth. The roses said: You do not have to choose.

—ROBIN MCKINLEY

Equanimity in the face of our struggles often comes from finding balance in opposing forces. Years ago I experienced a form of balance while practicing yoga, which embodies the marriage of tension and ease. We were in Malasana, a yoga squat, our butts sunk low between our legs, our hands together at the heart, our elbows pressed against the insides of the knees. I was feeling a lot of physical discomfort and felt that I had to get out of the pose—immediately! Just then, the teacher said, "You should be feeling pretty uncomfortable right now."

Instantly, I felt myself relax into the discomfort. It was okay. I could let my body experience the strain without having to escape it. My mind softened and my body continued to work as I experienced that union of opposites: tension and ease.

Even in the simple pose of sitting on the ground, we can experience opposition and balance. We can notice the weight of our bodies pressing down while our spines lift upward—a current of energy flowing between heaven and earth. We can hold our bodies in a way that balances tension and relaxation, neither slouching nor straining to sit up, coming into balance in both body and spirit.

INVITATION

Look for opportunities today to find ease in the balance of opposing forces. It might be something as simple as feeling your feet grounded on the earth as you walk and your head and shoulders lifting toward the heavens. Find your equilibrium as you move toward the harmony of opposites.

JUNE 22

I'm sure in your experiences in school, in applying to college, in picking your major, in deciding what you want to do with life, people have told you to make sure you have something to "fall back on." But I've never understood that concept, having something to fall back on. If I'm going to fall,...I want to fall forward. At least I figure that way I'll see what I'm about to hit. —DENZEL WASHINGTON

The year I was at Penn, Denzel Washington gave the commencement speech, from which today's quote is taken. I was struck by the philosophy—instead of playing it safe and having a fallback, act and risk falling forward.

Some of the best and most gratifying things in life involve taking a chance and being willing to fall. I pursued Emma when we were studying at St. Andrews, only to find out she wasn't interested in more than a friendship. Thankfully, after three months she came around and went on a date with me. Seth took a professional chance when he was unhappy but reasonably secure in his academic job. He's told me before that the transition to teaching and then to full-time clinical practice couldn't have been more rewarding. Friends have taken the chance together to have children, not knowing if it was even possible or how they would afford to raise a family or what it would mean to be parents. Falling forward is a risk, but it may open the door to great meaning and fulfillment.

INVITATION

I have no doubt there's something in your life that's worth trying, even at the risk of falling. Maybe it involves a professional move, a relationship, an athletic event, or something else. Why not take a chance and take the first step today?

JUNE 23

Even youths grow tired and weary, and young men stumble and fall;
but those who hope in the Lord will renew their strength. They will
soar on wings like eagles; they will run and not grow weary, they will
walk and not be faint.   —ISAIAH 40:30–31

When we decide to face a challenging task, we need something bigger than ourselves to fuel our efforts. The prophet Isaiah wrote about finding strength and stamina through trust in God. As legend has it, the Athenian runner Pheidippides ran twenty-six miles to alert his countrymen that their army had defeated the Persians at Marathon—all for love of country. After delivering the news, he died.

Civil rights leaders like Martin Luther King Jr. and Medgar Evers paid with their lives as they sought equality under the law for African Americans. Seth's ancestors fought a bloody war to secure freedom from England, as did Sir William Wallace in Scotland. In these cases and countless others, we're inspired to action in the service of something bigger than ourselves.

INVITATION

What are you serving beyond yourself that provides the passion to keep going when you feel like giving up? Take some time today to focus on what moves you, and to draw strength from that which is greater than you.

JUNE 24

In every end, there is also a beginning. —LIBBA BRAY

There's a sense of satisfaction that comes with endings, like completing a race, a workout, or a major project. We can step back and look at what we've done and appreciate the hard work that went into it. We can take a moment to finally relax after the effort.

Yet we may also feel a sadness. The joy I feel when a person "graduates" from therapy with me is laced with disappointment—disappointment that I'll likely never see them again, disappointment that I won't get to hear the rest of the story in which I played a fleeting role.

Everything ends. The best days and the worst nights will draw to a close. On the cold and starry Christmas Eve before our son Lucas's birth, Marcia had been in labor for more than a day but still had not progressed to the point where the hospital would admit her. Both of us barely slept for two nights. In the wee hours, I asked myself, *Why* did we think this was a good idea?

And then dawn came, and the sunrise had never felt so welcome. Marcia said, "It's time to go to the hospital." I grabbed our prepacked suitcase and we walked outside to the car through the crisp December air. About fourteen hours later, the pregnancy ended as Lucas took his first breath.

INVITATION

What's ending for you today? Maybe it's a project you've been working on for a while or a challenging workout or even a meal or your shower. Take a moment to reflect on how the ending feels and what it represents to you. What's on the other side of the ending? What begins?

JUNE 25

For where your treasure is, there will your heart be also.

—MATTHEW 6:21

O ur thoughts, feelings, and actions are closely related. By changing just one of these variables, we can change the others. When there's an action we want to take, we often wait until we feel ready. We might wait to give until we're feeling generous or wait to exercise until we're feeling motivated. But we might wait a long time if we're counting on our feelings to change. When we lead with behavior and invest our time or resources in a particular direction, our emotions tend to follow.

For example, when I was a doctoral student, I often needed to recruit research participants from among people waiting at the train station. I hated the idea of approaching them and would dread doing it as I sat in my office considering whether I should go. But once I was on my way, I invariably felt much less resistant. And once I was actually at the station, I was glad to be doing it.

We can embody actions that will fill our hearts with what we desire. We can give and feel more generous. We can exercise and grow to love it. We can hug and feel more loving. We can smile and feel more patient. We can give priority to time with our loved ones and feel how important it is. Through acts of service, we can develop a servant's heart.

INVITATION

What is one thing you've wanted to do but haven't had the heart? Maybe you've been waiting to feel sufficiently inspired. Take a definite step in that direction today, trusting that where your feet go, your heart will follow.

JUNE 26

He who has a why to live for can bear almost any how.
                                                    —FRIEDRICH NIETZSCHE

Recently, I undertook the challenge of running a sixty-nine-mile ultramarathon. I was hoping to raise awareness and money for a charity called Unite Against Cancer. The charity was set up in memory of Chris Smith, who lost his life to cancer in his midteens. Chris and my younger brother Cyrus were close friends. I have fond memories of them playing and joking together as children. One Halloween, I took them trick-or-treating in our neighborhood in exchange for 25 percent of their sweet earnings.

This ultramarathon route is one of the most scenic I've had the opportunity to run. Running across hills for hours on end with the sun pounding down is both grueling and exhilarating. At checkpoints and along the path, many runners end up dropping out as dehydration kicks in, injuries prevail, and the number of miles still to run becomes ever more daunting.

During the toughest moments, we all had to dig deep. I connected to the memory of Chris. I imagined his spirit flying alongside me as he encouraged me, smiling all the while. I thanked Chris for his loving support. The fascinating part was that these brutal times would pass, and then I'd enjoy deeply satisfying and appreciative moments of beauty and joy. The darkest and hardest phase was from mile sixty to mile sixty-eight. Remarkably, the easiest and most energetic part was the final mile. Late in the evening, as I stepped over the finish, Chris passed over with me.

INVITATION

Whatever you do today, remind yourself of your *why*. Connect to what is important. If it helps, draw on the support of family and friends, past or present.

JUNE 27

When you pray, move your feet. —AFRICAN PROVERB

There are many inspirational quotes about "charting your own course" and "following your dreams," and seemingly contradictory ones about "letting things come to you" and "releasing control." How can we distinguish between moving fearlessly toward our destiny and ego-driven striving toward an outcome we crave? If we're struggling toward a goal, when do we keep fighting and when do we accept that the universe is redirecting us?

In my own life, I had to reorient my career plan of being an academic psychologist. I was investing long hours, including nights and weekends, to write grant applications and research articles. Even so, I didn't feel that the articles really mattered, and reviewers rejected all my grant applications. I had to accept that my efforts were not paying off. It was time to pursue a different course.

We direct our efforts toward a goal, but we have to accept that the outcome is not under our control. We write our best grant applications, but the reviewers have the final say. We prepare for a job interview, but the manager decides who to hire. We train to run a race, but ultimately, it's not up to us whether we're able to finish. The distinction between effort and outcome can help us decide when to persist and when to change the plan.

INVITATION

Remember: the effort you put in toward your personal or professional goals is entirely in your hands. Also, keep in mind that your powers are limited. Find a sense of ease in these opposing forces as you extend yourself toward something you care about.

JUNE 28

Do not be daunted by the enormity of the world's grief.
Walk humbly now.
Do justly now.
Love mercy now.
You are not obliged to complete the work,
but neither are you free to abandon it.

—SHAPIRO

In the UK, there's a sense that we're living in turbulent times. Every few weeks, there seems to be another horrific tragedy that disturbs the nation. Two weeks ago, near where I work, a twenty-four-story tower containing public housing caught fire. Many people were unable to escape. Just over three weeks ago, a van drove onto the sidewalk along London Bridge, careening into pedestrians. The assailants wore fake explosive vests and attacked bystanders.

In our current society, news about acts of violence and loss of life are unavoidable, and the enormity of the world's grief can feel daunting at times. It would be easy to fall into hopelessness, fueled by the impression that our world is on the brink of ruin. It may provide little solace, but studies indicate that this may in fact be the most peaceful time in recorded history.

My wife often reminds me that every tragedy also holds tales of heroism. Strangers help one another; pedestrians risk their lives to protect others; communities fund-raise millions for the injured and the relatives of those who died.

When something tragic happens, perhaps what's most important is how we respond. We can turn inward and retreat from this world or we can try to do what we can to make it a better place.

INVITATION

Today, recognize any feelings of fear, worry, or pessimism. Feel them and take action nonetheless. Walk humbly now. Do justly now. Love mercy now.

JUNE 29

Think of all the beauty still left around you and be happy.
—ANNE FRANK

There are plenty of reasons to feel bad about what's happening in our world, including wars around the globe, violent terrorist attacks, senseless mass shootings, and widespread destruction of our environment. We need inspiration in these troubled times.

Whatever fears and uncertainties we face, we can choose to bring some beauty into the world. As rough as these times are, they're also filled with life and possibility. There is still love here. We can still find peace. Years ago I wrote to Elie Wiesel, a survivor of the Nazi concentration camps, to express my appreciation for his writings. In his reply letter, he wrote that, for him, despair was never an option. He chose hope and found ways to bring peace and beauty into the world in the years after his horrific experiences.

Bringing beauty into the world doesn't have to be grand or complicated. It might mean smiling at someone you pass on the street. It could involve cutting a flower and placing it in a vase on your counter. Maybe it's responding graciously when someone makes a mistake while driving. Recently, for me, it meant finally repairing the broken parts of our fence and arranging to have an overgrown corner of our garden cleaned up. Through small, simple actions, we can make our world more beautiful.

INVITATION

Plan two actions today that will bring beauty into your world. They could involve any of the senses, like the sight and scent of flowers, or the taste of a meal made with love. Find ways to brighten the world for yourself and others.

JUNE 30

Silence.
It has a sound, a fullness.
It's heavy with sigh of tree,
and space between breaths.
It's ripe with pause between birdsong
and crash of surf.
It's golden they say.
But no one tells us it's addictive.

—ANGELA LONG

A complete absence of sound in our daily lives is improbable. We live in a loud world. Some sounds are unwanted, like the screaming of children at the nearby table in the restaurant. Others are actively sought out, like the music or podcasts we might use to distract ourselves. We even have our own internal noise (talking to ourselves) and create external noise (for example, when Bruce Springsteen is playing on the radio and it's time to unleash our inner Boss).

Seeking pockets of quiet in our day can be a way to sink more deeply into the present moment. Through these moments, we can connect to the stillness and tranquility that exist within and around us. Research has shown that a two-minute quiet pause can reduce an individual's blood pressure and heart rate. We can find ways to cultivate moments of relative silence and peace by taking small actions throughout the day, such as silencing our phones or turning off the television, sitting quietly, and bringing our attention to our breath.

INVITATION

Today, explore what it's like to invite pockets of silence into your day. Complete noiselessness is virtually impossible. But there is often a space between sounds, whether between the thoughts in our heads, our in-breaths and out-breaths, or the cars that pass by in the night. Find the space between and see if you can experience the calm that rests there.

JULY 1

Let reality be reality. —LAO TZU

Our minds can terrify us with images of events that may never happen. My own terrifying visions often involve my children's safety. Earlier this week as I was walking home from work, I saw my family playing across the street. Our two-year-old, Faye, saw me and began running toward me, and the gate separating the park from the busy road was wide open. I love that Faye gets so excited to see me, but would she run into traffic? There was no way for me to get to her before she reached the road, and I held my breath for agonizing seconds as she approached the gate. *Please God, let her stop*. She did, just as she reached the gate.

At times, what we imagine can seem real. We may even feel the emotions we would expect if those things truly happened. In these moments, we can remind ourselves that these nightmarish images are creations of our minds—they don't exist in the real world. We can come back to reality, to what is here, to what we can see and hear and touch. We can return to earth, which, thankfully, is still mostly good.

INVITATION

Today, look for opportunities to ground yourself in the solid elements of this world, especially when the mind tries to pull you into imagined disasters. You might lay your hands on the bricks in a wall or lean against a door frame. You could rest your hands on a cold hard granite counter, or feel your feet pressing firmly against a wood floor. Reconnect with what's real.

JULY 2

Anything I cannot transform into something marvelous, I let go.

—ANAÏS NIN

Painful experiences can be the starting point of change. Those affected by adversity might act to promote awareness, make a positive difference, prevent future incidents, deal with their own loss, remember someone, or create a lasting legacy.

There may be events in your own history that you don't feel can be transformed. Painful parts of your past might creep into the present moment as thoughts, images, feelings, and emotions. What do we do with these pains? One option is to let go.

But how, you might be wondering, do we let go? The truth is, there is no magic formula. But here are a few strategies that can put you on the right track:

- Recognize the story that's causing the pain. While the tragic event has passed, our minds can replay thoughts about it. And it's these stories that cause the hurt, anger, or sadness now.
- Understand what's behind the story. Behind every story is at least one value. Behind anger might be the value of fairness, justice, or autonomy, which we feel has been violated. Seeing behind stories is a way to understand the way we feel.
- Decide to let the story go. We can easily fall into a trap of believing that we have no control over how much we invest in the stories that our minds relive. We have to consciously choose to let go.

We cannot undo the past. We can, however, make the best of the present.

INVITATION

Notice any pains or difficult emotions that arise today. See if you can recognize the story that is playing in your mind and any values that lie behind it. Is this story serving you or hurting you? Could it be time to let it go?

JULY 3

The ideal art, the noblest of art: working with the complexities of life, refusing to simplify.   —JOYCE CAROL OATES

Sometimes, we can let our disappointments color an entire experience. For instance, I recently took our kids on an outing in a state park while my wife was away. It was a beautiful day, and we were all excited as our outdoor adventure began. Then, during our prehike snack, my two-year-old, Faye, slipped off the picnic table bench where she was standing and slammed her head into the ground—an inauspicious beginning.

By the end of our walk through the woods, ninety minutes later, everyone was hot and exhausted. Faye needed to be carried; my six-year-old, Ada, was whimpering about the slimy mud inside her shoe; and my son Lucas was grouching at Ada to walk faster. The appearance of mosquitoes reminded me that bug repellent would have been a good idea, and then I remembered I'd forgotten to pack a diaper for Faye. *Boy, this turned out to be a mistake*, I thought.

Thankfully, something reminded me that there were also moments of beauty: the kids walking together on the trail, the toad we found, minnows swimming in the clear creek, sunlight sparkling on the water.

It's funny how our minds can reduce a rich and varied experience to a single up-or-down verdict. Was it a good trip or a bad trip? Is he a good person or a bad person? Are you a worthwhile human being? Most of the time, there is value in seeing complexity that defies simple categorization.

INVITATION

Today, look for complexity in what you bring to your world. Remember that missteps don't color everything about you. Be open to seeing the whole picture of who you are.

JULY 4

Let us celebrate the occasion with wine and sweet words.

—PLAUTUS

Happy Independence Day, friends! Since the eighteenth century, this day has been celebrated with parades, feasts, and fireworks.

There are major official and personal celebrations scattered throughout the year: birthdays, weddings, holidays, and other religious observances and secular events. These occasions provide opportunities to stop, reflect on the past, appreciate how far we've come, and look ahead to the future. They are a chance to celebrate the efforts, relationships, and achievements of the people closest to us.

The lovely part is that we don't have to wait for big events to celebrate. When my family gets together, whether it marks a special occasion or not, my dear mom calls it a "celebration of love and life." While this is now a family joke, my mom is a wise woman. Since being diagnosed with cancer, she's valued even more the joy and meaning that come from spending time together as a family. There's a clarity with which she sees what matters to her most.

INVITATION

Celebrate your own small successes as well as those of others. This could be as small as turning up for a meeting on time, fitting in a workout, or being patient or kind. Notice and enjoy the feeling as you connect to your successes and those of the people around you.

JULY 5

Many of us spend a lot of time looking at a screen, between work and social media and entertainment. There are obvious advantages to technology, like being able to communicate easily with people all over the world. But at the same time, when we're glued to our phones, tablets, and televisions, the view never really changes. Spending too much time in these activities can lower our mood and drain our spirits.

I've become more acutely aware of the cost of too much screen time during periods of depression. During these times, I often yearn to be outside using my hands. It's as though my mind and body know what I need, like working in my garden, hiking in the woods, preparing a meal, or building something tangible. Recently it was constructing a brick platform for our fire pit: digging out the sod, leveling and tamping the earth, covering the hole with a weed barrier, pouring in pea gravel, and placing two layers of bricks on top. Whatever our mood, we can nourish ourselves by spending time engaged in three-dimensional life, with all its textures, richness, and surprises.

INVITATION

What are your favorite parts of reality—parts you may not get to experience as much as you'd like? It could be anything: music, driving, walking, cooking, sitting, birding, hiking, etc. Can you make space today to find what feels real and feed your spirit?

JULY 6

We keep moving forward, opening new doors, and doing new things,
because we're curious and curiosity keeps leading us down new paths.
—WALT DISNEY

The main entrance of the British Museum in London resembles a Greek temple, with over forty huge columns and sculptures that depict the progress of civilization. As I sat outside in the central garden, I placed pencil to paper to sketch for the first time in over two decades.

When my friend invited me to sketch with him, the initial thoughts that arose in my mind were: *What's the point? You're not an artist. You don't know how to sketch. You'll be rubbish. It'll be embarrassing.* My mind wasn't far off. I was rubbish, but it wasn't embarrassing. We talked and laughed, and I sketched terribly. I loved it.

Trying a new activity or something that we've not attempted for some time opens up possibilities. It creates the opportunity to have fun, learn from others, surprise ourselves, develop our creative spirits, connect with strangers, deepen our friendships, build our sense of self-efficacy, bolster our confidence, and expand our identity in ways that we may not have previously considered.

INVITATION

Try something new or do something you haven't done in a long time. It could be completely random or an interest that you've harbored for years. Today is a chance to act on your curiosity and live with spontaneity and adventure! Don't worry about the outcome. This is all about the process.

JULY 7

It is a curious thing, the death of a loved one. We all know that our time in this world is limited, and that eventually all of us will end up underneath some sheet, never to wake up. And yet it is always a surprise when it happens to someone we know. It is like walking up the stairs to your bedroom in the dark, and thinking there is one more stair than there is. Your foot falls down, through the air, and there is a sickly moment of dark surprise as you try and readjust the way you thought of things.
                                                            —LEMONY SNICKET

We're rarely more conscious of what's precious to us than when confronted with the painful loss of death. I felt this recently when a friend of mine died. He and I had spent a lot of time together, though I'd seen him only a few times over the past couple of years. Our last communication was a text message exchange on Father's Day a few weeks ago.

It's disorienting when someone we know dies—how can they just stop existing? My friend's face continually comes to mind, triggering memories I haven't thought of in years: telling his family at the pool that we were expecting our first baby, seeing his new motorcycle, the way he would move his hands when telling a story.

Tragic losses underscore what we have, and often take for granted: life, friends, family, and love.

INVITATION

Reach out to someone you care about, whether it's someone you rarely communicate with or someone you see every day. Let them know you treasure their presence in your life.

JULY 8

Every day, think as you wake up, Today, I am fortunate to be alive. I have a precious human life. I am not going to waste it. I am going to use all my energies to develop myself, to expand my heart out to others, to achieve enlightenment for the benefit of all beings.

—DALAI LAMA

Big events often reorient our priorities. Through a wedding, birth, break-up, health scare, illness, injury, or death, we often come to realize, or remember, what matters most. After some time, we typically fall asleep again, seemingly forgetting the life-changing insights that struck us. The process of waking up begins once more.

We don't have to wait for disaster to strike in order to recognize the precariousness of life and appreciate the present moment. We can reawaken to whatever is most important to us on a daily basis. One way to do this is to connect to the breath: simply notice the abdomen rise and fall. Your breath can become a reminder that the gift of life is still with you.

INVITATION

The process of awakening will be unique to each one of us. In what ways today could you remember that life is precious? See if you can remind yourself at different points during the day that you are fortunate to be alive. Allow this realization to settle and move you in whatever ways seem most natural.

JULY 9

Physics depends on a universe infinitely centered on an equal sign.
—MARK Z. DANIELEWSKI

Our well-being in many areas depends on finding balance: being intimately connected to others without being engulfed, sticking to a routine that serves us well without being too rigid, working hard while allowing adequate time for rest and renewal. No matter what area we're addressing, learning to balance is closely tied to letting go. In a very literal sense, our physical balance improves when we let go, whether we're learning to bike, stand on one leg, or ice skate. Through letting go, our bodies learn to make microadjustments that keep us from toppling to one side or the other.

I've struggled in my own life to find balance, particularly in managing a recurrent health issue. I've tried many diets that were supposed to help and found endless opinions about the right approach—many of them with exactly opposite guidelines! I realized I was clinging to these authorities' recommendations even though they provided limited relief; there was some comfort in knowing I was "following directions." Finally, I decided I needed to trust my intuition, which felt a bit scary. What if I was wrong? I would have no one to blame but myself.

When we let go, we might fall, sometimes painfully, but every fall is an opportunity to learn. We can resolve in advance to get back up as we continue to find our center.

INVITATION
What can you let go of today to help yourself learn to balance? It could be practicing a balancing posture in yoga, trusting yourself at work or in a relationship, or something in any other life area. Look for opportunities today to find your equilibrium.

JULY 10

Accept—then act. Whatever the present moment contains, accept it…
Always work with it, not against it. Make it your friend and ally, not
your enemy. This will miraculously transform your whole life.

—ECKHART TOLLE

At different points in our lives, a major event can appear out of nowhere and create an overwhelming sense of uncertainty. It could be a financial crisis, finding out about infidelity in a relationship, losing a job, learning something unexpected about friends or family, or losing someone close to us. Our lives may be forced to change in ways we don't want. There can be a strong sense of unfairness and injustice, as the world seems to be doing something *to* us.

Rather than be swept away by our thoughts and feelings, we can temporarily stop, take slow, deep breaths, and check in with ourselves. It can be illuminating and liberating to be honest with ourselves on these occasions. Ask yourself,

- How am I feeling?
- What thoughts are dominating my mind right now?
- How do I feel in my body?

You might be experiencing uncomfortable bodily feelings: nausea, tension, or physical pain. See if you can stay with these feelings. In doing this, we often learn that the discomfort is unpleasant but bearable and that all sensations change. When you're feeling fragile, be gentle with yourself.

INVITATION

Notice whenever something doesn't turn out the way you expected it to. Take a moment to stop, step back, and check-in with yourself. Be courageously honest and see how you're feeling. From this new place of perspective, listen to your intuition as to what would be helpful for you right now and take action.

JULY 11

Nothing is worth diminishing your health. Nothing is worth poisoning yourself into stress, anxiety, and fear. —STEVE MARABOLI

We all need time to unwind. I often work with the people I treat on managing stress, and yet I was slow to accept the value of my own self-care. Early in my career, I took my mental and physical health for granted. I worked long hours, including nights and weekends. Eventually I gave up exercising to free up more time to work. I began to rely on alcohol to de-stress at the end of each day.

I didn't realize it at the time, but I was slowly and steadily draining my reserves as I started to dread my work. It came to a head on a bike ride one evening when I had a close call with a car that didn't see me. My first thought was, *Wow, they could've killed me*, and then I heard my mind say, *At least everything would've stopped.*

That got my attention. How had I reached a place where my own death didn't seem like such a bad thing? I realized what should have been obvious all along: that I'm human, and humans need downtime to recharge. It's kind of embarrassing that it took me nearly forty years to figure that out.

We don't have to wait until our health is seriously threatened before we tend to it. We can take care of ourselves proactively, finding ways each day to enjoy our lives and tend to our bodies, minds, and spirits.

INVITATION

Consider taking your well-being seriously as you think about the day you have ahead of you. What is one activity you could plan today to help reduce your stress level and nourish your well-being?

JULY 12

Out of suffering have emerged the strongest souls; the most massive characters are seared with scars. —KHALIL GIBRAN

When we have good mental health, it is easy to see mental illness as a sign of weakness or as the fault of others for not looking after themselves enough.

Our mental health is like a bucket. Pressures and stress from work, family, and other aspects of our lives are all water from hoses going into the bucket. What's happening in our lives influences the force and amount of water filling the bucket. If the bucket overflows, then we experience mental health issues, such as episodes of depression and anxiety.

Our self-care is the equivalent of scooping cups of water out of the bucket. The more we look after ourselves—with good nutrition, exercise, and rest—the less likely we are to become unwell. But just because others become unwell doesn't mean they're doing less to care for themselves than we are. The depth and width of the buckets we've been given vary. The size of our bucket depends on our genetic makeup and our early experiences as children, which are outside of our control.

When we're at work, the focus is often on productivity, efficiency, and output. The space for care can be squeezed out in order to try to maximize profit. The irony is that studies have shown that a happy and healthy workforce is a more productive, efficient, and profitable one! Whatever our goals or intentions, appreciating that mental health is a normal health issue and responding compassionately brings a multitude of advantages for all concerned.

INVITATION

Whether at work, with friends, or at home, practice empathy today. Be curious, listen, and understand another person's outlook and experiences.

JULY 13

How can I be substantial if I do not cast a shadow? I must have a dark side also if I am to be whole. —CARL JUNG

It can be easy to see people who are struggling, including ourselves, as fundamentally broken. Spells of anxiety, depression, or extreme stress can make it hard to find any enjoyment and lead to irritability and withdrawal. At these times, we may long to be ourselves, to be whole again.

But when I think about it more, I'm not sure *whole* and *broken* are necessarily opposites. I once heard a rabbi tell a story about a beautiful prayer book he received as a gift. He was furious when one of his young children drew in marker on one of the pages and angrily scolded the child. Years later, whenever he came across the page with the green scribbles, he said he saw it as "the holiest page in the whole damn book." What seemed to be damaged had in fact been consecrated.

The line we draw between being sick and being whole is a false distinction. Each of us is a complete individual, with interests, passions, loved ones, and dreams. At our lowest points, we can see ourselves and others as hurting rather than as defective. Instead of thinking of ourselves as sick, we can remember that we're healing.

INVITATION

However you feel today—well or sick, strong or weak, able or inept— remember that you are a whole human being. If you feel great, celebrate the feeling of being alive and the sense of vitality that animates you. If you're battling despair, remind yourself as often as you need to, "I am healing. I am whole."

JULY 14

Try something different. Surrender. —RUMI

As human beings, a whole suite of emotions is available to us, including happiness, sadness, fear, anger, surprise, and disgust. Throughout the week—and even within a single day—we will experience a range of feelings.

However we're feeling, there is deep wisdom in meeting ourselves at this place, wherever we are. Rather than feeling the pressure to immediately change how we feel, we can welcome these sensations. We can roll with them, like a surfer gliding on top of waves.

When I'm feeling very tired, I love the feeling of slowing down and going at the pace that feels right for my body. Even the speed at which I walk becomes slower and I use slower, deeper breaths to connect to my body. When feeling happy, there is a loveliness and splendor about cherishing that moment, holding it delicately like a flower and appreciating the fragrant scent that it gives off. If there are powerful feelings of frustration or disappointment, there is comfort, too, in accepting them.

Lightness can be brought by allowing ourselves to feel whatever is arising in that moment. No judgment, just kindness. No struggling, just peace.

INVITATION

Today meet yourself wherever you are. Welcome the sensations in your body as though you are greeting old friends. Allow them to arrive and leave of their own accord. Remember that all feelings pass. Notice any changes in tone or intensity. See if you can appreciate the diversity and colors of the different emotions you are experiencing in the present moment.

JULY 15

You will be your best self when you take time to understand what you really need, feel, and want. —DEBORAH DAY

We've all heard the invitation to "be where you are," focusing awareness in the present. Part of present awareness is accepting the reality of our current needs. Unfortunately, it can be hard to recognize what our minds and bodies are asking for. Part of the difficulty is that our needs change. What served us well at one time might not at another.

I had a conversation with an arborist once that underscored this point. When we bought our house, there was a small ornamental tree that was oddly positioned in our yard. I expressed my reluctance to remove it because we liked that variety of tree. He replied, "It's never going to be the right tree if it's in the wrong place."

In the same way, an activity is "right" only if it fulfills our current needs. We might enjoy certain technologies, for example, and then find that our relationship with them changes. I loved the first smartphone I got years ago, and then found that it was draining the life out of me; still, I struggled to curtail my use. Finally, I took what is probably considered a drastic step and traded it in for a "feature phone." I had worried I would miss my smartphone, but instead I felt liberated.

We can prioritize our well-being by asking ourselves what we need in order to be our best, listening for the answer, and acting on what we hear.

INVITATION

What would nourish you today? Is it adventure, a challenge, a break, a bath, communion with others? Prioritize what you need on this day, and release that which no longer serves you.

JULY 16

A mountain is the best medicine for a troubled mind.
—FINIS MITCHELL

At any point in the day, we can use parts of a mountain meditation to feel more grounded.

Whether you're standing or sitting, notice the parts of your body that are in contact with the chair, bed, or floor. Sense the support that is being provided. Tap into the flow of your breath as it finds its own relaxed and natural rhythm.

Now, imagine a magnificent mountain. See its edges and contours. Does it have a snowy peak, towering trees, sparkling waterfalls, or tumbling streams? Try to feel the qualities of the mountain: its raw strength, majestic stillness, and natural balance.

When you feel ready, see if you can bring this image into your mind and body, as though you and the mountain have become one. Absorb the positive qualities of the mountain as you sit or stand in harmony.

Bring your awareness to the thoughts and physical sensations in your body. Note how they come and go like clouds passing by the mountain, sometimes slowly and at other times more quickly. See how feelings can surge in intensity, like the rising sun, or simmer down, like the falling evening temperature. Whether ice melts or plants blossom, the mountain sits there and watches. The mountain is not the weather or the wildlife or the seasons. In the same way, you are not your thoughts or your emotions or your bodily feelings.

INVITATION

Try parts of the mountain meditation today. Whether you're enduring a violent storm of emotions or a gentle day of ease, see if there's a sense of stillness and peace with which you can connect.

JULY 17

That's what people do who love you. They put their arms around you and love you when you're not so lovable.   —DEB CALETTI

Images of mountains trigger different associations for each of us. When I was young, my dad would occasionally drive us up into the Trinity Alps of Northern California, the air gradually cooling and noise receding as we gained elevation. When we stepped out of the car, he invited us to listen to the stillness.

Mountains have punctuated my relationship with my wife too. In the summer after we graduated from college, we traveled to the mountains of Maine where we worked on the Appalachian Trail. Later that fall, Mount Desert Island became our home, where mountains look to the sea. It's there, on Dorr Mountain, that I want to have my ashes scattered when I die.

In recent years, I've become much more aware of what my dad must have gone through when we were young. He was still sorting through the aftermath of his own dad's suicide while working hard and raising five sons. Through my own struggles with depression, I now understand much better the lows he went through, the impatience and irritability at times directed at us, the yearning for peace in the midst of a storm. I think back to those drives into the mountains, standing in the cool of the forest, straining to hear what he heard. Now I know what I was listening for.

INVITATION

Bring to mind someone who loves you even when you're struggling. Show that person your love today, perhaps in words or through a warm embrace. Let this person know as best you can what it means to have them in your life.

JULY 18

I have come to know that [death] is an important thing to keep in mind—not to complain or to make melancholy, but simply because only with the honest knowledge that one day I will die can I ever truly begin to live.
                                                        —R. A. SALVATORE

L ast night out at supper, Emma and I played a game—one where we told each other what we think should be written on the other person's gravestone. It was more difficult than I imagined! It jumped out to me that Emma is much more than my life partner and soul mate. She is also a daughter, cousin, niece, granddaughter, colleague, friend, and perhaps one day, a mother herself.

As we drove home, we saw a very old couple walking up the mountain path together, arm in arm. We commented that it would be nice to be like them at their age. I felt a strong desire to live to be old and gray with Emma—to have the privilege of enjoying a long and full life with her. The strange truth is, of course, that I do not know if this will be the case. None of us knows what the future holds. All that matters is that we make the most of each moment, showing our love for and appreciating our time with the people in our lives.

INVITATION

If you learned that you only had a little time left on this earth, with whom would you want to spend it? What would you want them to know? What would you like to do? See clearly and feel what matters most to you. The blessing is that you still have the chance to weave what you know into the day ahead.

JULY 19

How often have I lain beneath rain on a strange roof,
thinking of home. —WILLIAM FAULKNER

All of us want a place that feels like home—a place that not only shelters us and those we care about from the elements but also provides refuge from the pressures and problems of the world.

Earlier this week my wife and I considered moving our family into a new home close to where we live now. It was somewhat bigger than our current house, with a lovely new kitchen, a large patio surrounded by beautiful landscaping, and was right next door to some of our very close friends.

When we decided not to make an offer on the house, I felt a deep appreciation for the home where we've lived now for nearly eight years. Two of our children were born during that time, and it's the only house our oldest remembers. Even more than for the house itself, I was profoundly grateful for the lives that fill it and make it truly a home.

The familiar tends to become invisible, whether it's our home or the people closest to us, and we stop noticing the richness that surrounds us. When we practice looking with fresh eyes, we can experience what's right in front of us.

INVITATION

Consider today the place where you live; what makes it home for you? Perhaps it's sharing the space with others, or if you live alone, it might be the touches you've added that make it your own. As you interact today with the space you inhabit—whether bathing, eating, dressing, working, or relaxing—take time to notice the specifics that make it yours.

JULY 20

Strange, isn't it? Each man's life touches so many other lives. When he isn't around he leaves an awful hole, doesn't he?

—IT'S A WONDERFUL LIFE

I n my early twenties, I trained as an actor. I was first cast for a role in a stage version of Frank Capra's 1946 Christmas classic, *It's a Wonderful Life*. You probably know the story: An angel takes a suicidal man called George Bailey on a journey to see life as it would've unfolded had George never been born. The angel opens George's eyes to the precious gifts in his life by showing him a world without those blessings.

A recent study named after the film investigated this premise. The researchers found that individuals reported more positive feelings when considering what life would be like had events for which they were grateful never occurred. The wonderful part is this: we don't have to wait for an angel to fly into our lives. Simply thinking about how the world might look had certain events never occurred can open doors of happiness and gratitude today.

INVITATION

Choose an event or part of your life for which you're grateful. Take a few minutes to think about the circumstances that led up to it. Now, think about all the ways in which this event might never have happened. Imagine what your life would be like without it.

Shift your attention to the present moment. Recognize that this event did occur and reflect on all the positive benefits that have arisen as a result. Repeat this process throughout the day, with as many events as you like, allowing feelings of gratefulness to flow through your body.

JULY 21

The opposite pole to narcissism is objectivity; it is the faculty to see other people and things as they are, objectively, and to be able to separate this objective picture from a picture which is formed by one's desires and fears. —ERICH FROMM

It can be exceedingly hard at times to really hear someone. We tend to be good at listening for what we expect to hear or for a chance to work in what we want to say—or at not listening at all. All too many conflicts are based on misunderstandings that arise from failing to listen.

This point seems self-evident, yet I often don't take the time to listen, especially to my kids. For example, I was recently getting my two-year-old ready for bed and she refused to let me brush her teeth. I immediately felt irritated and said, "You *have* to brush your teeth every night, Faye, even if you don't want to. Do you want your teeth to rot?" The more I insisted, the more she refused, until she started crying. Finally I asked her, "Faye, why don't you want me to brush your teeth?"

She replied that she doesn't like how the spray from the toothbrush gets on her face, so we decided she could cover her face with a cloth while I brushed. Such a simple solution—and all I needed to do was listen.

When we take the time to understand another person's point of view, we're in a much better position to work with them collaboratively.

INVITATION
Look for opportunities today to truly hear what another person is trying to communicate. Set aside preconceived ideas about what you'll hear and open up to what's in front of you.

JULY 22

If love is the treasure, laughter is the key. —YAKOV SMIRNOFF

After I left medical school and during my bachelor's psychology degree, I performed in improv comedy troupes. You might be familiar with the set-up from the program *Whose Line Is It Anyway?*, in which comedians improvise characters, scenes, dialogues, and songs on the spot based on the audience's suggestions. At the University of St. Andrews, we had weekly shows. We even performed at the Edinburgh Fringe Festival, where we were delighted with five-star reviews. The best part of the whole process, though, was the laughter.

There's a freedom and an electric aliveness in not having a script or safety net. Every moment is do-or-die. I learned that the key to the most moving and hilarious improv is giving full attention to your partner. Magic can arise from truly listening and allowing yourself to be affected by the other person's words and actions. Attempting to control the scene or the other performer simply produces something limp and contrived.

Life and laughter naturally flow out of spontaneity, acceptance, and presence.

INVITATION

Today, enjoy the gift of laughter! Be present and give yourself permission to be spontaneous! It's a wonderful life when you're laughing.

JULY 23

If you can eat with mates or friends or family, I mean, it's such a
brilliant thing isn't it?   —JAMIE OLIVER

Food facilitates connection. No wonder that a French word for "friend"
is *copain*: *co-* (together) plus *pain* (bread). We design meals to celebrate momentous occasions, like wedding feasts and holiday spreads.
Christians partake of bread and wine in the sacrament of communion,
while the Friday evening Shabbat meal ushers in the day of rest in the
Jewish tradition.

Of the thousands of meals I've eaten in my lifetime, a few stand out:
a special birthday dinner with my wife many years ago, the Thanksgiving
dinner we ate in the hospital the day after our middle child was born, and
the last time I ate with my grandfather before his death.

I've shared many meals with Aria over the years, none more memorable than dinner the night I arrived in Newcastle, England, for his wedding. Several of us staying at a retreat house gathered to eat around a large
wooden table, evening light pouring in through the windows. Our salmon
was deeply satisfying, and I was introduced to apple crumble with warm
custard. I've never felt more content while eating or more connected with
those around me.

The food we eat becomes our bodies and brains. It fuels every experience
and interaction. To share food with others is, fundamentally, to share life.

INVITATION

Today, allow food to be a vehicle that connects you to others—to those
who grow it, sell it, prepare it, and eat it with you. You might also think
back to meals you've shared that have been especially memorable and
meaningful.

JULY 24

Love is patient, love is kind. It does not envy. It does not boast, it is not proud. It does not dishonor others, it is not self-seeking, it is not easily angered, it keeps no record of wrongs. Love does not delight in evil but rejoices with the truth. It always protects, always trusts, always hopes, always perseveres. —1 CORINTHIANS 13:4–7

Recently Emma and I attended the wedding of two close friends. Weddings always remind me that the most important thing in life is love. Love has different faces: patience, kindness, respect, peace, protectiveness, trustworthiness, hope, perseverance, and many others.

You can love your partner, your parents, your children, your pet, your friends, your career, or some other passion or pursuit in life. Love is more than a feeling; it is also a commitment to give openly and generously. To love takes courage because whenever you open your heart, you open yourself to potential hurt and disappointment. It's extremely important to continue to take that risk because love is the foundation of a rich, meaningful, and fulfilling life. It truly is better to love fully than never to love at all.

INVITATION

Choose a word that describes an element of love—for instance, kindness. Let this be your directing force for the day. Bring your attention to your breath and imagine breathing in kindness and breathing out kindness. Check in to your breath and repeat this several times during the day. Allow love to guide you.

JULY 25

The life of every man is a diary in which he means to write one story,
and writes another.
                                                    —J. M. BARRIE

One of the most reliable ways to have a more fulfilling life is to live with greater intention. Unfortunately, our automatic reactions often lead us away from how we truly want to live. We might spend entire days—or even a lifetime—acting mindlessly and automatically in line with our conditioning.

Each of us has mindless habits that don't serve us well. I often stress myself out about being on time, like getting dinner on the table by six thirty, even when there's no real cost to being late. Recently I had a surprising moment of clarity when I was worried that our son would be late to his Saturday tennis camp. I had a vague sense it would be a very bad thing to be late.

And then I realized that the worst possible outcome was that the instructor might be a little annoyed, although even that was unlikely. On the other hand, I did know the costs of letting myself get stressed out: anxiety, tension, and irritability. By relaxing into what was happening, I avoided the tightening in my chest and throat that happens as the tension builds. I also spared those around me my impatience.

Without deliberate planning, we'll be disappointed by how we meet the day's challenges. Through greater awareness we can align our actions with the life we want and the person we want to be. Each day is a canvas waiting to be painted. Who holds the brush?

INVITATION
Bring greater intention to one challenging area. How can you plan to raise the odds of acting in ways you feel good about?

JULY 26

One of the most tragic things I know about human nature is that all of us tend to put off living. We are all dreaming of some magical rose garden over the horizon—instead of enjoying the roses blooming outside our windows today. —DALE CARNEGIE

We can fall into the trap of idealizing the future. We may think that we will be happier once we are ten pounds lighter, our house is bigger, our car is newer, or our bank balance is greater. We may chew on feelings of dissatisfaction and discontent right now because "things are not going as they should." Even though we may know it, we can frequently forget that research consistently shows that while a new car, bigger house, or job promotion might initially result in a peak of pleasure, we become accustomed to our new circumstances and our level of happiness typically returns to what it was beforehand.

Our dreams of a better life can tragically prevent us from enjoying the beauty that exists right here, right now.

INVITATION

Today, notice when your mind fantasizes about the future. While it can be motivating to have goals and move toward them, be aware of the possibility that comparing your current situation to an imagined rosier future can leave you feeling deflated. Explore what happens when you think of the future as a blank canvas waiting to be painted. Turn your attention to the present moment and note three good things about your current situation.

JULY 27

Worry does not empty tomorrow of its sorrow, it empties today of its strength. —CORRIE TEN BOOM

Worry is an interesting process. When we can't control an unknown outcome, we're prone to engage in mental activity that gives us some illusion of control. So, though it may feel like the same thing as anxiety, worry is actually an attempt to cope with our fear of uncertainty.

And yet, worry isn't worth what it costs. Almost everything we worry about turns out fine—and not because we worried. What's more, worrying fuels anxiety because we can't mentally manage an unknown future when uncertainty is woven into the fabric of life.

The antidote to the excessive mental activity of worrying is not more mental activity. Nor is it trying to reassure ourselves that everything will be fine. The antidote is letting uncertainty be. It can be hard at first, but in the end, we'll feel less anxious when we stop trying to make sure things will work out. The mental grip will loosen even though we don't know for certain that things will be okay.

INVITATION

When you notice the mind trying to worry something into being okay, can you interrupt the process and deliberately lean into the unknown? You might say to yourself something like, "I can't completely control the future—I'll just have to see when I get there." It will take practice doing this before you find any relief. Stick with it! You can break the grip of worry.

JULY 28

It's just about being you and being cool with that. And I think when you're authentic, you end up following your heart, and you put yourself in places and situations and in conversations that you love and that you enjoy. You meet people that you like talking to. You go places you've dreamt about. And you end up following your heart and feeling very fulfilled.
—NEIL PASRICHA

Accepting ourselves doesn't mean that we think we're perfect individuals. Accepting ourselves is not egotistical or narcissistic. Accepting ourselves is not an absence of progress. Accepting ourselves equates to being okay with who we are. We can see both our strengths and our flaws. We can sit with our quirks and idiosyncrasies.

The inherent irony is that we cannot change what we do not accept. Acceptance therefore creates fertile ground for growth. It is the unexpected fertilizer of personal development. There is a natural flow to this way of living.

When we're authentic, we acknowledge and accept who we are. We're more likely to follow our passions and intentionally choose meaningful and rewarding activities with people whose company we enjoy. We can even act in line with our valued goals despite our fears and anxieties. We still grow, adapt, and progress. But taking action becomes for us a matter of preference rather than of need. We're happy with where we are, and we're also enjoying making progress.

INVITATION

Take a few moments to recognize your unique personality, qualities, and quirks. Simply be yourself throughout the day! Enjoy the release and relief of knowing that you are enough just the way you are. See where this takes you, and have fun along the way!

JULY 29

When I fully enter time's swift current, enter into the current moment with the weight of all my attention, I slow the torrent with the weight of me all here. —ANN VOSKAMP

One of the most important parts of accepting who we are is accepting *where* we are. We often look ahead to what's next, feeling that we should be there already. I noticed this tendency during our recent travels to Kansas City for a family wedding. At each leg of our journey—car, bus, moving walkway, plane, bus, car—I had a feeling that we needed to be *there*, at the next step. Yet each stage had its rightful place. Whatever step we were taking at the time was the only one we could and should have been taking just then.

Traveling is a good metaphor for life. How often do we tell ourselves we should be somewhere other than where we are? Thinner, stronger, richer, healthier, more patient, more loving, more successful—the list goes on. It may be a constant mental refrain we don't even put into words—more a general sense of discontent, of restlessness.

Sometimes we're afraid that accepting where we are will lead to stagnation, which doesn't have to be the case. When I accepted that we were in the airport, I didn't drop my bags and tell the family, "We're here! Now we live at the airport!" No, being where we are means inhabiting this step of the process, even as the journey continues to unfold.

INVITATION

When you have the feeling today that you should be somewhere else, whether literally or metaphorically, consider this simple three-word response: "I am here." Whatever your expectations, whatever your goals, you are here. See how it feels to fully inhabit where you are.

JULY 30

Friendship is the only cement that will ever hold the world together.
—WOODROW WILSON

Happy International Friendship Day! The United Nations named this day to mark the spirit of human solidarity.

In 1998 Nane Annan named Winnie the Pooh as the world's "Ambassador of Friendship." In honor of this, here are three Winnie-related ideas about friendship.

1. Like honey for Winnie, friendships make us happy! Having close relationships is one of the strongest predictors of happiness.

2. Winnie once said that rather than sitting in the forest waiting for others to reach out to you, sometimes you have to make the first move. It can be easy to sit back, expect others to call us and chide those who haven't been in touch. We forget that the other person could apply the same thinking to us! Friendship involves putting our egos aside and connecting to the people we care about.

3. Winnie often gave others the benefit of the doubt. If a friend didn't appear to be listening, Winnie would wonder if he might have a piece of fluff in his ear! Rather than jumping to conclusions about others being uncaring, he remembered that there may be external factors at play. We often don't know what others are going through. If we did, we would probably find it easier to be patient.

INVITATION

Today, celebrate friendships!

Here are a few ways to do this:

- Tell your friends how much they mean to you
- Reach out to an old friend
- Be open to making new friends
- Post a photo with friends on social media
- Dedicate a song to a friend on the radio

The gesture can be as big or as small as you wish.

JULY 31

*Above all, love each other deeply, because love covers over a
multitude of sins.* —1 PETER 4:8

Nothing in this life matters more than our relationships. Good ones
will relieve at least as much pain as bad ones create. As I look back
on more than twenty years of marriage, I can see how love has kept Marcia
and me bound together through major heartaches and petty squabbles. It
feels miraculous that we've weathered them all. And we've done it through
the grace of a force stronger than either of us: the power of love.

Love is real and honest and sometimes raw and painful. It requires us
to grow—and to keep growing. And it's much more than a feeling—to
love means to act. Love compels us to extend ourselves again and again for
the ones we care about.

Many emotions can threaten our closest connections—fear, anger,
grief, hurt, envy, bitterness—yet love is stronger than all of these. By
meeting others in love, we can transform our individual pain into compassion. When we step into love's current, feeling it around us and in us,
we can forgive, we can heal, and we can grow together and not apart.

INVITATION

When do you feel most loved, and when do you feel most loving? Take
a moment to sit in stillness and close your eyes. As you breathe in, allow
yourself to open to love—to receiving love, to feeling loved. As you
breathe out, allow the love to flow out of you toward others. Breathe in: *I
am loved.* Breathe out: *I love.* Return to this practice throughout the day
as often as you like.

AUGUST 1

Clothe yourselves with compassion, kindness, humility, gentleness, and patience. Bear with each other and forgive one another if any of you has a grievance against someone. Forgive as the Lord forgave you. And over all these virtues put on love, which binds them all together in perfect unity. —COLOSSIANS 3:12–14

Physical appearance is important to most people. We spend a huge amount of money and energy trying to achieve a certain look—going to the hairdresser, regularly exercising, buying make-up, having nails done, buying clothes even when there's no more wardrobe space. We take the time to decide what to wear each day, particularly on special occasions. We choose the colors and combinations that make us feel good, are appropriate to the situation, and represent who we are. Saint Paul encourages us in his epistle to the Colossians to do the same with our values.

What values make you and others feel good? What values are appropriate for the situation and represent who you are? If you need some ideas, compassion, kindness, gentleness, and patience could be a solid place to start. And when we don't treat others the way we would like to, or others don't act the way we would hope, perhaps forgiveness is the way forward.

INVITATION

Consider what values you'd like to have represent you today. The wonderful thing is that this is up to you! See if you can enjoy the process as you decide what to wear on the inside as well as the outside.

AUGUST 2

The reason many people in our society are miserable, sick, and highly stressed is because of an unhealthy attachment to things they have no control over.
        —STEVE MARABOLI

I t's hard to let go of control—control of how someone treats us, of the outcome of our efforts, of scary medical possibilities, or of any other unknowns. We want things to work out the way we hope they will and don't like to imagine our ultimate powerlessness over outcomes we care about.

On our recent trip to a family wedding, I had to remind myself over and over that most of the things I was worrying about were not under my control: how long it took us to get through security, whether the next bus to the parking lot would have enough room for all of us, if our fellow riders were annoyed at how long it took us to load and unload, or even if the planes landed safely.

One thing we do have control over is where we place our attention. Without awareness, attention might seize around a worry and crowd out other things, including the love we want to show those around us. But we can wake up to what we're doing and let go of control that was never ours to begin with. By attending to the present, we're able to connect with others in a more meaningful way.

INVITATION

"I let go of that which I cannot control"—what would happen today if you made this statement your mantra? You can repeat it anytime you find yourself trying to force reality to bend to your will. Allow yourself to let go of a false sense of control.

AUGUST 3

Make the best use of what is in your power, and take the rest as it happens. Some things are up to us and some things are not up to us.

—EPICTETUS

Throughout history, sages with varying philosophical and religious backgrounds have spoken about control in everyday living.

In the eighth century, the Buddhist monk Shantideva asked, "If there's a remedy when trouble strikes, what reason is there for dejection? And if there is no help for it, what use is there in being glum?"

Around three hundred years later, the Jewish philosopher Solomon ibn Gabirol proclaimed that "at the head of all understanding is realizing what is and what cannot be, and the consoling of what is not in our power to change."

Perhaps the most well-known version echoing this sentiment is the Serenity Prayer by Reinhold Niebuhr: "God, grant me the serenity to accept the things I cannot change, courage to change the things I can, and wisdom to know the difference."

A recent study found that those with the greatest well-being changed their way of thinking about a situation depending on the level of control they had over it. When faced with lower controllability, they tended to shift the way they and dealt with the situation—for instance, toward finding silver linings. When a situation was more controllable, they reappraised less. Flexibility with the strategies we use appears to be central to our wellness.

INVITATION

If you're feeling frustrated, upset, or stressed about a situation, pause for a moment. Judge how much control you actually have in this instance. Is it time to change your outlook or to act and change the situation?

AUGUST 4

All that is important is this one moment in movement. Make the moment important, vital, and worth living. Do not let it slip away unnoticed and unused.   —MARTHA GRAHAM

S ometimes it can feel exquisite simply to move—to stretch, to bend, to kneel, to twist, even to stand. There are benefits to mindful movement besides the sheer pleasure of it, like avoiding senseless injuries from moving awkwardly. A little bit of awareness can go a long way.

Practices like yoga can help our minds tune into what our bodies are doing. Years ago I took a yoga class with my younger brother. Toward the end of the class, we were standing side by side in Warrior II, one of my favorite poses: front knee bent, back leg straight, torso upright, arms extended front and back. Before we transitioned to our next pose, the instructor told us to be aware of the sensation of *preparing* to move our arms before we actually moved. This simple instruction taught me that we can access a deeper connection with our physical experience than we may be accustomed to in our typical rushing-and-doing mode.

Thankfully we don't have to limit our awareness of movement to times we're on a yoga mat. We can bring greater presence to our body at any time, even right now.

INVITATION

Take an upright posture either sitting or standing. Turn your palms face up and breathe in as you lift your arms as high as is comfortable. Feel the movement. Turn your palms over and lower your arms as you exhale, again with a conscious awareness of the sensations. Do this five times. Throughout the day, look for opportunities to reconnect with your body and all the ways it moves.

AUGUST 5

Above all things physical, it is more important to be beautiful on the inside—to have a big heart and an open mind and a spectacular spleen.
—ELLEN DEGENERES

We all have different relationships with our bodies. There may be some parts that you like and others that you like less or even dislike. Western societies pay homage to physical beauty and build multibillion-dollar industries on "improving" looks. The sad, inherent message is this: Right now we are not enough. We are inadequate and maybe even unworthy.

Part of leading a happier life may include becoming conscious of external cultural and societal pressures. By noticing the messages that bombard us, we can recognize beliefs that we've unwittingly internalized. We can develop greater awareness of the unrealistically high expectations we hold or the abuse we hurl at ourselves for being the way we are. With this realization, we can try to extend to ourselves a little bit more love, compassion, forgiveness, and acceptance. We can tap into what is most important in our lives and let our values lead the way.

INVITATION

There may be parts of your body with which you are dissatisfied. Today, try to show a little love and kindness to these parts. If you notice your mind making harsh comments, see if you can offer a compliment instead. If you're feeling down about any way you look, ask yourself what really matters, what values are important in your life. See if you can connect with these values and extend them to the way that you act and feel toward yourself.

AUGUST 6

A sense of life meaning ensues but cannot be deliberately pursued: life meaning is always a derivative phenomenon that materializes when we have transcended ourselves, when we have forgotten ourselves and become absorbed in someone (or something) outside ourselves.

—IRVIN D. YALOM

People often come to me for therapy because something is getting in the way of what's most important to them. Maybe the daily press of life has led them away from what they really care about, or the things that gave them a sense of meaning and purpose no longer do so. I've certainly been there myself—a crisis of meaning led me toward mindfulness-based living.

Still, I'm not exactly sure what it means to say that "life has meaning." We all die in the end, and any influence we have will certainly be erased with the passage of time. Eventually the earth will be swallowed by our sun's expansion into a red giant, and it will be as though life as we know it had never happened. Where's the meaning in that?

And yet countless people I've worked with have shared with me the local meaning they find in their lives—usually nothing grand—and it's heartbreakingly beautiful. It's found in the experience, in the living and breathing and sharing and doing and being. More often than not, the question of what all this is *for* simply fades into insignificance, eclipsed by a felt awareness of what it is to walk this earth for a few short years alongside those we love.

INVITATION

What can you do today that you would love? Finish a big project? Spend time connecting with someone you care about? Do something nice for someone in your life, even yourself? Allow yourself to feel what it's like to connect to what you value.

AUGUST 7

The eternal stars shine out again, so soon as it is dark enough.
                                            —THOMAS CARLYLE

The dark, forbidding clouds loomed above us. Intense shades of gray blanketed the skies, hiding the sun and any hints of blue. As we ran down the side of the mountain, loose rocks and stones gave way underfoot.

It was then that misfortune struck. The scene played out in front of me in slow motion as my running partner fell to the ground. A severe twist tore the ligaments in his left ankle. The injury looked excruciating.

Once the pain had settled enough, we strapped up his ankle with a bandage from the emergency kit in his rucksack. We had another two miles to travel before we'd reach the closest village. There was certainly no mobile phone reception in the vicinity.

The journey was slow and exceedingly painful for my partner. What struck me was his reflection that it could have been a lot worse: we could have been even farther away from help; he could have been on his own; his ankle could have broken; he could have been at the side of the ridge and toppled over the edge. Despite the pain and unexpected end to our run, there was an underlying feeling of relief and gratitude. There were silver linings around the dark clouds that still loomed above us.

INVITATION

The day ahead may bring challenges, rewards, joy, and even unexpected pain! Whatever unwelcome events you face today, ask yourself in what ways could the current moment be worse? You might find that gratitude exists in even the most unexpected places.

AUGUST 8

When you're lost and you're alone and you can't get back again,
I will find you darling and I will bring you home.
And if you want to cry, I am here to dry your eyes.

—SADE

We all know the most important thing in life is the people around us, and then there are times when we feel it acutely. I recently spoke to the mother of a childhood friend who'd had a serious medical diagnosis. She told me she couldn't imagine making it through this ordeal without the loving support of her husband and friends.

I know that sentiment well. Over the weekend I had had a return of fatigue and depression, and I was able to talk through my frustrations on a Sunday walk with my wife. It's hard to describe how good it felt to have someone supportive to open my heart to. Afterward, it felt like I'd ridden out a storm that had left behind a deep sense of peace, even as I was still in pain.

We all face major challenges in our lives—maybe even right now—like a health crisis, the loss of a loved one, or losing a job. Hopefully, there is someone at those times that we can turn to for emotional and practical support—someone who can make things okay even when they aren't. And inevitably there will be times when we can be that person for someone else.

INVITATION

As you look back on your life, who has helped you through the biggest challenges you've faced? Notice any feelings of gratitude as you consider what it meant to have their support. Allow that feeling of gratitude to radiate into your interactions with others today. You could make all the difference in someone's life.

AUGUST 9

We rise by lifting others. —ROBERT G. INGERSOLL

Our relationships can be a source of light and courage in bleak and troublesome times. We can rise out of the darkness through love, by receiving *and* giving it.

When I was in my late teens, my father was diagnosed with advanced cancer. The prognosis was poor. Doctors told us that the probability of him surviving more than six months was slim. It felt as though a rug had been pulled from under my feet. The possible loss was like a blow to my stomach. Hope for a bright future seemed to drain from my thoughts like sand passing through the neck of an hourglass.

My younger brother unknowingly came to my rescue. I moved back home to help out. The responsibility to look after him was what helped most. Getting him up in the morning, making him breakfast, dropping him off and picking him up from school, assisting with homework, and playing together provided a sense of normality, certainty, and structure. The love that I was giving and receiving was the air in my life jacket.

Pulling through emotional challenges is undoubtedly easier when we have someone else by our side.

INVITATION

Show your love to someone who would support you right now if you needed it. See if you can choose a specific action, like calling them or buying them some flowers. If you can't think of anyone, perhaps it's time to consider who that person could be, reach out to them, and build a strong relationship based on receiving and giving love.

AUGUST 10

Suffering has been stronger than all other teaching, and has taught me to understand what your heart used to be. I have been bent and broken, but—I hope—into a better shape. —CHARLES DICKENS

Suffering is part of what it means to be fully alive and fully human. While we can't escape pain and disappointment in this life, we can share it with others.

I recently sat with a couple in my office, the wife there to support her husband. I felt tears in my eyes as I witnessed the love between people who had shared a life. My patient's wife described how much she had depended on him throughout their relationship, and how happy she was now to return the favor.

And yet her husband felt guilty for hurting and needing to lean on his wife, which was a sentiment I could relate to. We forget that because difficulties are an inextricable part of life, all of us need extra love and encouragement at times. For example, Marcia reminded me recently of how I helped her through our difficult years of trying to have a baby.

We often think we're experiencing something extraordinarily unfair when we go through difficult times, yet they are an inextricable part of life. The Buddha spoke at length about suffering. Similarly, Jesus promised, "In this world you will have trouble." Even if there's nobody by our side to offer support, there are countless others in this world who are suffering too. We never truly suffer alone.

INVITATION

Consider for a few moments all the other people in this world who are suffering in some way, including individuals you know. Whatever your current situation, breathe with awareness as you connect with them in that shared human experience.

AUGUST 11

When everything seems to be going against you, remember that the airplane takes off against the wind, not with it. —HENRY FORD

D ifficult periods in our lives can be distressing and bewildering. When we get knocked down, it can take time and huge effort to find a way to stand back up.

Some people come through challenging periods with a greater sense of meaning in their lives. Post-traumatic growth might involve seeing yourself as stronger and wiser, developing a profound appreciation for being alive and for your close relationships, and learning that you can endure traumatic events and emotional pain.

The potential for positive change is something that's unlikely to come from others. Trying to encourage someone else to "see the bright side" or "find that silver lining" can cause more harm than good. This type of growth comes from within, from personal insights that might arise suddenly or develop over time.

I wonder if we can help ourselves now, though, by recognizing some of our strengths, reflecting on how we've come through challenges already, and being open to the possibility that we can grow through the bad times and the good.

INVITATION

Looking back over your own troubling times, in what ways have you grown since then? Consider your relationships, how you feel appreciation, your personal courage, your spirituality or religion, or your sense of possibility. See if you can recognize your positive qualities and the strength that is deep within.

AUGUST 12

Like all magnificent things, it's very simple. —NATALIE BABBITT

Times of deep contentment tend to involve simplicity, yet many of us create lives that are hectic and cluttered. I once spoke with a young man who had a very promising career ahead of him in finance. He described being drawn to the outward signs of success—a mansion, fancy cars, lavish trips—but feared that the stress and anxiety from work would be unmanageable. He longed for a simple life but worried for his financial security and about others' perceptions of his success.

Simplicity can seem insignificant, even boring. But when we have time to really notice our everyday experiences, we might be amazed, as I was yesterday morning. I had lowered an egg into simmering water and was mesmerized by how the bubbles moved around the shell. There was something perfect about the clear water enveloping the brown egg in the silver pan. I felt like I could stare at it for the full five minutes I was letting it cook.

Even in our busy lives, we can discover moments of connection with the ordinariness of our everyday experience. Anything we truly perceive can be breathtaking—the line where a wall meets the ceiling, a ripe tomato growing on the vine, the weight of an apple, the feel of our child's hand in ours. Simplicity can be spectacular.

INVITATION

Look for opportunities today to dwell in simplicity. It could be anything—noticing and appreciating a simple food, really experiencing an object with your senses, feeling your body as it moves, fully seeing another person. Perhaps you can find rest in that place.

AUGUST 13

Success in life means living by your values. —RUSS HARRIS

I have an affinity for simplicity. Freedom from complication can bring an ease of being. It seems ironic that sometimes we need to find creative ways to make our lives simpler. As E. F. Schumacher stated, "Any intelligent fool can make things bigger, more complex, and more violent. It takes a touch of genius—and a lot of courage—to move in the opposite direction."

In the final few months of writing my doctoral thesis, increasing amounts of my time, energy, and attention were dedicated to the project. Despite working longer than usual, there was a loveliness and freshness about focusing on a single endeavor. Most of my efforts and actions were aligned, bringing a feeling of simplicity.

Simplicity can come in many forms: having less, doing less, thinking less. But it can also involve being extremely active and productive, as we move in the direction of our most valued goals and dreams.

INVITATION

Identify the values behind your actions. If you're making breakfast for your children, you might be tapping into love, responsibility, or care for others. If you're doing exercise, you may recognize the importance of health or living longer to be with your family. At work, the values that are important may differ. They will be unique to you. As you become aware of the values behind your actions, see if you notice a simplicity that is present: the simplicity of being guided by your values, whatever you happen to be doing.

AUGUST 14

It took a world of trouble, took a world of tears.
It took a long time, to get back here.

—TOM PETTY

There's peace in finding a close connection to what's most important to us. Yet if you're like me, it's easy to drift away from what you value. We may start with a clear-eyed intention about where we want to focus, and then drift away from that intention or add unnecessary layers to our lives.

In recent weeks I've felt strongly that the only question that really matters in my life is this: Have I shown love?—talk about simplicity! Then my mind gets pulled in familiar directions: *What if I'm not feeling well tomorrow? What if that gets in the way? What if I don't get everything done?* When I'm connected to my basic sanity, I can remember that nothing else is important. I always have the option to show love.

There's something profound about coming full circle and rediscovering our long-held fundamental values. The ones I'm reconnecting with have inspired me throughout my professional life—indeed, they inspired me long before I knew I wanted to be a psychologist. The solid ground of our values is always present, even when we're not consciously aware of it. When we're feeling scattered or unsure or afraid, we can return to that foundation. We can come home.

INVITATION

As you look back on your life thus far, what have you held most dear? Where do you find the greatest sense of meaning and of transcending yourself? Today, consider ways to come home to your values and intentions, dwelling in those things that make your spirit expand.

AUGUST 15

We can't help everyone. But everyone can help someone.

—RONALD REAGAN

As a child, I was extremely shy and quiet. I was less confident than most children my age, but I loved to laugh with others. Little, laughing, quiet Aria found it difficult to express himself vocally. On a couple of occasions, when I had finally built up the courage to speak up and tell a story, I noticed others shifting their attention away from me. This could have been for any number of reasons, but the one I took to heart as a child was that I was uninteresting. I learned that my stories were boring and that my opinions weren't as important as others'.

Over the years, different people have helped me find my own voice. A momentous occasion for me was performing as an improv comedian in a sell-out, five-star show at the Edinburgh Festival Fringe, the largest arts festival in the world. Comedy improvisation forced me to speak up in front of others and gave me the great pleasure of making others laugh.

I'll always be grateful for those who have supported me in my journey. I've also come to realize that I'm happiest when I'm making a positive difference in others' lives, even if it's simply by making them laugh. Contributing value to the lives of others imbues our own with value.

INVITATION
See if you can connect with and act on the value of helping others. Be the reason someone else smiles today.

AUGUST 16

Thou know'st 'tis common; all that lives must die,
Passing through nature to eternity.

—WILLIAM SHAKESPEARE

Life is uncertain. Yesterday evening on my way home from work, I discovered a man lying facedown in his garden and knew something was terribly wrong. When he was unresponsive, I called 911; an EMT came on the phone and gave me calm, firm instructions: "Check his breathing. Roll him over. Place the heel of your palm on the center of his chest, your other hand on top of it. Now give hard, fast compressions, about two per second. Don't stop until we get there and take over."

I kept pumping his chest, but his color was all wrong, and he showed no signs of life. Soon I heard sirens approaching. A minute later the emergency teams arrived. A small crowd gathered to see what all the flashing lights were about.

There were still no signs of life fifteen minutes later as they loaded him into an ambulance. I found his broken glasses and asked an officer if they wanted to take them with him to the hospital; he said it wasn't necessary. I learned later that the man was pronounced dead at the ER.

Earlier in the week, I'd said hello to this person in passing. I couldn't have known it would be the last time I'd see him alive. I like to think he died doing something that brought him joy—he was still wearing his gardening gloves as they took him away.

INVITATION

Today why not feast on life? Once we're gone, this world will go on without us in almost exactly the same way, just as it did before we arrived. Feel what it's like today to fully inhabit this life. This is your time.

AUGUST 17

Wake up and live! —BOB MARLEY

There is a tenderness and fragility to life that we seem to lose sight of most of the time. Losing someone close to us can be a sobering reminder of this.

If you're reading this, then you have another chance.

You have the chance to wake up to whatever you're taking for granted.

You have the chance to see the magnificence that exists all around.

You have the chance to remember all the wonderful qualities of your partner, brother, sister, mother, father, child, cousin, or friend.

You have the chance to remember what life is really about and what truly matters to you.

You have the chance to breathe, take in the world, and act in whatever way you choose.

INVITATION
Wake up and live today.

AUGUST 18

Beauty is life when life unveils her holy face.
But you are life and you are the veil.

—KAHLIL GIBRAN

We often take for granted the people we see all the time until something sharpens our ability to appreciate them. When my six-year-old woke up recently feeling unwell and then vomited blood, I became acutely aware of how much I appreciated Ada and her health. But over the coming days, I found it virtually impossible to sustain that heightened awareness and I returned to my baseline feelings of love mixed with occasional irritation.

Yet there are moments of full awareness that surprise us. A couple of days ago I was sitting in the living room with the rest of my family. Suddenly I saw beyond my normal seeing and was astonished by the high-lights in Lucas's blond hair as he sat next to me. I took in Ada's handsome face and look of concentration as she read. I saw Faye's big blue eyes and sweet smile. I felt the love that Marcia gives to these children. And I felt in my own eyes tears of amazement.

It's hard to be amazed without giving ourselves opportunities for presence, to look and hear and feel. At the same time, we can't deliberately create these experiences, which is part of what makes them amazing. What we can create, however, are the conditions that make space for being stunned. By opening to what's already with us, we can find magic in our everyday lives.

INVITATION

Make a point today to notice the people you see regularly. Notice the color of a person's eyes, the way they move their hands, their facial expressions. Allow yourself to be with someone just as they are, taking in all of them. Make room for amazement.

AUGUST 19

The key to creating health is figuring out the cause of the problem and then providing the right conditions for the body and soul to thrive.

—MARK HYMAN

I feel less happy, grounded, and confident when a lot of things in my life seem out of my control. Sometimes I find it useful to make sure the small things are in order, such as the tidiness of my office. By taking control of this and having a clear space in which to think, I feel as though I'm in a better place to prioritize and tackle my commitments. This is a very literal illustration of shaping the conditions in which we can flourish.

This week two of my clients had a similar insight. They are two very different individuals in very different circumstances and are experiencing very different problems. Yet both said they've come to realize that one of the most helpful strategies in their lives is to "stop and think." Rather than be driven by automatic thoughts and emotional responses that tie them to unhelpful ways of behaving, they've each found value in simply stopping—stopping what they're doing and thinking consciously—and asking themselves what's important in that moment, if this is a balanced way of seeing the situation, if there's another way of viewing it, or what they can be thankful for in their lives right now.

INVITATION

Stop and consciously consider what aspects of your day contribute to your good health—such things as the following:

- Sleeping for a certain number of hours each night
- Having a specific pattern of eating
- Making room in your day for certain activities
- Spending time with particular people
- Responding to your mind's thoughts with compassion
- Allowing yourself the time to just be

Choose one and create that condition today so that your body and mind can thrive.

AUGUST 20

The purpose of life is to live it, to taste experience to the utmost, to reach out eagerly and without fear for newer and richer experience.
—ELEANOR ROOSEVELT

The daily grind of work and other responsibilities can wear us down, and we need to refresh our spirits. Sometimes we need to rest to find refreshment, and other times we need to move, to travel and explore and find something new.

I was reminded of the need for adventure on the road trip we're on to witness the total solar eclipse. So far, it's been hours of driving late into the night as we journey south through several states—not the relaxing time I'd imagined when I decided to take a week off. So far, it's been more inconvenience than convenience, more unknown than predictable—including whether, due to cloud cover, we'll even be able to see the eclipse.

And yet there's something about this trip that already feels rejuvenating. Last night we drove through the aptly named Blue Ridge Mountains, the nearer peaks a deep green and the farther ones progressively lighter and bluer. Lingering clouds from a storm made for a sublime sunset that was unlike any I've ever seen.

New experiences can enable us to see the world with fresh eyes, including seeing the people around us more clearly. Through adventure we can find our way home.

INVITATION

Could you use a little adventure in your own life? It could involve travel or even just a bit of novelty in your typical day, like taking a different route to work, mixing up your routine, trying a new restaurant, or saying hello to someone new—the possibilities are endless. Take a chance on the unknown today.

AUGUST 21

Raise your words, not your voice. It is rain that grows flowers,
not thunder. —RUMI

When my brother and I were growing up, we avidly watched a British television game show called *The Crystal Maze*. It involved a team of players undertaking a series of physical and mental challenges set within a crystal labyrinth. We would both imagine being on the show, heroically completing the games. Recently we had the opportunity to play out this childhood fantasy with our family and friends in a live-experience version of the show!

Throughout the day there was something that continually struck me. While it was the competitive element—each of us racing against the clock to complete our designated challenge—that drove our adrenaline and created the exciting buzz, the most enjoyable part of the experience was helping one another. While one person was undertaking a challenge, the others peered into the room from side windows, offering advice, observations, or words of support. The extra pairs of eyes and shared creative ideas were immensely helpful. The encouragement was uplifting. It truly was a team effort. The whole was indeed greater than the sum of its parts.

INVITATION

Our words can bring others up or tear them down. They can be empowering or hurtful. It is amazing the power we hold with our tongues. We can choose cooperation over competitiveness and kindness over cleverness. Today, use your words as gifts of encouragement, gratitude, appreciation, and inspiration. Raise your words—and others along with them.

AUGUST 22

Acknowledging the good that you already have in your life is the foundation for all abundance. —ECKHART TOLLE

Relationships are central to our well-being, and one of the healthiest things we can do in relationships is to express our gratitude. Everyone likes to feel appreciated, so it's no surprise we get a boost when people tell us they're grateful for us. But research has found that expressing gratitude is a "two-for-one" bargain, benefiting both giver and receiver. In fact, the lower our mood, the more we benefit from telling others we're grateful to them—more so than from simply reflecting on what we're grateful for.

Throughout our trip to see the eclipse, I've been thankful to my wife for her enthusiasm that inspired our travels. My first reaction when she raised the possibility of traveling to see the eclipse was that it sounded stressful and complicated. But I keep being struck by what a great adventure it is, and I've expressed my gratitude to Marcia for prompting us to do it.

We often stop seeing and appreciating the people we're with every day. Over time we can lose sight of the good we find in those we love and start to notice only the things that annoy us. Our need to be acknowledged, however, is not diminished by the length of a relationship. By looking for opportunities to say what we're grateful for in others, we nourish our closest connections.

INVITATION

Look for opportunities today to tell at least one person what you appreciate about them. Consider doing it face-to-face, if possible, and notice how they react. What effect does more deliberate gratitude have on the quality of your connections with others?

AUGUST 23

If you look at what you have in life, you'll always have more. If you look at what you don't have in life, you'll never have enough.

—OPRAH WINFREY

Yesterday I followed the invitation to express my gratitude to others. I thanked Emma for her patience listening to my thoughts and uncertainties about the next stage of my career. I noticed that being honest in this way brought us even closer together. I know intellectually that she deeply values open communication, but it still surprises me how much it means to her when I share my vulnerabilities with her. Hearing the belief and confidence that Emma has in me and the future has been uplifting and inspiring. Reminding myself of what I do have in life has provided the faith and fuel to move toward my goals rather than become afraid of them.

I thanked Seth for his friendship. I thanked him for his openness in his entries and his dedication to this collaborative process. As the rest of the day progressed, I noted the things that I have right now: my health, my supportive family, my loving wife, my good friends, clothes to wear, work that I find meaningful, money to buy a delicious sweet potato hot box.

INVITATION
As your day unfolds, notice what you have in your life. Try to spot when your mind drifts to scarcity rather than abundance. Gently and kindly allow those thoughts to pass by, creating space for you to see the good that lives right here, right now.

AUGUST 24

And above all, watch with glittering eyes the whole world around you because the greatest secrets are always hidden in the most unlikely places. Those who don't believe in magic will never find it.

—ROALD DAHL

There is so much to take in when we open our senses to this universe, as I was powerfully reminded earlier this week. Three days ago we sat in a small park in Greenville, South Carolina, to await the total solar eclipse. By early afternoon the moon made "first contact" in our area, taking a tiny bite out of the sun's disk. Over the next hour and a half, the sun became a thinner and thinner crescent. As totality approached, the light became strangely dim and the air turned cool. I lay on the grass with our kids and we stared upward as the last sliver of sun was covered up.

There was a collective gasp as safety glasses came off. Some people cried. My own eyes filled with tears. The sun's pulsing corona behind the blackness of the moon was glorious and surreal—an unbelievable sight that words cannot capture. It was a reminder that our universe is filled with more mystery and magic than we know.

Thankfully we don't have to see an eclipse to marvel at this universe. This magic is present in our everyday lives, whether we notice it or not, from the fiery ball that heats our planet to the fact that anything exists at all.

INVITATION

Notice the magic that's inherent in your life—the profound effects we can have on one another, the bacteria that turn milk into yogurt, or anything else. Open yourself to the mystery that pervades existence.

AUGUST 25

Act without expectation. —LAO TZU

Recently I shared some uncertainties that I feel about my career with my younger brother. I was bowled over by his compassion and wisdom. He said that one of the first things he would advise is to stop and see all the wonderful and important elements in my life, two of which he named straight away: my health and my supportive wife. He then said I should release the expectations I was placing on myself. Later, when I spoke to my older brother, the first piece of advice he gave was the same: to take off the pressure I was placing on myself.

We can all create internal expectations of what we should have achieved by certain stages in our lives. As the arbitrary deadlines approach, and the realization that we aren't going to meet them sinks in, we can feel disappointed with ourselves. There's a tension to our being, rather than an ease. Thankfully, during these moments we can pause and take a step back. We can recognize that we may have created unrealistic expectations and goals.

Our own internal constructs can tie us down. We can become prisoners to our own beliefs. The magical part is remembering that we can rip apart what we have created. We can change what we believe right now. We can free ourselves from expectations and start afresh tomorrow.

INVITATION

Have you created beliefs or expectations that are weighing you down or holding you back? The goals and expectations we construct can drive action or quell it. Tear down the mental constructs that are disempowering you today and build new empowering ones in their place.

AUGUST 26

If I speak in the tongues of men or of angels, but do not have love, I am only a resounding gong or a clanging cymbal. If I have the gift of prophecy and can fathom all mysteries and all knowledge, and if I have a faith that can move mountains, but do not have love, I am nothing.
—1 CORINTHIANS 13:1–2

Freedom comes, paradoxically, from being tied to an overarching sense of purpose. When our actions are connected to something meaningful, we can rest in the knowledge that we're doing enough. Without that sense of purpose, we'll probably feel that there's something else—something more—we need to be doing.

One way of identifying the purpose that inspires us is to ask what the necessary and sufficient elements of our lives are. "Necessary" means that nothing else could make up for its absence; "sufficient" means that this one thing alone would be enough.

When I think about the essentials in my own life, I arrive at *experiencing love*, both giving and receiving it. Am I allowing myself to feel loved and acceptable? Am I helping others to experience love? If I'm doing these things, it's enough. If what I'm doing is not coming from a place of love, it will never be enough. This recognition feels so simple: Love is enough.

Each of us must decide for ourselves what's most important; possibilities other than love may include being present, connecting with others, feeling grateful, opening to what is, or anything else that inspires us. By centering our lives on this intention, we can find rest.

INVITATION
When you're most awake, in moments of stillness and awareness, what are your necessary and sufficient conditions for having spent your time well? Find ways to embody this intention today.

AUGUST 27

A man is a success if he gets up in the morning and gets to bed at night, and in between he does what he wants to do. —BOB DYLAN

In the West, we tend to build our idea of success on the value of attainment and base our self-esteem on our level of achievement. Dylan starts his idea of success with being able to get up in the morning. The fact that we have the force of life pulsing through our veins is a miracle in itself. We've been given the privilege of another sixteen or so waking hours to take in the beauty and majesty of this world.

What about the time in between? To do what we want to do, to have the ability to make our own choices and act on those decisions—framing the day this way is a reminder that although it might not feel like it, each and every day we've been granted the ultimate power: to be autonomous and in control of what we choose to do.

With each action we take, we can act from love. If we can wake up in the morning, give love, receive love, and go to bed at night, then perhaps that's success. And that's something to be celebrated.

INVITATION
Today, focus on love. Become aware of your heart and any feelings of love or resistance to love. See if you can act from a place of love with each and every action.

AUGUST 28

Do not waste time bothering whether you "love" your neighbor; act as if you did. —C. S. LEWIS

Feeling love often follows loving behavior, whether toward ourselves or other living creatures—as I experienced yesterday. As my kids and I walked home from a nearby park, I was alarmed to see a beautiful hawk partway under a car. I thought it was dead, but it turned its head as we stood looking at it. I was inclined to keep walking because I wanted to get home and make Sunday brunch, but honestly, I knew my wife would be surprised I hadn't tried to help him (we found out it was a male). A woman from a wild animal rehabilitation center told me I could capture him and bring him in, adding, "Just watch out for the feet."

It was an emotionally intense experience. The hawk's yellow-green eyes stared at me in terror as I approached him, afraid he might claw my eyes out. After several failed attempts, I managed to wrap him in a towel and slide him into a cardboard box. As we drove him to the center, I remembered my words as I'd captured him: "It's okay, I won't hurt you. Come here, I got you, you're safe." I do not have a particularly soft spot for birds of prey, yet I felt love for this creature as I cared for him.

The same is true for our relationships with other people: when we practice acts of love, we can change the state of our hearts.

INVITATION

Find ways to express care to others today—even if you're not feeling particularly loving at the time. What happens to your mind and emotions when you lead with action?

AUGUST 29

Hope is being able to see that there is light despite all of the darkness.
—DESMOND TUTU

We never know how a situation will turn out until it's actually happened. It's easy to fall into pessimistic patterns of thinking, believing that we're being "realistic." Sure, it can be prudent to know when the odds are stacked against us. But as my wife Emma often reminds me, a 90 percent chance of one outcome means there's still a 10 percent chance of another.

Yesterday, Seth wrote about caring for an injured hawk. This reminded me of a time in Tuscany when we came across a baby bird that had fallen from its nest. Emma spotted it and said that we should do something. I didn't think there would be anything we could do and didn't have any hope for the bird. It looked severely injured and wasn't moving. Without hope, the most humane suggestion I had was to put the bird out of its misery. Emma, on the other hand, had a stronger caring instinct, compassion, and hope. She insisted on speaking to a worker on the land who came over and saved the day. He gently picked up the bird and took her to the main house to care for her. We found out later in the week that the bird had made a full recovery and had flown away successfully. I was amazed. I learned two things in that moment: First, to always listen to my wife's gut instinct. Second, to have hope.

INVITATION

Choose hope, whatever that may mean to you, at different points throughout your day.

AUGUST 30

Every accomplishment starts with the decision to try.
—JOHN F. KENNEDY

Every day we face many choices—what to eat, what to buy, what to say, and countless others—by one estimate, an incredible thirty-five thousand each day. Some of our decisions lead to good results, and others don't. We might pick the wrong traffic lane or the slow grocery checkout line; we might order a meal we're not crazy about or say something well-intentioned that offends another person.

Research has shown that we're prone to "hindsight bias," meaning we factor our current knowledge into decisions made in the past. In sports, for example, we might criticize athletes' real-time decisions based on knowing how they turned out—a tendency known as "Monday morning quarterbacking."

We often criticize ourselves in a similar way when a decision didn't work out the way we had hoped, telling ourselves we "should have known." For instance, I recently started a new medical treatment that could help or hurt, and I can sense my readiness to criticize myself if it ends up making things worse, as if I expect myself to be clairvoyant. Yet, in truth, all we can do is make the best choices possible given our current knowledge.

It's freeing to remember that while we can choose as wisely as possible, we can never know in advance what the outcome will be. And despite the limits of our knowledge, we can act with confidence, knowing we're doing our best.

INVITATION

Use the decisions you make today to practice compassion with yourself, recognizing that your power to know the future is limited. Know that you can't control every outcome and give yourself a break when something doesn't go the way you hoped.

AUGUST 31

So many of our dreams at first seem impossible, then they seem improbable, and then, when we summon the will, they soon become inevitable. —CHRISTOPHER REEVE

The way we frame the future can lead to feelings of hopefulness or helplessness.

Lately I've been thinking about my future career. It's helped to take a step back and let go of the pressure of having to make the "correct" decision for the next step. Rather than perceiving this period in my life as one characterized by uncertainty and insecurity, I'm beginning to view it as a chance to reconnect to what's most important.

We rarely take the time to consider the type of future we'd like to build. We seldom give ourselves the freedom to think creatively about the rest of the year. Part of this involves allowing ourselves to dream a little. You might notice resistance to this. Daydreaming is often associated with being indulgent or fanciful. Behind this may be a fear of losing touch with reality or being viewed as flighty.

Giving ourselves permission to think about our aspirations can be liberating and motivating. Instead of focusing on the "right" or "wrong" thing to do next, we can work to align our passions and our goals. Whether we will reach these goals, and whether they will change along the way, is unknown. But the journey will probably be a little bit brighter, lighter, and more exciting.

INVITATION
Daydream a little today! Give yourself permission to imagine a future that inspires and excites you, without needing to judge what this looks like or know how it would be attained. Let your mind roam free.

SEPTEMBER 1

There are many tenets of Wholeheartedness, but at its very core is vulnerability and worthiness; facing uncertainty, exposure, and emotional risks, and knowing that I am enough. —BRENÉ BROWN

I've spoken with countless people in my therapy office who struggle to go for the things they really want in life. When we climb, there's a chance we could fall, so we might prefer to stay in the basement, where we're safe. Unfortunately, it's dark and damp down there, and the view is lousy.

It might be especially intimidating to tell others what we're aiming for. I was quite guarded when I wrote my first book about cognitive behavioral therapy, keeping it private from most people until I knew it would be published. What if the editor hated what I'd written and rejected it? I wanted to avoid the embarrassment of having to explain why my book had never materialized.

I've always admired people who put themselves out there, like a good friend of mine who lives in Denver. When we were twenty-one years old he told me his long-term career plan, which involved a succession of jobs, a law degree, and eventually owning his own business. Ten years ago he moved with his family across the country to start a company, which has been thriving even through major downturns in the economy. I suspect his willingness to share his vision for the future had a lot to do with his success in moving toward it.

INVITATION

Consider with whom you might talk today about your aspirations. Supportive family members or close friends might be a good place to start. You could let people outside your closest circle know too—potentially a greater risk, but also a way of underscoring your commitment.

SEPTEMBER 2

If I had a single flower for every time I think of you, I could walk forever in my garden.   —CLAUDIA ADRIENNE GRANDI

Our relationships are one of the most poignant sources of meaning and joy we have. Experiences become richer, brighter, and more fulfilling when we share them with someone.

We all forget this simple truth. We often take the people we love the most for granted. We get caught up in other aspects of life. Our thoughts become consumed with getting more stuff: more clothes, a new phone, another pair of shoes, a better car, a bigger house, a higher income, and the list goes on. Once we have an idea in our heads, it can feel as though our life won't be complete until we have that new thing. Yet we were perfectly happy before we came across that material object.

We don't have to judge ourselves as superficial for enjoying shopping. We don't have to renounce material objects. If we're trying to find lasting contentment through acquiring more possessions, however, we're going to be continually disappointed. Our belongings and our happiness are two separate matters.

A wiser source of happiness is our relationships. When we invest time, care, and attention in the people or pets in our lives, the return is great. When we think about the beings we love, we can experience immense joy in the present moment and feel inspired to act with love.

INVITATION

Think of a person or animal that makes you feel relaxed, happy, or comforted. Bring an image of them to mind throughout the day. See if you can connect to feelings of love, peace, and gratitude, allowing these feelings to guide your actions.

SEPTEMBER 3

Home, let me come home
Home is wherever I'm with you.

—EDWARD SHARPE
AND THE MAGNETIC ZEROS

What makes us feel connected to certain places? Most of us connect most deeply and durably to the places we've shared with the people we love. This is certainly true for me. I have warm memories of Columbus, Indiana, because of the friends and family I spent time with there as a teenager. At the end of each day, I would gather with my parents and four brothers for dinner around our small dining room table, our home a refuge from whatever might be happening in the rest of the world.

I love Strasbourg because it's where my future wife and I met and lived for the first few months of our relationship. It's been nearly twenty years since we were last there, yet memories of the smells on the street, the feel of the air, the squeak of the old floorboards in our dorm, the night we first kissed—all of these feel so close.

I feel the same about Maine because we lived there for two years after college and have returned several times for vacation with our kids. The neighborhood where we now live feels like home because of the friendships we've built here.

No matter where we live, home isn't just a place that's familiar; it's the location for countless moments shared with those we care about.

INVITATION

Think about some of your favorite places. Which ones connect you to the people you love? Take a few moments to savor the warmth you find when you're in those locations.

SEPTEMBER 4

Let us be grateful to the people who make us happy; they are the charming gardeners who make our souls blossom.

—MARCEL PROUST

Our weekend with our new puppy, Alfie, has been glorious. On our first day with him, Emma and I had a memorable conversation:

ME: *I think this is the greatest day of my life.*
EMMA: *Really?*
ME: *Yes, definitely.*
EMMA: *Really? (Sounding somewhat more annoyed.)*
ME: *Yes, I really do. How come?*
EMMA: *You mean after our wedding day, right?*
ME: *Ah. Yes. Of course.*

Right now Emma and I are in the sitting room of our home, with Alfie fast asleep at our feet. I wonder how we'll look back at our time here in the future. While I can imagine living in a bigger house with a kitchen we both fit inside, I know deep down there's nothing materially that will truly make us happier in the long run. The joy that overflows derives from my time with Emma, and now with our little pup. We could be in a smaller or bigger house, and the joy would be just the same. Despite being continually bombarded by societal and cultural messages to earn more, buy more, and have more, it's people (and animals) and our relationships with them that truly drive our happiness.

INVITATION
Bring to mind two or three of your fondest memories. Who were you with? Where were you? What did you feel? If it's appropriate, share these memories with someone—perhaps the person who's in the memory. Allow the glow of your positive memories to lift your heart and radiate out into the rest of your day.

SEPTEMBER 5

I can only note that the past is beautiful because one never realizes an emotion at the time. It expands later, and thus we don't have complete emotions about the present, only about the past.

—VIRGINIA WOOLF

I used to do research on emotional memories—memories that connect us powerfully with our past. When I would ask people to write about any event from their lives, they often described the arrival of a child. Wedding days were also common.

The practice of mindfulness is about the present, yet savoring our memories is perfectly compatible with a commitment to mindful living. We can do anything with awareness, including thinking about the past—and thank goodness. When we're young and most of our life is ahead of us, we have more dreams than memories. As the slider of time moves forward, and the amount of life behind us grows bigger than that ahead, we exchange our hopes and dreams for memories.

I anticipated the arrival of each of our children with excitement and fear, and now I'm left with three memories of magical and terrifying births. More recently I looked forward to yesterday morning's bike ride and the breakfast afterward, and later I anticipated the evening's preparation for our older kids' first day of school.

As we experience each minute and hour and day and year, we trade our imagination of what might be for a trace of what was.

INVITATION

Today is the only September 5 of this year the world will ever know and the only one you'll have in your memories of a life that once was. As you cash in today's potential, how might you create memories that are magnificent to look back on?

SEPTEMBER 6

Success? I don't know what that word means. I'm happy. But success, that goes back to what in somebody's eyes success means. For me, success is inner peace. That's a good day for me.

—DENZEL WASHINGTON

What does success mean?

What would a successful life look like to you? Does a specific car, size of house, level of income, or career pop into your head? Does a particular way of living come to mind?

Is it about being able to provide for your family or to live with minimal financial pressures and constraints?

Is success fulfilling your potential, whatever that is, or is it living life as authentically as possible and feeling comfortable with who you are?

Does success involve aligning your actions with your dreams, ambitions, and goals? Or does it simply mean achieving them?

Is success having inner peace? being able to lay your head down on your pillow with a clear heart and a clean conscious?

We all have our own ideas about success. What is success to one person may not be so to another. We often forget that our ideas about success are exactly that: ideas. They don't exist anywhere but in our heads. Without realizing this, we're far more likely to swallow the most prevalent societal definitions of success, striving toward constructed ideals that may not fit with our values. When we see our thoughts and ideas as internal events that arise in the mind, we free ourselves to create our own notions of success.

INVITATION

Take a moment to consider what you would like success to mean to you. Allow this to guide your life today.

SEPTEMBER 7

All the possibilities of your human destiny are asleep in your soul. You are here to realize and honor these possibilities.

—JOHN O'DONOHUE

When we start something, like building a career or having a child, it can feel like an exciting new adventure. Over time, we might become a bit disillusioned. Maybe practical constraints like budgets and bureaucracies set a lower ceiling on the possibilities we can imagine, or the daily routine of caring for children feels humdrum and tedious.

We all need inspiration to breathe life into our souls. A few years ago, I had become quite dispirited by my endless hours of research—work that I was sure wouldn't make a difference in anyone's life. During that period, I attended my first classical music concert in many years. As the first notes from the solo violinist reached my ears, I thought, *What a thing to create this kind of beauty!* I had to ask myself, *What beauty have I added to the world through my work?*

And then I saw the faces of the many survivors I had treated in the aftermath of traumas and tragedies and knew that if I had done anything of beauty in my professional life, it had happened through the intimate work of therapy. I knew I needed to focus on work that would make a direct difference in the lives of others. That realization inspired me to open my practice, determined to do work that mattered.

INVITATION

Spend some time today reflecting on your motivation for the work you do. Take in the bigger picture as you remind yourself why your efforts matter.

SEPTEMBER 8

We hold these truths to be self-evident, that all men are created equal,
that they are endowed by their Creator with certain unalienable rights,
that among these are Life, Liberty, and the pursuit of Happiness.

—THOMAS JEFFERSON

Cultural influences have a powerful impact on the way we think and act. Modern Western society currently equates professional roles with merit. One of the first questions that people ask at social events is, What do you do? A hundred years ago, someone's standing in society was more dependent on what family that person came from. It was simply another social construct.

We can fall into the sad trap of judging individuals and their worth by the job they have during the week. I'm sure you know people who have treated you differently from those in positions of greater power. You may find it demeaning and vexing. But before we throw stones and chastise others, it might be worth asking if we ever treat those who earn less than us with less courtesy and consideration than we do those who earn more or have a greater social standing.

How liberating and empowering it would be to treat others equally, with respect and kindness; to free ourselves from societal expectations and stories that tell us that how we act toward someone should be determined by their social standing; to remember that all men, women, and children were created equal, that integrity and worth is the birthright of every one of us.

INVITATION

Today, see beyond titles, roles, and labels. Go past the superficial layers that automatically blind us with unhelpful judgments. See the person in front of you and become aware of their right to be recognized and treated with dignity.

SEPTEMBER 9

Everybody can be great because anybody can serve. You don't have to have a college degree to serve. You don't have to make your subject and verb agree to serve. You only need a heart full of grace. A soul generated by love. —MARTIN LUTHER KING JR.

It's easier to see love in some actions than in others. I used to think love meant reaching out to "those less fortunate." But a conversation years ago changed my way of thinking.

I'd been working a series of jobs in Maine and felt like I needed career direction, so I arranged to meet with my college mentor, Dr. Mitchell. He asked me what I was interested in doing, and I said I wanted to help people. His reply stuck with me: "There are lots of ways to be helpful, like driving a delivery truck or being an attorney. What are you drawn to?" His words helped me see that I'd had an overly narrow definition of what it meant to help others.

Love is all around us—in the plumber who works twelve hours on a Sunday so we'll have water and flushable toilets; in the instructors who teach our kids to read, make art, do gymnastics, and hit a tennis ball; in the EMTs who tend to our loved ones in medical crises; in the fishmongers who carefully select our seafood and hand it to us with a smile and a friendly word. It's found in countless daily deeds from others that make our lives better, and in more of our own actions than we realize.

INVITATION
See if it's possible today to notice the love that drives your everyday behaviors, whether doing laundry, making food, working, or anything else. Self-love counts too! Practice seeing love's many faces.

SEPTEMBER 10

If life were predictable, it would cease to be life, and be without flavor.
—ELEANOR ROOSEVELT

The viva voce is the final examination of a doctorate. Examiners carry out an academic interview in order to confirm that the candidate can defend his or her thesis verbally. It's an ancient institution that often instills fear and apprehension into candidates, who have typically invested at least three years into their research.

I was nervous the night before and the morning of my viva. But despite my fears, it went very well. Dare I say it was even enjoyable! In spite of my preparation, however, none of the topics I specifically reviewed came up; the questions were much more adventurous and insightful. It was a rare occasion: two experts in their own field had taken the time to read tens of thousands of words that I had written and had gone to the effort to come up with thoughtful questions and astute comments. I was delighted when they informed me I'd passed.

We all feel anxious about the unpredictability of what lies ahead from time to time. How many times have you worried about something only to find your fears unfounded? If you could know about every event that will unfold in your life, would you actually want to? As much as we may fear the unknown, perhaps it's the unpredictability of life that provides its flavor and richness.

INVITATION

Find your own way to embrace the unpredictability of the day ahead. See if you can appreciate the fullness of the unknown.

SEPTEMBER 11

The only way to make sense out of change is to plunge into it, move with it, and join the dance. —ALAN WATTS

Today will not be like any other day in your life, or exactly what you expect it to be. On this day in 2001, I was walking with my wife on a gorgeous Tuesday morning to my first week of classes at the University of Pennsylvania. I was surprised when I entered the class building to find students crowded around televisions in the lobby that showed a smoking tower in New York, plane wreckage in a Pennsylvania field, smoke billowing from the Pentagon, and images of Osama bin Laden. America had been attacked.

It was a day like any other, until it wasn't. The world changed profoundly for the thousands who died that day and their loved ones. They had no idea when they woke up that it would be their last day, or that their spouse, brother, sister, parent, or child would not be coming home.

The flow of life continues. There are ongoing episodes of terror and tragedy. Our worlds continually evolve as people move away, children are born, dogs are adopted, parents pass on. The quiet, comfort, and freedom we enjoy can be wiped away in an instant. This realization, the thought of losing what we love, can provoke fear. Our only options are to cling to life as we know it and diminish our happiness in the process or to embrace the flow and change that is life.

INVITATION

Enjoy what you have today, fully and completely, without clinging to it so fiercely that it robs your peace of mind. Hold it lightly. Move and flow with the inevitable changes in life.

SEPTEMBER 12

Never take anything for granted. —BENJAMIN DISRAELI

An old family friend passed away a few days ago, and the feeling of loss is still fresh in my heart. He had a joy for life and always made me laugh.

One of my fondest memories is visiting him in my early twenties. He picked me up at the airport in his Cadillac, shortly informing me that he'd left his driving glasses at home. "It'll be an adventure," he said cheekily, with a glint in his eye.

At one point, he misjudged a stop and halted in the middle of an intersection. I imagine the other drivers expected we'd reverse or drive out of their way. But my friend, midstory, was completely oblivious to the situation. I was too shy to interrupt or correct him. So we sat there. The other drivers sat there too, becoming increasingly frustrated, hollering out of their windows and pumping their horns. Eventually, the cars began driving around either side of us, shouting rather impolite phrases and making ungracious gestures as they passed. My friend looked at the other drivers, looked at the red stoplight, and looked back at me. He then said something that made me laugh and that I'll never forget: "What am I meant to do? It's a red light!"

INVITATION

What are we supposed to do? Perhaps all we can do is live each moment we have with as much joy and passion as possible. Today, try not to take anything for granted. See if you can appreciate the present, whether that's the walk to work, the conversations you have, or the food you eat.

SEPTEMBER 13

There's a common misunderstanding among all the human beings who have ever been born on the earth that the best way to live is to try to avoid pain and just try to get comfortable...

A much more interesting, kind, adventurous, and joyful approach to life is to begin to develop our curiosity, not caring whether the object of our inquisitiveness is bitter or sweet. —PEMA CHÖDRÖN

In every challenging moment, we have a choice: to resist what is happening or to roll with it. So often we say no to reality, trying to push it away or force it to be different. Yet sometimes we find that what we're resisting turns out to be better than what we were hoping for.

In fact, life seems to be filled with times when something "bad" ends up being very good. For example, a person who loses her job when the economy goes belly-up may subsequently find her true passion and calling. Yesterday's bad news becomes today's good news.

Even if we find no silver lining in our disappointments, perhaps we still can be open to them. If nothing else, they expand our understanding of what it is to be alive and invite us to connect with others who may be hurting in similar ways. We don't have to shut down when we face challenges and surprises. We can continue to open ourselves to the unfolding of our experience.

INVITATION

Each time you find yourself starting to shut down against your experience today, ask yourself this question: Can I open to this? Focus on your breath if that helps you to meet reality as it finds you. Feel the grip of resistance loosen as you practice being with what is.

SEPTEMBER 14

The pessimist sees difficulty in every opportunity. The optimist sees the opportunity in every difficulty. —WINSTON CHURCHILL

Our minds have evolved to scan the environment for threats. For our ancestors, danger came in the form of saber-toothed tigers. In modern times, our internal thoughts about what could go wrong and what others think are our most prevalent threats.

Recently, I was speaking to a friend who had just returned to work in finance following maternity leave. In her first few days back, she noticed something from an "outside perspective," aided by her time outside the corporate environment. She called a director's meeting to bring it to the forum. In the days leading up to the meeting, she had a barrage of worries: *What if no one turns up? I've been out of the company for nine months, and now I'm calling a director's meeting in my first week back! What will people be thinking about me? What if I can't chair the meeting well? What if the meeting goes horribly wrong?*

Her mind was jumping from negative thought to negative thought, like a monkey swinging between trees. She held her nerve, though, and the meeting went ahead. It turned out to be a great success! All the other directors had noticed this point personally, but no one had aired their concerns publicly. The meeting gave everyone the chance to have an open, honest, and productive discussion with the potential to lead to substantial improvements. The directors were impressed, and she'd shown her value in her first week back. Opportunity lay there for the taking.

INVITATION
When your mind dwells on what could go wrong today, consider the ways that same event could go well. See if you can balance your thoughts of threat with ones of opportunity.

SEPTEMBER 15

When what you value and dream about doesn't match the life you are living, you have pain. —SHANNON L. ALDER

How can we align our daily activities with what's most important to us? Time management specialist Steve McClatchy addressed this question in a talk I attended years ago. He underscored the idea that there are only two things that motivate: winning and avoiding loss. Most of our days are filled with trying not to lose: *Don't be late. Don't disappoint. Don't get stuck in traffic. Don't embarrass yourself. Don't miss your train. Don't fail.* The focus on not losing crowds out our efforts to move toward our life goals—the things we care about most of all. Fear crowds out love.

Steve had a very concrete solution to this crowding-out problem: First, we identify tasks that will move us toward our treasured goals. Then, we block off time in our calendar and protect that time as if it were sacred—because it is. It's hard to imagine something worthier of investing our time in than activities that move us toward our dreams.

The contrast between the loftiness of our life's biggest goals and the humbleness of a daily calendar may seem jarring, but these two fit together perfectly: the living out of what we most care about happens in the daily allotment of our time.

INVITATION

What is a life goal you'd be sorry to leave this earth not having given your all? Is it writing a book? making a bold career move? a profound deepening of your relationships? relocation to a place that inspires you? Take time today to plan ways to move toward this goal as you allow your values to drive your calendar.

SEPTEMBER 16

Your life will become better by making other lives better.

—WILL SMITH

When we serve others willingly, we tend to feel happier and experience more purpose than when we solely focus on our immediate self-interests. We also add value. We're making others' lives better, so we'll likely experience a multitude of benefits that flow from this.

Work is one domain in which we can give to others. Here are three simple ways to adopt a mind-set of service and derive more meaning from your work:

1. Become aware of the positive impact of your efforts. Notice how your work has contributed to the greater good or has made someone else's life happier or easier. Celebrate your small successes!

2. See yourself as part of the team. When you view yourself as part of a team with a common goal, you're more likely to put the group's interests first. Focus on building your relationships at work: Find out how someone else's day is going or what's happening in his or her life outside work. Take the time to have a coffee break or lunch together. We've all experienced how much more enjoyable a job is when we have colleagues we genuinely care about and who care about us.

3. Align your work with your strengths and passions. Find ways to apply your strengths to the work you're doing or volunteer for projects you're particularly enthusiastic about. This will make it easier to give more and affect others positively.

INVITATION

Put on your service hat today. Find ways to give to others and enjoy the benefits that follow!

SEPTEMBER 17

Bowing helps to eliminate our self-centered ideas. This is not so easy. It is difficult to get rid of these ideas, and bowing is a very valuable practice.
—SHUNRYŪ SUZUKI

In many countries, bowing is a traditional display of respect. In their book on mindful parenting called *Everyday Blessings*, Myla and Jon Kabat-Zinn describe bowing inwardly to one's children, "bowing from your true nature to theirs." I've bowed to my own children as they slept, signifying my intention to honor them in their waking moments as much as I do when they're sleeping like angels.

There are many ways to bow; here are some examples:

1. While sitting or standing, press your palms together in front of your heart, and allow your head to bow forward as your chest stays upright. Alternatively, lift your pressed palms to your forehead with your thumbs lightly pressing against the space between your eyebrows.

2. While standing, bend forward at the waist as your arms extend down toward your toes and the weight of your head relaxes. In yoga this is known as the "Forward Fold" position.

3. Kneel on the floor and bring your big toes together with your knees apart. Drop your buttocks and lower your torso over your thighs until your forehead reaches the floor. Extend your arms in front you, palms resting on the floor. In yoga this is called the "Child's Pose."

INVITATION

Today, choose a way of bowing that fits your physical abilities. Bowing could be a way of embodying your commitment to another person, to your faith, to your highest self, or simply to an awareness of that which is beyond you. If it feels awkward or silly, stick with it. See what emerges as you spend a few quiet moments in this posture.

SEPTEMBER 18

When you dance, your purpose is not to get to a certain place on the floor. It's to enjoy each step along the way. —WAYNE DYER

This weekend, we went to a wedding. It was one of the most enjoyable days of the year. The sun was shining, the bride and groom were happy, everyone in the wedding party was in great form, the food was delicious (always a win), and the speeches were heartfelt and hilarious.

The evening ended on a high note as Emma and I literally danced for hours, together as well as with friends and new acquaintances. I haven't danced with such carefree abandon and joy for some time! We even played a game where we assigned each other dance moves. For instance, I gave Emma the challenge of dancing like a shark, as though she were lost, and as if she were a detective trying to discover the identity of a murderer. From Emma's reactions, I can only assume that my own impressions of a giraffe and a candle were equally amusing.

As we grow older, we can lose our sense of childlike playfulness. Life is so much brighter, lighter, and more joyful when we let go of certain expectations, rules, and limitations and allow the dance of life to take center stage.

INVITATION
Today, bring a sense of playfulness, humor, and fun to your day!

SEPTEMBER 19

If you're reading this … Congratulations, you're alive. If that's not something to smile about, then I don't know what is.

—CHAD SUGG

We invest a great deal of energy trying to ward off what we fear, sometimes getting lost in our fantasies of what might be. In the process, we can become quite glum, as though we're already living out what we fear.

Over the weekend, I found myself doing just that. We were visiting my in-laws and our two-year-old woke up crying with the barking cough of croup. My thoughts began to spin as I drove blearily to the pharmacy around midnight: *I'll be lucky if I get four hours' sleep. I'll probably get sick. What if I lose my voice? What if I can't work for a few days?*

My body was tense, and I noticed I was frowning. But when I tried to identify an actual problem, I couldn't. My car worked, the pharmacy would be open, and I could afford the medicine. I decided to smile as I drove, and suddenly things seemed lighter. None of the things I was afraid of would mean the end of the world. I smiled again as I felt the grip loosen.

Faye was up about a dozen times that night, barking like a seal. And it was okay. Yet how easy it would have been to ride that train of fear and resistance. As hard as it can be at the time, we can allow the grip to loosen as we smile, remembering that it's all experience.

INVITATION

Take a moment right now to smile gently to yourself. What do you notice? When you have tense moments today, is it possible to bring a smile to your face? See how your mind, body, and heart respond.

SEPTEMBER 20

Listen with curiosity. Speak with honesty. Act with integrity. The greatest problem with communication is we don't listen to understand. We listen to reply. When we listen with curiosity, we don't listen with the intent to reply. We listen for what's behind the words.

—R. T. BENNETT

Yesterday I attended a lecture exploring the ingredients of psychological therapies associated with positive change. The professor presented data showing that the outcomes of therapy vary considerably depending on the therapist being evaluated. This is to be expected: in every profession, there will always be those who are more and those who are less effective than others.

Analysis showed that a therapist's experience was linked to the outcomes of therapy. But the relationship was not in the direction one might predict. It turned out that therapists with less experience had better results with their clients. Why might this be?

Therapists at the start of their career may begin from a place of curiosity. Clients are seen as individuals with unique experiences. The goal is to learn about them and to understand their internal worlds and emotional experiences. As therapists gain more experience, however, they may begin to make more assumptions, placing individuals into diagnostic categories: *Oh, I've seen this type of person before. They're bipolar / psychotic / depressed.* Understanding ceases the moment such sweeping judgments about a person are made. The diversity and idiosyncrasies of that unique individual are lost. Curiosity leaves the room, and presumption takes its place.

INVITATION

Today, move from a place of curiosity. Listen with curiosity. Look with curiosity. Taste with curiosity. Smell with curiosity. And if you're going to touch with curiosity, just make sure you have the other person's permission first!

SEPTEMBER 21

Spring passes and one remembers one's innocence.
Summer passes and one remembers one's exuberance.
Autumn passes and one remembers one's reverence.
Winter passes and one remembers one's perseverance.

—YOKO ONO

Now is the time of year we say goodbye to summer and hello to fall in the Northern Hemisphere. It doesn't seem that long since the transition to spring, and now we're at the other equinox, 180 degrees around the sun. When we pay attention, we'll start to notice signs of the coming fall—the copper-colored leaves lining the streets, the smell of the air.

In contrast to light and airy spring, fall has a weight to it, a seriousness that perhaps goes along with the start of a new school year. Even the foods seem more serious—root vegetables and thick-skinned squashes take the place of the asparagus and strawberries of spring and the tomatoes and zucchini of summer.

We might look forward to putting away summer's frivolity and focusing on school and work. It's also common to feel a sadness as summer ends, and with it our more relaxed schedules and extended time with family. Maybe we thought we would have time to do more. As with every transition, fall offers an opportunity to experience the change as we straddle what was and what will be.

INVITATION

Take stock today of what this summer meant to you. What were the best parts? What memories will you carry with you? Are there parts of it you'd just as soon forget? As you look ahead to the fall, consider what intentions you will carry with you—when the winter solstice rolls around and fall becomes winter, what do you want to have done this season?

SEPTEMBER 22

New beginnings are often disguised as painful endings. —LAO TZU

Each year is marked by seasons. Similarly, our lives often fall into chapters. As my doctorate draws to a close, I've been reflecting on this past phase.

I realized that my most significant experiences have been grounded in relationships—relationships with my clients, colleagues, and supervisors. It hit home that we're all human: we all share over 99.9 percent of our DNA; we all have passions, worries, fears, dreams, good days, and bad days; we're all trying our best given the hand we've been dealt; and we all deserve to be treated with compassion and understanding.

We're often on our own at the moment any big occasion gets underway, whether sitting for an exam, being interviewed, graduating, being promoted, buying a house, or achieving an important goal. But there's always a support network that made it possible. It's people and the memories we have with them that make life so meaningful and valuable.

At any moment in our lives, we can ask ourselves,

- What have I learned about myself?
- In what ways have I changed?
- What will I miss about this chapter in my life?
- What will I be glad to leave behind?
- What will I take with me?

INVITATION

Take stock of where you are at this point of your life. Consider when this chapter began and when it might end. In what ways have you changed since it started, and who's been involved along the way? Pause to recognize where you are, acknowledge the others that are playing their part, and celebrate your successes so far, no matter how big or small.

SEPTEMBER 23

Death and life are in the power of the tongue.

—PROVERBS 18:21A

Our words can have powerful effects, for good and for ill. We can use them to tear people down and build them up. My mom used to encourage us as kids to "speak to one another unto edification." I love the idea of edifying others with our words—of helping them to be better. It's a miraculous thing that by moving our tongues and lips and vibrating our vocal cords, we can create patterns of activity in others' brains that improve their lives.

I've benefited from that phenomenon many times, even in the past week. During a particularly trying moment, even a few words of encouragement can bring us back from a point of despair. Needless to say, there are times when we do the opposite, saying things that hurt others or even reduce them to tears. I can think of multiple mornings when I've left for work after making more than one child cry through my careless or impatient words.

One of the things I became acutely aware of during a long process of recovery from a vocal injury is how consequential our words can be. What a shame to waste the voice we're given, or even worse to use it as a weapon of destruction. Talk may be cheap, as the expression goes, but our words are precious. How will we use them?

INVITATION

Bring your palms together and raise your hands to your mouth, allowing the backs of your thumbs to press lightly against your lips. Allow your eyes to close. Take a moment to set an intention for how you will speak today. How can your words impart life to others?

SEPTEMBER 24

The best of us must sometimes eat our words. —J. K. ROWLING

My mom used to say that our words are like swords: they can protect or hurt others. When I was growing up, she encouraged my brothers and me to think about our words going through three gates—the gates of truth, necessity, and kindness:

- Are my words true?
- Are they necessary?
- Are they kind?

It's common to consider only the first gate. We can place a huge value on truth but easily overlook necessity and kindness. I'm sure we can all think of times when we've said something unnecessary or unkind and then justified it with, *But it's true.*

One of the hardest things in life can be to admit when we're wrong. We forget that we're all fallible. We all say and do the wrong thing. We all make mistakes.

This presents a conundrum: do we admit our mistakes or hide them? In disguising mistakes by rationalizing them, we might think we're protecting ourselves. We may hope that others will accept the legitimacy of our actions rather than think worse of us. We overlook that people generally see through this, however, and we'll probably be coming across as defensive.

When we admit our mistakes and truly intend to make amends for any hurt we've caused, even inadvertently, we show that we care. We place the other person above our own ego. We free ourselves and heal others.

INVITATION

Remember that you're human and that it's natural to make mistakes. If you say or do something that hurts someone else today, open up to the possibility that there may have been a better way of handling the situation. Allow humility and compassion to guide what you do next.

SEPTEMBER 25

Part of me suspects that I'm a loser, and the other part of me thinks I'm God Almighty. —JOHN LENNON

I t often feels like we face two possibilities: either we're perfect and therefore acceptable or we're flawed and unacceptable. This dichotomy is most apparent in narcissistic personalities, in which individuals inflate their sense of self-importance because they feel completely worthless on another level. We fear that being imperfect will cause others to think less of us or even reject us. And so we try to be angels while fearing we're devils and to defend against even the suggestion that we're less than perfect.

In the thousands of mistakes I've made in my relationship with Marcia, not once can I remember her admiring me for my defensiveness or criticizing me for admitting a mistake. Our sixteenth wedding anniversary comes to mind. I grew impatient while she was taking pictures and expressed my annoyance passive-aggressively. For the rest of the night, I tried to act like it was an innocent remark, which kept us stuck in an argument. And yet, as pointless as my defensiveness is, I'll probably do the same thing many more times.

Thankfully, there's a way out of this ego trap. We can practice opening more fully to who we are, including our imperfections. We can even accept that we're defensive about our defenses—it's just another layer of ego. And it doesn't mean we're unlovable—people love us more for being fully human, and for being willing to admit it.

INVITATION

Embrace your imperfections today, looking for opportunities to freely acknowledge when you've made a mistake by speaking unkindly, misremembering something, showing poor judgment, or whatever it may be. Can you feel that you're still fully acceptable, lovable, and fundamentally complete, even in your imperfections?

SEPTEMBER 26

Live as if you'll die today. —JAMES DEAN

A close friend of mine just found out that his father died. It came out of the blue. The two of them had a complex relationship and it's brought up a mixture of complicated issues and emotions to process.

The old proverb that "life is short" is easily overlooked. Life and death can arise unexpectedly. We don't know when we'll go, or when the people closest to us, or even furthest away, will go either. But what we can do is make the most of the time we have right now.

If you did pass away today,

- Is there anything you'd wish you had said or done?

- Are there people you'd regret not being in touch with?

- Is there anyone you'd want to forgive?

- Is there someone you'd want to have apologized to?

- Are there people, places or activities you'd wish you had engaged with?

INVITATION

Take some time to think about any regrets you might have if you passed away today. Tap into a place of gratitude for being alive and use these insights to act in any positive ways you can right now.

SEPTEMBER 27

Dare to seize every opportunity on your life's journey.
                                        —LAILAH GIFTY AKITA

Death cannot be avoided or ignored. With life's finitude in mind, how shall we live? The answer seems to be to do just that: live.

I had an opportunity over the weekend to say yes to life when my wife suggested we spend the day at our favorite nearby beach. I've learned the value of following Marcia's lead when she has an idea for diving into life, so I immediately said yes.

After a big brunch, we packed up the car and the kids and drove two hours to Cape May, the southernmost tip of New Jersey, where the Delaware Bay meets the Atlantic Ocean. The sky was a deep blue, and a lovely breeze made the beach just the right temperature. An occasional monarch butterfly flitted by. It felt like a perfect day as I took in the beauty around me and watched the kids build castles in the sand.

As a creature of habit, *no* is my default response when given the option to deviate from my routine. My mind immediately thinks about the difficulties, the inconvenience, the complications, and the opportunity costs. Yet being home on this day would have meant saying no to an invitation to boldly seize the day—saying no, perhaps, to being fully alive.

Life is continually inviting us to jump in—to seize opportunities, take chances, risk rejection, say what we mean, follow our dreams, drive to the beach. Who knows where our *yes* will take us?

INVITATION

Make *yes* your default response today each time life beckons you. It doesn't mean you have to say yes to everything, but do tip the balance toward embracing all of life.

SEPTEMBER 28

Everything has to come to an end, sometime. —L. FRANK BAUM

The last week has been a whirlwind. In six days we had sold our house and had had an offer accepted on a new one.

This unexpected opportunity and surprisingly quick process have made me appreciate our current house. It's our first home as a married couple, and we have wonderful memories here. Before this week I was living as though we'd always be here. Little frustrations about the tiny kitchen or other imperfections would rear their ugly little heads. Now these things don't seem to matter as much.

It's easy to live as if our current situation will continue forever. When we do, we take aspects of our lives for granted. We focus on deficiencies and overlook blessings. But if we can see past this illusion and recognize the transience of the world, we're much more likely to appreciate what we have and cherish the present moment.

INVITATION

Consider the possibility of various parts of your life coming to an end. This could be the job that you're in, the car you're driving, relationships with people, the city in which you're living, or anything else you might be taking for granted. Allow the realization of impermanence to settle. It might just change your outlook and experiences for the better.

SEPTEMBER 29

Wisdom is merely the movement from fighting life to embracing it.
—RASHEED OGUNLARU

The things we like and dislike about our circumstances are often as closely connected as the two sides of a coin. For example, I love having all our kids living at home and feel sad realizing that our oldest child is more than halfway toward being out of the house. I can't imagine ever being ready for our cozy family unit to be broken up as the kids head off to college and build families of their own.

On the other hand, I often find myself wishing to get through these early years of parenting as quickly as possible. I can't wait till the kids can make their own breakfast, do their own dishes, brush their own teeth, make dinner, stay home by themselves. I know this time goes so quickly, yet I would love a break—and the opportunity to do things alone with my wife, like going out to dinner more often or taking walks together.

Our life situations are a package deal. We can't have kids in our daily lives without the strain and constraints of raising them. We can't do meaningful work without taking on some degree of stress. We can't be in committed relationships without forgoing other opportunities.

Whatever situation we find ourselves in, perhaps we can move toward celebrating all of it—our gains and our losses, our joy and our pain, our struggles and our triumphs. It's all experience. It's all life.

INVITATION

Today, if you find yourself rejecting something that's happening because it's annoying, inconvenient, tedious, painful, or difficult, ask yourself if it's the flip side of something good in your life. Practice welcoming your full reality.

SEPTEMBER 30

Finish each day and be done with it... You have done what you could;
some blunders and absurdities no doubt crept in; forget them as soon
as you can. Tomorrow is a new day; you shall begin it serenely, and
with too high a spirit to be cumbered with your old nonsense.

—RALPH WALDO EMERSON

It's wonderful when we have little insights in the middle of an experience. But we often only see the fullness of a situation on reflection.

For instance, yesterday I was taking our puppy, Alfie, out to tinkle when Emma called. The smoke detector then went off full blast. I ran back into a smoke-filled kitchen to see my tortilla wrap burning in the toaster. (Our oven stopped working, and we don't have a microwave, so the toaster seemed like a good idea at the time.) With Emma still on the phone asking me to send over an important document and the alarm still blaring, Alfie ran back into the kitchen with me, became startled, and peed all over the floor.

This is just one small event that was flustering at the time but which had another side. I realized that I'm very fortunate to have a home, a toaster, food, and an adorable little pup that likes to follow me around, even when an alarm is going off.

There are often blessings hidden in every difficulty. The challenge—or opportunity—is to find them.

INVITATION

Today, bring forgiveness to your day. Try your best, learn from your mistakes and let them go. Forgive yourself, and others, for shortcomings. We are all just human after all.

OCTOBER 1

Tonight I'm drinkin' in the forgiveness
This life provides.

—BRUCE SPRINGSTEEN

There's good news and bad news today: The bad news is that you and someone you love might cause each other pain before the day is over. But the good news—the great news—is that you'll most likely forgive one another.

How is it that we can move past hurts and failures at the hands of those we love? How can our kids smile and hug us minutes after we've spoken harshly to them? How do parents let go of the perfectly aimed insults their teens hurl at them? How is it that Marcia still loves me as much as she does after the countless conflicts in our many years together?

In our closest relationships, forgiveness seems to be standard issue and somewhat automatic. It's built into our connections to others, just as our immune systems respond routinely to the invisible invaders that attack us. If we're upset about something, we'll almost certainly feel less upset about it after some time has passed.

This is not to say that we don't run into major challenges to forgive others, just as our bodies run into extraordinary difficulties managing serious illnesses. Major hurts like neglect, abuse, abandonment, or assault are akin to the cancers or systemic infections that at times overwhelm our bodies, and forgiveness in these contexts is a different matter.

But letting go of others' daily faults feels to me like something our minds just do for us, to our great benefit. We can breathe with the lightness of this awareness that forgiveness is woven into life's fabric.

INVITATION
Drink in life's forgiveness today, whichever side of it you find yourself on. Savor forgiving and being forgiven.

OCTOBER 2

It is during our darkest moments that we must focus to see the light.

—ARISTOTLE

Sometimes it feels as though we have no control over how we feel and act. But it may be that we are holding onto certain feelings that are directing our actions.

The other night, Emma and I were having supper. Halfway through, she stopped eating and said something along the lines of, "Okay what's wrong? You're not being yourself. I feel like you're being mean to me." She was absolutely right. I was grumpy. A few things from earlier in the day had annoyed me, and I was holding onto the frustration and taking it out on Emma.

At each moment in time, we all have a choice: we can keep our focus on ourselves and what's going wrong or we can turn our attention toward others and make a conscious effort to be more loving. Past events do not have to dictate the tone of days moving forward. We do not have to be slaves to our circumstances.

INVITATION

If you find yourself in a place of frustration today, notice where your attention is falling. Rather than looking inwardly, direct your attention to the people or place around you. If you'd like to be more loving or kind, make a conscious decision and see what happens!

OCTOBER 3

Nothing is harder to bear than a succession of fair days.
                    —JOHANN WOLFGANG VON GOETHE

There are few things that feel as good as having a problem resolved, like when we or someone we love returns to health after a significant illness. When I had an issue with my voice, I wanted nothing more than to talk freely, or socialize, or chat with my kids, or even read to them. When I was able to do those things again, I was filled with gratitude to have this basic function of living and loving restored.

Our minds are built to notice contrast and to figure out whether things are improving or getting worse. We're aware of our health when we get sick and when we finally feel well. But accordingly, the sameness of fair weather or bodies that work or peaceful relationships doesn't stand out to us. As Goethe suggests, we appreciate the sun much more after it has been hidden by clouds.

At some point, we almost inevitably take for granted the sun or our health or the people who love us. Our connection to what we have fades, and we must remind ourselves to appreciate the good things in our lives. Deliberately noticing what's going well is like turning our faces to the light of the sun.

INVITATION

Think back to three concerns you've had that have since been resolved—times you've been sick and recovered, times you were worried about something that turned out well, or times you faced a problem that got fixed. Don't worry about making yourself feel grateful; simply remember what is going well now that once was not.

OCTOBER 4

The word maybe *was beginning to annoy me, because the only thing that was fixed was that* maybe *would be with me forever.*
—MARKUS ZUSAK

There's an ancient Taoist story. One day, an old farmer's only horse ran away. The news spread to his neighbors, who came round to convey their condolences: "What bad luck," they said. "Maybe," the farmer replied. The following day the horse returned with three other wild horses trailing behind. "How lucky!" his neighbors exclaimed. "Maybe," the farmer responded. The next morning the son of the farmer was attempting to ride one of the wild horses but was thrown off and broke his leg. The neighbors came to express their sympathies: "How unfortunate that was." "Maybe," the old man replied. That afternoon the military entered the village to draft eligible young men into the army. Upon seeing that the farmer's son was injured, they excluded him from the draft. "How wonderfully that worked out!" The farmer said once more, "Maybe."

We often label events as lucky or unlucky as they happen. While it might be difficult to see circumstances any other way, at the time, we're often unable to see the full story. For instance, my father's cancer seemed like the worst thing that could happen at the time, but it brought us together as a family and changed the trajectory of my life. It made me realize how important it is to be true to yourself and follow your own passions and values rather than being led by the expectations of others.

INVITATION

As little concerns or frustrations arise, see if you can let go of the temptation to label them. If your mind does declare something as positive or negative, try replying, "Maybe," and see what happens.

OCTOBER 5

Go after what you really love and find a way to make that work for you, and then you'll be a happy person. —TOM PETTY

All of us have things we would like to move toward in life. They might be small changes like trying a new exercise class or big ones like a midlife career move. We can spend much of our life waiting for an invitation to do what we really want to do, not realizing that life itself is that invitation.

One of the best parts of pursuing goals we're excited about is that we're more likely to throw our talents and energies into reaching them. In my own life, I know that I have struggled to bring passion and creativity to work I found uninspiring, like when I was doing research that didn't seem meaningful.

What holds us back from trying to build the life we want? Fear of failing is one of the most common barriers. We worry that we'll embarrass ourselves if we don't succeed or that we will have wasted time and effort. But when all is said and done, most of us would prefer to have failed at something close to our hearts than to have succeeded at something we didn't really care about.

Oh, and there's another possibility: to be daring and succeed gloriously. All that's required to move toward our dreams is deciding to take that step.

INVITATION

Consider for a moment what you've been holding yourself back from. It could be something small that you could complete today, like tackling a new running route or fixing something around the house. It could also be a big project that will take weeks of planning and preparation, like major home renovations or jump-starting a new career path. Choose today to live your life more fully.

OCTOBER 6

You build on failure. You use it as a stepping-stone. Close the door on the past. You don't try to forget the mistakes, but you don't dwell on it. You don't let it have any of your energy, or any of your time, or any of your space. —JOHNNY CASH

When we're trying to achieve a goal, it's tempting to want the end product right now. We might secretly wish that we could fast-forward our lives to future success. It can be painful imagining failing. But we're all human and thus fallible by our very nature. We will inevitably make mistakes, and we will all fail at times. It's easy to overlook that the most successful people in their areas fail too. A key differentiator is that they then learn from their mistakes and keep going. They fail forward!

Charles Darwin, one of the most influential scientific minds in history, dropped out of university—twice—and was considered a failure by his father. The Wright brothers, the fathers of aviation, nearly killed themselves trying to fly. Michael Jordan didn't make his high school basketball team. Stephen King's first manuscript to be published was rejected by thirty different publishers before someone bought it.

Failure is inevitable, but the way you view it isn't.

INVITATION
Fail forward, my friend, fail forward! Try to see failure as a process. Aim for success in whatever you do, but be prepared to make mistakes. Learn what you can, and move forward.

OCTOBER 7

The most basic of all human needs is the need to understand and be understood. The best way to understand people is to listen to them.
—RALPH G. NICHOLS

How do we communicate our support to someone who's going through a difficult time? Humanistic psychologist and therapist Carl Rogers posited that effective support is "person-centered," meaning we meet the person where they are. We acknowledge the person's emotions and validate how they're feeling, even if we feel differently ourselves. We might also elaborate on the person's feelings, doing our best to make them feel understood.

My research colleagues and I explored what person-centered communication looks like in practice. Our work suggested that the following four actions are the most effective when supporting someone who's hurting:

1. Acknowledge the person's feelings. Explicitly recognize the person's emotional experience, such as by saying, "You must be so disappointed."

2. Communicate understanding. Express empathy by validating the person's experience. You might say, for example, "No wonder you're angry."

3. Take their side. Let the person know you support them, even if they're partly to blame in the situation. Rogers calls this stance "unconditional positive regard," and it's powerful in relationships.

4. Resist rushing to problem solve. Meet the person where they are, which likely involves dealing with difficult emotions. Men and women alike generally prefer to talk about their experience rather than moving immediately to problem solving.

It doesn't take a psychologist to know that it feels good to be heard and to be met exactly where we are.

INVITATION

Is there someone you can aim to really hear today? It could be a significant other, another family member, a friend, or a coworker. It could even be a stranger who decides to share something with you. Practice opening your ears and your heart.

OCTOBER 8

Let your aim be to come at truth, not to conquer your opponent.
—ARTHUR MARTINE

Conflict in relationships is natural. In a well-known study, researchers observed married partners argue in a lab for fifteen minutes and then were able to predict which marriages would end in divorce with over 90 percent accuracy. By observing thousands of couples interacting during conflict, researchers identified a number of factors that predicted divorce. One of them was criticism.

Criticism was defined as attacking the whole identity of the other person. It's healthy to share your thoughts and feelings about an aspect of a relationship with which you feel dissatisfied or unhappy. But while a complaint focuses on a specific behavior, criticism moves into the realm of character assassination:

- **Complaint:** "Last night at your friend's house, I felt left out. I didn't know anyone else there. We'd agreed that we'd include each other in conversations and not leave each other for long periods of time."
- **Criticism:** "Last night you spent the whole time with your friends and left me out the entire night. You never think about me when we're out. You're so selfish."

It's easy for criticism to seep into relationships. We get used to criticizing one another. We could literally spend the whole day noticing "flaws" or suggesting "better" ways of doing things. Even with good intentions, this can leave the person we love most feeling rejected, hurt, and not good enough.

INVITATION
Notice when you criticize someone else or feel the urge to criticize. Take a moment to see if you can express how you feel without taking down the other person's whole being. At other times during the day, try expressing what you admire and respect about them too!

OCTOBER 9

To accept ourselves as we are means to value our imperfections as much as our perfections. —SANDRA BIERIG

The way we treat others is often a reflection of how we treat ourselves, and the more self-critical we are, the more harshly we tend to judge others. Yesterday, for me, was a case in point. We had traveled to a nearby botanical garden, and I approached a staff member at what looked like an information desk. She preempted my question by saying, "Sir, the line for tickets is over there." When I asked her if we needed our e-tickets for admission, she said, "No, and they can help you with that *in the line for tickets,*" pointing in that direction.

As I walked away, I heard her say to the people behind me, "I'm so sorry about that." I was furious—I didn't want to be the "that" she was apologizing for! I felt like I needed to punish her in some way to even the score. In time, I realized I felt embarrassed, afraid I'd missed a "members only" sign at the desk or had accidentally cut in line. My response was to despise the staff member, telling myself she was a phony who acts nice to some people but is, in fact, uptight and unfriendly.

It's more than likely that each of us will fall short in some way every day, even today. When we treat ourselves gently, we're more likely to extend that same kindness to others. We can plan to treat our shortcomings as understandable imperfections that come with being human.

INVITATION

Plan right now for a kind response to yourself when you mess up—something like "Everyone makes mistakes. You're human!" Breathe in, breathe out, and release any sense of condemnation.

OCTOBER 10

A person lives a false life whenever they are afraid to make contact
with his or her authentic self. A sensitive ego—one that protects a
person from pain—can also prevent a person from maturing mentally
and emotionally by causing a person to distort truths and refuse to
admit unpleasant facts.   —K. J. OLDSTER

In the last book of the Christian scriptures, the Four Horsemen of
the Apocalypse represent harbingers of the end of the world: Con-
quest, War, Famine, and Death. According to extensive research by John
Gottman, the four horsemen that betray the end of a relationship are
Criticism, Contempt, Stonewalling, and Defensiveness.

In my relationship work with clients, the pattern of defensiveness
frequently surfaces. We're all defensive at times. When we feel attacked,
judged, criticized, or misunderstood, we often try to explain why we've
made a specific decision or acted in a certain way. The downside is that
this strategy is rarely effective. The other person usually sees this as a stub-
born act that justifies a behavior and serves as an excuse not to change.
"You're being defensive" is hurled back, which typically leads to more
defensiveness and justification. Could it be time to break this cycle and
find a new way of relating to the people we love the most?

INVITATION

See if you can explore the function of your justifications. Are you trying to
protect yourself from the pain of admitting a mistake? Are you attempting
to avoid confronting an unpleasant fact? Is there a fear that you're somehow
not good enough? Notice if you can separate making a poor decision from
being a bad person as you travel on your unique path of self-discovery,
acceptance, and growth.

OCTOBER 11

I will show you, you're so much better than you know. —SADE

There may be no greater gift we can give another person than helping them feel utterly lovable. I don't mean begrudgingly or selectively lovable—I mean worthy of love in an inalienable sense.

Perhaps some of us have memories of this profound love from a parent. Despite our imperfections, our mom or dad let us know that our superficial faults didn't make us inadequate in any deep sense. Or maybe we've had this experience through our spiritual faith. This kind of love can't be gained or lost based on what we do.

How can we help others to feel worthy of love? Avoiding negative behaviors like attacks on their basic character is one obvious way. There are also many positive steps we can take, like showing love through small acts of service, physical touch, encouragement, or just asking the person directly: "Do you know you're absolutely worthy of love?"

When we know deep in our gut that we're fundamentally okay—that nothing can shake our essential standing in the universe—we're less likely to respond to potential criticism with defensiveness and counterattacks. We'll have an easier time reacting to what others say rather than to our projected fears of being unacceptable. And perhaps best of all, we'll have a chance to share that love with others.

INVITATION

What might you do today that could help someone you care about feel completely lovable? You might choose one of the examples given above or plan your own way to invite them to rest in a place of absolute acceptance.

OCTOBER 12

Every day we have plenty of opportunities to get angry, stressed or offended. But what you're doing when you indulge these negative emotions is giving something outside yourself power over your happiness.
                                                            —JOEL OSTEEN

Over the weekend, we went to a restaurant to celebrate Emma's birthday. As the meal progressed, I became more and more disappointed with what I deemed poor service. I could feel myself becoming increasingly frustrated as the meal failed to unfold the way that I had hoped. I wanted the meal to go perfectly. Minor inconveniences, like waiting longer than I expected for courses to arrive or the wrong order coming twice, affected me more than usual. And even though Emma seemed perfectly happy, I became tense.

The irony was that because I was tied so tightly to my hopes and expectations, I had blown little incidents out of proportion and ended up being Emma's one source of stress. Later, while discussing it in the car, I came to realize that I was acting from a place of defense: "But it's the principle," I said to Emma, and she agreed. "But is it worth getting upset over?" she asked. A worthy question, indeed.

INVITATION

Today, if something begins to frustrate you, try asking yourself, Is this worth getting upset over? It may be something that's important and needs to be addressed. But it's also possible it's something that won't matter in a year, a month, a week, or even a day. Let it go, and focus on what's going right instead.

OCTOBER 13

It is a wonderful day in a life when one is finally able to stand before the long, deep mirror of one's own reflection and view oneself with appreciation, acceptance, and forgiveness. —JOHN O'DONOHUE

Wouldn't it be great if we could create a perfect version of ourselves? Mine would be more patient, more present, more daring. And yet, our efforts toward perfection are prone to backfire as striving for an unattainable goal only leads to stress and frustration. Thus we face a catch-22: accept that we're going to be imperfect or aim for perfection and create the very conditions we're trying to avoid.

I don't know why the intimate relationship we have with ourselves can breed contempt, making it hard to love ourselves wholly and unconditionally. But what I do know is that the few moments we manage to greet ourselves with acceptance or even appreciation are heavenly. We can truly rest in those moments, breathing in deeply and letting go of any sense of fighting what is. In that space, we are okay just as we are.

Each of us may despise aspects of ourselves, whether physical, emotional, or mental. When we're focused on fixing our faults, we're not at our best, neither for ourselves nor for others. It takes deliberate effort to cultivate a more loving attitude toward ourselves. Our world will change for the better as we foster that sense of being absolutely accepted as we are.

INVITATION

Practice radical acceptance of yourself today, embracing all of you—even your faults and foibles. Remind yourself that you are worthy of love exactly as you are.

OCTOBER 14

It's just about being you and being cool with that. And I think when you're authentic, you end up following your heart, and you put yourself in places and situations and in conversations that you love and that you enjoy. You meet people that you like talking to. You go places you've dreamt about. And you end up following your heart and feeling very fulfilled.
—NEIL PASRICHA

L ife is about progress, not perfection. The very idea of perfection is itself debatable! We can, however, try to live authentically each and every day.

There is great power in being honest with ourselves. Embracing our imperfections does not mean condoning unwanted behavior. Accepting ourselves does not mean that we have to hold onto our flaws forever. It just means that we're okay with not being perfect.

The paradox is that, by being authentic, by owning our mistakes and our shortcomings, we free ourselves from having to act in a certain way. We can see each moment as a chance to try something new. By recognizing each new act, we might even start to see ourselves in a different light.

INVITATION

Today, identify one aspect of yourself you wouldn't want to admit to someone else. Just see it for what it is, without adding judgment into the mix. Look for opportunities to demonstrate the opposite of this "short-coming." Notice the power that comes from realizing you're not constrained to act in any particular way. You are free. You are powerful. You are you.

OCTOBER 15

Patience is a conquering virtue. —GEOFFREY CHAUCER

It can be hard, in our busy lives, to allow things the time they require. Many situations can trigger our impatience: having to sit through a red light, a child not immediately complying with a request, someone explaining in detail something we already know, a meeting going past the designated end time. Anything we perceive as a delay can trigger a strong sense that "this is taking longer than it should!"

I've often wondered what causes the near-panic I feel when I'm being held up. When a child takes an extra thirty seconds to get in her car seat, for example, why does it feel like an eternity? Maybe it's tied in part to a vague awareness that our time on earth is finite, and a resulting sense of not wanting to waste any of it. Whatever the cause, I often recognize a belief that this should not be happening: *I should be there already; I should've made that light; we should be on the road by now; things should be moving quicker*; and any number of other "shoulds."

"Shoulding" like this makes time the enemy, and our expectations the standard by which we judge reality. *Did my fantasy of getting an early start come true? Did this person behave as I wanted them to?* It's hard to find peace when we feel like the universe isn't cooperating. By making friends with time, it's easier to be friendly to ourselves and to others.

INVITATION

Where might you exert your patience today? Decide to surprise yourself with patience when you're tested. Use a slowly exhaled breath to settle into what's happening, letting go of the rushing and shoulding. Feel unnecessary strain and tension dissolve.

OCTOBER 16

Patience is a virtue,
Virtue is a grace.
Grace is a little girl
Who would not wash her face.

—DICK KING-SMITH

Most of us will feel impatient at different points in our lives when we're not where we think we should be. We should be kinder or more loving. We should be more productive. We should lose weight / exercise more / eat better / drink less.

But what would happen if we stopped focusing on how we "should" be? Perhaps we're afraid that we'll become mean, lazy, entitled, fat individuals. I'm not sure about you, but having written this down, it seems to me that maybe we're all being a bit harsh on ourselves.

It may come down to thinking that we're not good enough to be fully happy, content, and fulfilled. Instead, we find ourselves chasing after an imaginary perfect self or perfect moment that simply does not exist.

INVITATION

Try to notice when you feel that something, or someone, should be different from the way it is. Rather than resisting reality, welcome it. Rather than fighting yourself, embrace yourself.

OCTOBER 17

Your work is yours to choose, and the choice is as wide as your mind.
—AYN RAND

It's satisfying to finish tasks and cross them off our to-do lists. However, with a nearly endless number of things to do and finite time, it can feel like we've never done quite enough. What's more, all this *doing* can get in the way of *being*—being connected with ourselves, others, and our experience. As we continually think ahead to the next task, rest can start to seem like an impossible luxury.

It can be helpful, when we're awash in a sea of activities, to plan our days more carefully. By defining what we can accomplish in a given amount of time, we're more likely to feel satisfied when we've met the mark. If we're overly ambitious and can't get to everything we'd planned, we can make adjustments.

This approach shifts our mind-set from "How much can I cram into today?" to "Let me use my time well." The first step is making a list of what we need to do; then, we simply find a time in our calendar for each task.

When we look back on any period of time in our life—a day, a week, a year, a lifetime—we want to feel like we made good use of it. We can rest when we know we've used our time well, pausing in our productivity as we allow ourselves simply to be.

INVITATION

Write down the things you want to accomplish today, and then find time in your schedule for each one. You may discover that everything will not fit into one day and you'll have to put some things off till later. Allow yourself to rest in the evening as you look back on what you did.

OCTOBER 18

When we think we're multitasking we're actually multi-switching. That is what the brain is very good at doing—quickly diverting its attention from one place to the next. We think we're being productive. We are, indeed, being busy. But in reality we're simply giving ourselves extra work.
—MICHAEL HARRIS

For the first time in my life, I'm a business owner. My to-do list sometimes seems endless, as I learn about aspects of a start-up I know virtually nothing about, from business and accounting to brand creation and marketing. It's easy to feel overwhelmed with the amount still left to do.

We can easily find ourselves jumping from one task to the next and worrying about the project we're working on. When this happens, we're often thinking about the future and what lies ahead or looking back to the past and regretting how little we accomplished earlier. But we only have this one moment. This is it. We can stay in our heads or live in the present. We can jump between ships or sail this one boat forward right now. The choice is ours.

INVITATION
When you find yourself feeling overwhelmed with the day ahead or notice that you're mentally multi-switching, take a moment to pause. Bring yourself back to the present and remind yourself that this is the only moment you have. Choose one task and stick with it. As the Russian proverb goes, "If you try to chase two rabbits, you'll catch neither one."

OCTOBER 19

Decide what to be and go be it. —THE AVETT BROTHERS

We often hold ourselves back from doing what we really want to do in life. We want to make changes, pursue a passion, or start something new, but we don't. We find reasons we can't do it, when in fact fear is getting in our way—*What if I give it my best shot and fail?*

We might also fear the opposite outcome: *What if I succeed?* Change is rarely easy, even when it's positive, as it brings new demands and expectations and problems to solve. And so, we might convince ourselves we'll do it later, and the weeks turn into months and then years—even a lifetime—and still our dreams sit on the shelf.

I had many fears and uncertainties as I began my private practice a few years ago. Would there be a need for my services? Would anyone call? Would I be able to pay down my start-up costs and meet my monthly overhead? Sometimes I feared that starting a practice would be just a big charade in the end, and the joke would be on me.

We can move boldly toward our dreams. It starts by declaring what it is we intend to do. Then, the biggest step we can take is simply deciding to start. Once we do, we'll find ways to remove any obstacle in front of us.

INVITATION

Identify something that you've wanted to pursue but haven't. What's stopping you? What is a small step you can take today in that direction?

OCTOBER 20

You are never too old to set another goal or to dream a new dream.

—LES BROWN

Dreams are magical and enchanting. They exist somewhere else, outside of our current reality. Imagining a desired future can provide excitement and escape. In dreams everything is possible. And there's something comforting about the fact that I *could* potentially be a music star. With dreams the end product is clearly visible. What's less apparent is the hard work required to *actualize* them. For me, this would involve learning how to sing, play the guitar, and write songs, for a start.

When we don't take steps toward a dream, the dream is preserved. We can always think, "I could have been … If only …" When we start to move toward our dreams and truly consider the actions required, however, certain dreams might appear less attractive. We can let go of any regret for not chasing these dreams. We can see the dream for what it is.

It's often helpful to look at our dreams with clarity and honesty. There may be dreams that we feel truly motivated to achieve. We might not know all the steps that will be involved, but we believe that we'll enjoy the process and work hard at it. We'll be doing what we love. We'll be living the dream.

INVITATION

If you have any dreams or ambitions, ask yourself,

1. Is this something that I truly wish to achieve?
2. Is it something that I'm prepared to work hard at, day-in, day-out, without guarantee of success?
3. Will the journey itself bring joy to my days?

If your answers are yes, then perhaps this dream is one worth pursuing. If not, it's never too late to dream a new dream.

OCTOBER 21

Every day, you can offer a devotional love to your own body. When you take a shower, when you take a bath, treat your body with all your love, treat your body with honor, with gratitude, with respect. When you eat, take a bite, close your eyes, and enjoy the food. That food is an offering to your own body, to the temple where God lives.

—DON MIGUEL RUIZ

We often hear about the importance of self-love, but it can be hard to enact. Though often not easy, taking care of our bodies is a great place to start since it's relatively straightforward.

I recently met with a dear friend who had lost nearly two hundred pounds—more than I even weigh. Having not seen her in years, I barely recognized her when she walked through the door. We talked about her journey to better health and how it involved many episodes of losing weight only to gain it all back.

She described finally starting to "eat for joy"—choosing foods that were quite literally filled with life, rather than ones that were stealing years from her. Through it all, I heard a deep appreciation for her own body and the desire to be a good caretaker of it. This mentality of caretaking resonated with me, especially with my ongoing health struggles. I'm more thankful for my body than ever and want to honor it.

Physical care is foundational to self-love—the better we feel physically, the better our ability to do everything else that matters to us.

INVITATION

How might you take loving care of your body today? What can you offer that your body will thank you for? Pay your body its due respect, as it carries the light inside you.

OCTOBER 22

But the fruit of the Spirit is love, joy, peace, forbearance, kindness, goodness, faithfulness, gentleness, and self-control.

—GALATIANS 5:22–23

When I was training as a clinical psychologist, one of my first supervisors was an insightful therapist with decades of experience. In cognitive therapy, clinicians often work with clients to help them to identify automatic thoughts—thoughts that pop up in their minds. My supervisor advised me to find out about the emotional tone of the client's inner voice. Was it harsh, soft, melodic, judgmental, kind, unforgiving, or encouraging? As she taught me, the way that we say something is just as important as what we say.

Similarly, the way that we do something is just as important as what we do. We can eat nutritious food, but if we're filled with anger at the time, the benefits seem to diminish. We can go for a walk in the countryside, but if we're arguing with our partner at the time, the beauty is lost. We can take a break from work, but if we're judging ourselves for being lazy, the potential for rejuvenation dissipates. There are different ways to do the same thing. The emotional textures that we bring to how we move, eat, drink, and even go to sleep are powerful.

INVITATION

Bring awareness to the way you do things. You might be eating, driving, reading, speaking, working, kissing, preparing food, or even thinking. What qualities would you like to bring to whatever it is that you're doing? compassion? kindness? love? patience? thoughtfulness? softness? empathy? Choose one that resonates with you and see if you can cultivate it in this moment.

OCTOBER 23

The greater part of our happiness or misery depends upon our dispositions, and not upon our circumstances.

—MARTHA WASHINGTON

How willingly we give away our happiness at times, not even realizing we have a choice in the matter. Thankfully, we don't have to be quick to part with our contentment—even when things don't go our way, as I was reminded during a recent dinner out with my wife.

We'd had great experiences at the restaurant in the past, but this time things were off. My field greens salad was filled with grit, which must have been the "field" part. It was the first time I've ever sent back a dish. I then felt my mood sour as we waited more than an hour for our main courses. *This is our first evening out in three years*, I thought bitterly, *and they're spoiling it.*

Thankfully, I realized my mood wasn't in the restaurant's hands. Maybe a gritty salad and a longer-than-usual wait weren't the end of the world. Besides, how many truly hungry people would give anything for such a meal? And I was enjoying an uninterrupted conversation with my wife. All was well.

Without this realization, I would have kept feeling that the restaurant wouldn't *allow me* to have a good time on our rare night out. Instead, I enjoyed the rest of our evening together and didn't ruin things for Marcia. On the drive home we had a heartfelt conversation rather than a rehash of the meal's lowlights.

When people or circumstances annoy us, we can find a sense of buoyancy that carries us through these daily hassles.

INVITATION

What kind of day do you want to have? Look for opportunities to choose your response when things don't go as you want them to.

OCTOBER 24

The best-laid schemes o' mice and men
Gang aft agley,
An' lea'e us nought but grief an' pain,
For promis'd joy!
—ROBERT BURNS

Rabbie Burns is widely regarded as Scotland's national poet. Today's quote is from "To a Mouse," which I learned at school for Burns Day when we'd read his works to celebrate his birthday. In this poem, the Scots author is plowing the fields, when he accidentally destroys a mouse's nest—a nest it needed to endure the cold of winter.

As the mouse experienced firsthand, sometimes life throws a wrench in the works. Even daily, life gives us mini-lemons: a crying baby on a flight, a tissue in the pocket of an item in the wash, rain on a vacation and sunshine back home. We can't avoid this. We can, however, choose how we respond.

We can hold onto thoughts of unfairness. We can ruminate as to why this has ruined our day, journey, or vacation. We can catastrophize about all the possible future negative consequences. But another option is to stay grounded in the present—to be alive to the gifts that exist right now, to take in the good aspects of our current situation, like the fact that we're on vacation and not at work or that the crying baby isn't ours! There's always a way to find that sense of buoyancy in the present moment.

INVITATION

Ask yourself this question throughout the day: Am I focusing on what is going right at this moment or what is going wrong?

Whatever the answer, you have the choice to direct your focus and open up to the joy that exists right now.

OCTOBER 25

When you hear your heart guiding you to your happiness, then make a choice and stick to it. —DON MIGUEL RUIZ

A friend of mine once said, "Being miserable is easy. It's hard work being happy." It always amazes me how readily we slip into a negative frame of mind and set up camp there. We find much more joy when we focus on the positive, yet this is often not our natural inclination. It seems we're programmed to pay attention to perceived problems: *What don't I like about this? What could be better? What are my shortcomings? What are others not doing for me?* In the process, our happiness goes out the window.

When we feel that downward pull, what stops us from saying, *That doesn't feel good—let me come back to a place of contentment?* We reflexively withdraw our hand from a hot stove; why is it different in our emotional lives? More often than not, we seem to seek out emotional "hot stoves" and, having found one, deliberately place our hand on it—then leave it there despite the pain. That is, unless and until we decide to take our emotional well-being seriously.

No matter how many times we've freely given up our happiness, we can make a different choice. We can choose to smile; to take a slow, cleansing breath; to remove the negative filter that biases our thoughts; to pursue activities that bring us joy; to stop doing things that deplete us. We can decide in advance to guard our peace of mind.

INVITATION

When you notice you're leaving a place of contentment today, do what you know is likely to bring you back. Do the work required to be happy.

OCTOBER 26

Joy does not simply happen to us. We have to choose joy and keep choosing it every day.
                                                              —HENRI NOUWEN

Over the weekend, I was at a wedding. I was sitting at a table with a group of people I didn't know and was feeling distinctly antisocial. I then realized that I had a choice. I could be Mr. Self-focused for the evening and keep to myself. I could also shift my attention to the woman to my left and the man to my right and learn about them. I could be curious, finding common ground and interesting differences. Thankfully, I ended up choosing the latter and had one of the most entertaining and interesting evenings in a long time. It all started with the awareness that I had a choice. I chose to bring the joy.

The way that we live our life is our responsibility. Where we place our focus is our responsibility. Becoming aware of the way we're thinking and feeling is our responsibility. Even the way we interpret this responsibility is our responsibility! We can perceive it to be a burden that hangs around our neck, or we can see it as the ultimate freedom.

INVITATION

As you enter each new situation today, remind yourself that you have a choice as to how you engage with this moment. In whatever way seems most natural and authentic to you, bring the joy!

OCTOBER 27

Whoever is not in his coffin and the dark grave, let him know
he has enough.   —WALT WHITMAN

We often see ourselves from a one-down position, making our value conditional on reaching some goal: *I'll be good enough if I get this job. I'll be beautiful enough if I lose weight.* Without realizing it, we may be continually judging ourselves as inadequate, with a nagging sense of not measuring up.

I noticed this tendency as I was heading to my office yesterday. As I thought about the many things I wanted to work on, I was gripped with anxiety. Would I get to them all? Would I do a good job? The deeper fear driving these questions seemed to be, What if I'm not good enough? I was seeing myself as starting from a deficit and hoping I could claw my way back to zero over the course of the day. It was an uninspiring mind-set coming from fear and a feeling of inadequacy.

Thankfully, on this occasion my mind caught the lie. And as it did, I felt the tension drain from my body.

We are already sufficient. Our worth is not dependent on what we accomplish. Each day is an adventure to be lived, not a test to be passed or failed. We can drop unnecessary self-judgments, even as we hold onto our goals. It's easier to meet life's challenges without the unnecessary weight of chronic feelings of inadequacy.

INVITATION

Notice if your mind tells you that you're not measuring up in some way. Remind yourself that you are already enough. You have everything you need. Anything you might accomplish is a bonus. Allow this awareness to energize your efforts today.

OCTOBER 28

We must accept finite disappointment, but never lose infinite hope.
—MARTIN LUTHER KING JR.

E mma and I were shocked to hear that a family member is in critical care. The consultants prepared us for the worst in the next twenty-four hours. When we visited him, he looked remarkably serene despite the intubation mechanically supporting his breathing.

What Emma found most difficult was that he appeared completely well a week ago and was making jokes as usual. When something like this happens, it's a difficult pill to swallow. Any notion of fairness simply evaporates.

At times like these, I have a deeper appreciation for the importance of hope. We can accept reality and still have hope for the future. Hope can be protective and comforting. Hope can dampen the fire of suffering to which the mind seems drawn. Hope can allow us to be there for others and help them in the ways they need. Hope can save our day.

INVITATION

Today, ignite a little hope. Choose to be open to the possibility that all will be well. It may be exactly what you need to carry you through the day and allow you to take action to support yourself and others.

OCTOBER 29

Be kind; everyone you meet is fighting a hard battle.
—REV. JOHN WATSON

Anyone who's suffered has probably felt alone at some point. Our private pain is ultimately unknowable by others, and our tendency when we're unhappy is to turn inward. It can start to feel like our suffering is uniquely personal.

But when we expand our awareness, we realize we're never alone in our pain. Countless others are suffering at any moment. We can start to recognize a community of suffering: our fellow students facing final exams, our fellow commuters trying to get to work on time, our fellow couples wondering why it's so hard to get pregnant.

Just yesterday I found myself feeling exhausted and uninspired in my spin class. My legs felt heavy, I couldn't get comfortable, and I wondered how I'd make it through the hour. Then I realized that the man next to me was probably as uncomfortable as I was. Indeed, everyone in the class was probably in pain. While I didn't take pleasure in their discomfort, I did feel more energized, as though we were parts of a single organism working together.

Just by being alive, each of us is engaged in a daily battle. Even the rude cashier, the jerk in the big car who cuts us off in traffic, and the inconsiderate office mate are fighting battles we know nothing about. The company of those who suffer alongside us can be immeasurably comforting.

INVITATION

Open your mind and your heart to others' struggles today. If you feel antagonism toward someone, remember that this person's life consists of joy and pain, hope and disappointment. Maybe it's even possible to feel some sense of connection with the other person through the pain that unites us all.

OCTOBER 30

Perhaps the greatest charity comes when we are kind to each other, when we don't judge or categorize someone else, when we simply give each other the benefit of the doubt or remain quiet…Charity is expecting the best of each other.

—MARVIN J. ASHTON

Yesterday we had family friends over to visit. One couple told a story that I perceived as being prejudiced. It hit a nerve in me, and I ended up saying that we should be wary of the way we describe others. I was trying to speak out for those who are often discriminated against. Unfortunately, my emotionally charged response meant that I came across as "that guy" on his moral high horse. Naturally, this went over like a lead balloon and tanked the previously jovial atmosphere.

While I think it was important to speak out, I could have pitched my response in a less preachy way. I realized that I was judging the couple for what they said. Ironically, I was making attributions about their whole characters while internally condemning them for doing the same to others.

By appreciating that numerous factors can lead individuals to hold certain attitudes and by seeing that one opinion, remark, or story does not define a person, we can let go of thoughts and feelings of judgment. We can give others the benefit of the doubt. We can start to see people as whole, complex human beings trying their best. We can accept and relax into the present moment.

INVITATION
Give yourself, and others, the benefit of the doubt today! See if assuming the best in others makes a difference.

OCTOBER 31

Forgiveness is an act of the will, and the will can function regardless of the temperature of the heart. —CORRIE TEN BOOM

People will hurt us in this life, in big ways or small. Drivers will behave badly, bosses will treat us unfairly, spouses will be unkind. In these instances, we always have an invitation to forgive, which is no small thing. How do we let go of the unfairness, the injustice, the desire for retaliation?

I've never gotten to forgiveness without having to let go of a resisting "but": *But she hurt me. But he's wrong. But I need to even the score. But he'll get away with it. But I don't feel like forgiving.*

Psychologists who study decision-making describe a phenomenon called the "endowment effect": things are worth more to us once we own them. We may be willing to pay three dollars for a mug, for example, but if someone gives us the mug for free, we wouldn't think of parting with it for less than seven dollars.

Perhaps forgiveness works the say way: When we're on the steep side of forgiveness, wanting to get there but unable to, we undervalue what it will feel like on the other side. But in truth, I can't recall ever being sorry I forgave; without exception, it's felt like a relief from an unnecessary weight. Once we let go of a slight, an insult, a personal injustice, or other hurt, we're transformed, and we know how much forgiveness is worth.

INVITATION

Is there something you could let go of today? Maybe it's an old hurt you've been carrying for years or a new petty grievance you could choose to forgive. While you're offering up forgiveness to others, remember to forgive your own shortcomings too.

NOVEMBER 1

Somebody should tell us, right at the start of our lives, that we are dying. Then we might live life to the limit, every minute of every day. Do it! I say. Whatever you want to do, do it now! There are only so many tomorrows.
—POPE PAUL VI

I'd like to send hearty congratulations to anyone who's celebrating a birthday, anniversary, or special occasion today. It just happens to be my birthday too!

We often save the things we most enjoy doing for special occasions. I find the steam room so relaxing but rarely go. I love going to the cinema—it makes me feel like a child for some reason—yet I seldom go. And we all have these things—things we enjoy doing, but don't regularly do.

The irony is that this moment is the only one we have. Each day is unique and as special as the next. We just happen to confer symbolism to certain dates. Which is lovely. It's wonderful to mark, acknowledge, and celebrate specific occasions. I wonder if we ever put certain aspects of our life on hold, though, waiting for a "worthy" occasion. Could we be preventing ourselves from living fully today?

INVITATION

Whether it's a special occasion or not, find a reason to celebrate today. If you can't think of a reason, celebrate anyway! You might want to put on one of your favorite outfits, prepare and savor your favorite dish, or do any number of things that you would ordinarily reserve for a "special" day. Today is special enough.

NOVEMBER 2

You should always be taking pictures, if not with a camera then with your mind. Memories you capture on purpose are always more vivid than the ones you pick up by accident. —ISAAC MARION

Frames can have a sharpening effect on our experience, like when a landscape seems more stunning when viewed through a window. Photos or videos are another type of frame; many times I've looked back at images of our kids, and the most ordinary moments seem magical. Even the smallest details seem momentous.

Narrative frames can function the same way. For example, I was recently talking with my wife after our family's Sunday brunch, watching the birds come and go from our finch feeder. I thought about what it would be like to recall sitting there with her and watching the birds as though I were telling a story as I looked back: *Marcia and I would sit at the table, watching the goldfinches and house finches as they ate niger seed from our bird feeder.* Those seemingly inconsequential moments suddenly felt so tender when told as a story.

We can put that frame around any episode in our lives, like taking the kids to the playground or making Saturday breakfast. Whatever the experience, seeing it in the past tense underscores that it's a time that can't last forever, making it more poignant in the present.

INVITATION

Think about the run-of-the-mill things you'll do today with someone you love or even alone. Imagine looking back on some of those times when this period of your life has passed. Notice what it does to your experience of those events.

NOVEMBER 3

I think everybody's weird. We should all celebrate our individuality and not be embarrassed or ashamed of it. —JOHNNY DEPP

A number of Christmases ago, my brother suggested that, rather than watch a movie, we play one of our dad's camcorder tapes. Our dad filmed virtually every possible occasion when we were growing up: school plays, birthday parties, sports days, holidays.

After the slow process of figuring out how to play an old camcorder tape on the television, we sat down to watch one of a family holiday in Malaysia. It was hilarious seeing our younger versions all together and fascinating to watch moments of which I had no recollection. I then turned around to see my father holding the camcorder. He was recording us watching the home movie. "Dad, why on earth are you videoing us watching the video?" I asked. "I just want to capture this moment," he replied. A few minutes later, I saw him pointing the camcorder at the television screen; now he was filming the old home video! I burst out laughing.

My dad's propensity to film and photograph so many moments used to frustrate me. Now I consider it one of his most endearing qualities. I love how serious he becomes when trying to "capture" the perfect moment, often disrupting it in the process. We all have peculiarities that make us who we are. When people eventually leave our lives, their idiosyncrasies will probably be the things we remember most about them.

INVITATION
Recognize the quirks of the people around you. See if you can appreciate and even enjoy those little oddities that make them unique.

NOVEMBER 4

Self-deception always manifests itself in terms of trying to create or re-create a dream world, the nostalgia of the dream experience. And the opposite of self-deception is just working with the facts of life.

—CHÖGYAM TRUNGPA

Why is packaging sometimes nearly impossible to open? Why is the cabinet of baking sheets crammed so full that I can't get things in or out of it? And why did I have to be wearing my favorite pants and shirt when I spilled food all over myself?

Most of us spend a lot of mental energy wishing life were better in some way. We might even start to feel like we're getting a raw deal in this whole *life* thing with all its surprises and inconveniences.

We forget that we can embrace the gift horse of life—all of it, just as it is. For better or worse, we don't get to pick the parts we like and send back the rest. Maybe most of our suffering comes not from the things we don't like but from our resistance to what is. For example, being cold is unpleasant; fighting the cold is miserable.

We would probably give anything for one more day of minor hassles if we knew our life were ending. With this awareness in mind, we can smile at life's inconveniences rather than curse them.

INVITATION

If you're reading this now, life in all its fullness is still available to you. Can you open yourself to all of it today, embracing even the unpleasant parts? Remind yourself that, no matter what else happens, if you have your breath, you still have life. Open. Smile. Breathe.

NOVEMBER 5

The only thing more important than your to-do list is your to-be list.
The only thing more important than your to-be list is to be.

—ALAN COHEN

Most of us have to-do lists. I have ones for work, research, the house, and personal tasks. They can be remarkably helpful in prioritizing items of urgency and importance, as well as being simple reminders of what needs to be done.

There are a few quirks about to-do lists. First, they never end. Even when we attack one with gusto and achieve everything on it, the list soon regenerates. Even so, we still seem to fool ourselves into thinking that the list will soon be finished forever. Second, we rarely seem to congratulate ourselves when we tick something off of one. Completing items on a list seems to be a given, as though it's just something that's required of us in order to be human. Third, no matter how much we achieve, it's seldom enough. Usually we've still fallen short in some way, or there's just that one extra item we could, or should, have completed too.

If we're not careful, each part of our day can be consumed by the illusory need to *be productive*, rather than the joy of just *being*. It's wonderful to be productive, but if we squeeze the bliss out of every moment in the process, is it worth it?

INVITATION

Experience the joy of just being. Notice if thoughts about what you "need" to do pull you away from the present. There will always be more to do and accomplish. That will always be there. For now, enjoy this moment. For now, just be.

NOVEMBER 6

Once we truly know that life is difficult—once we truly understand and accept it—then life is no longer difficult. Because once it is accepted, the fact that life is difficult no longer matters.

—M. SCOTT PECK

Acceptance can bring such peace, especially in difficult circumstances. Years ago I worked with someone who was famously critical and inconsiderate. Many times I would find myself upset at how she had treated me or someone else and would rack my brain to figure out why she was so difficult. I kept feeling like something was amiss and that she shouldn't be so hard to work with.

One day I saw so clearly the answer to my question: Because she's difficult. That was it! There was no mystery or mistake. She was just being who she was—someone who could be quite hard to work with. This realization didn't make working for her any more pleasant, but it did remove a lot of unnecessary stress from my job. I could let reality be what it was. Whew!

Acceptance lightens our load, but it's rarely easy. Most of us are very reluctant to give up the illusion that we have control over all aspects of our lives. But true acceptance helps us reclaim the control we do have. When things don't go the way we want them to, we can roll with the unexpected.

INVITATION

You probably have a forecast for how you hope and expect the day to go. Today, hold those expectations lightly. If you find yourself asking why things aren't going as you'd hoped, consider an obvious answer: Because that's how things are. See what it feels like to move toward acceptance.

NOVEMBER 7

Adopt the pace of Nature. Her secret is patience.
—RALPH WALDO EMERSON

Recently I returned home from an afternoon walk with my dog, Alfie. When I went to put Alfie in his cage at the end of his "lunch break," he scampered under a chair and showed me the biggest puppy eyes possible. Alfie didn't want to go back into the cage. This is how things were. Instead of instantly fighting reality, I lay down on the ground. Alfie slowly crawled over and lay down on top of my chest. He nuzzled into my neck and breathed softly. After about ten minutes, I sat up, and he promptly walked into the cage of his own accord.

It's a minuscule example, but there was something lovely about being able to allow the process to take the time that was required. We are often rushing toward deadlines and commitments. If only we could make peace with time. If only we could allow the world to unfold just as she intends. If only …

INVITATION

Today, make peace with time. See if you can allow each part of the day to take the time it requires. Give the world permission to unfold as she wishes! Allow nature to flow at her own pace.

NOVEMBER 8

Being under stress is like being stranded in a body of water. If you panic, it will cause you to flail around so that the water rushes into your lungs and creates further distress. Yet, by calmly collecting yourself and using controlled breathing you remain afloat with ease.

—ALARIC HUTCHINSON

Life offers countless opportunities to practice how we respond under pressure. We often become harried as our bodies and minds respond to stress, but we can aim for a sense of ease and grace whatever our circumstances.

Ease doesn't necessarily mean easy, of course—we can marry ease with great effort. Yoga practice is an embodiment of effort with ease. In the Crow Pose, for example, we place our palms on the floor and balance our knees on the backs of our upper arms with feet suspended off the floor. It takes strength, but it's not a matter of "muscling through" it. Attention to proper form—placement of the hands and knees, engaging the core muscles—brings grace to the pose.

Ease means working with things as they are. We can invite ease as we drive, letting the trip unfold in front of us. Ease is available as we walk, bringing a sense of uplift to our head and neck. We can bring grace and ease to our work, whether we're talking with someone, responding to email, or puzzling over a tough problem. Ease is the antidote to letting our challenges overwhelm us.

INVITATION

Find a sense of ease today. Maybe it means finding physical ease and dropping your shoulders each time you notice you're holding unnecessary tension. Maybe it's in the way you move. Perhaps you find ease in your responses to others, even those who challenge your patience. Wherever it's available, find ease and grace.

NOVEMBER 9

Contrary to what we usually believe, moments like these, the best moments in our lives, are not the passive, receptive, relaxing times— although such experiences can also be enjoyable, if we have worked hard to attain them. The best moments usually occur when a person's body or mind is stretched to its limits in a voluntary effort to accomplish something difficult and worthwhile.

—MIHALY CSIKSZENTMIHALYI

About halfway through last night's run, I noticed a cascade of thoughts had infiltrated my mind. I was mentally constructing lists of what needed to be done as different tasks popped into my head. As my attention moved from what I was doing now to "more important and pressing matters," my running pace began to slow. Planning for the future began to take away from my ability to fulfill my potential in the present. I returned my attention to what I was doing: running. The rest of the run was hard, fast, exhilarating, and rewarding.

In each moment, we can only ever try our best. But mental distractions can detract from our current level of effort, commitment, resourcefulness, creativity, and playfulness. When we fully immerse ourselves in an activity, we experience a sense of flow. We feel energized, focused, and in control. The challenge inherent in the current moment can raise our game and our spirits if we give ourselves the opportunity to grow.

INVITATION
Become absorbed in whatever you are doing. See if you can live in the present moment and simply try your best!

NOVEMBER 10

There are two tragedies in life. One is to lose your heart's desire. The other is to gain it. —GEORGE BERNARD SHAW

Our brains are good at tricking us into thinking that happiness exists at some future endpoint. We continually chase an "if only": *If only I had my driver's license, then I'd be happy. If only I were with that person. If only I had that house. If only I could stop working.* These expectations are false as true contentment doesn't come from gaining something we lack.

Yet these fantasies about what will bring us happiness are powerfully compelling, and so we continually fall for them. I often find myself chasing an idealized state of "more happy" through the foods I crave and my drive to eat past the point of being comfortably satisfied. "Just have a bit more," my mind tells me, "then you'll feel *completely* satisfied." Except I don't.

Pleasure, possessions, and accomplishments can enrich our lives in certain ways, but they can't make life fundamentally better. There isn't some essentially happier place, no matter what we do, who we're with, where we live, or how much money we make. This is it—the full deal.

That realization might seem like bad news on the one hand. But the good news is that we can direct our energy toward our best shot at contentment—not in getting or having, but rather in doing and being.

INVITATION

See if you can notice today when the mind tells you to grasp for something that will finally satisfy. Can you open yourself to the experience of longing—seeing and feeling your desire—without getting lost in it or necessarily acting on it? Having acknowledged it, is it possible to rest in what is?

NOVEMBER 11

This is it. —THICH NHAT HANH

We all have ideas about what will bring us happiness. I remember writing to Santa one Christmas for a Star Wars lightsaber. I knew that if I had a lightsaber, I would be content *forever*. I was pretty happy (though I wouldn't say I attained a transcendental state of bliss) when I received a torch, or flashlight, instead. It was big and relatively powerful, so it looked a little like a lightsaber when all the lights were off. It didn't cut through objects, though, which was probably for the best since I was seven at the time and the living room furniture might not have lasted long.

As the Zen Master Thich Nhat Hanh writes, "This is it."

This is it my friends. No more, no less.

This is life, in all her beauty and glory.

We'll all have sparkling moments and stinky moments, and both will pass. The only thing constant is change. Our mantle, then, is to flow with the world and see the joy, beauty, and meaning in each moment.

Life has offered us this gift. All we have to do is receive it.

INVITATION

Today, embrace the gift of life. Whatever reality brings to your doorstep, try to see the beauty, joy, and meaning that are here! This is it.

NOVEMBER 12

Technology is a useful servant but a dangerous master.
                                          —CHRISTIAN LOUS LANGE

Almost every area of our lives requires us to use the internet—work, school, shopping, home repairs, communication. When I finally gave in and got a smartphone, I planned to use it for the phone, calendar, and occasional email. And yet, somehow I've amassed more than a hundred apps. Some of them are quite handy, like the one that reminds me when it's time to do my physical therapy exercises.

At the same time, useful apps also provide a good excuse to be on our phones. While we have them out to check the weather, we may as well check our email, and social media, and the news, and on and on. Our screens have a way of pulling us in. I often find myself staring blankly at my array of apps, thinking there must be something there to entertain me.

Our time on this earth is limited, and it sickens me to think of wasting precious moments hoping my phone would provide some elusive sense of satisfaction. At times, I imagine the freedom I would feel from hurling it into the depths of the ocean. Unless we commit to living apart from the mainstream, however, technology is going to be part of the reality of our lives. Thus our relationship with technology will need periodic tending in order to check the inevitable sprawl of screen time.

INVITATION

Take stock of your relationship with your phone, computer, tablet, and television. Has the use of your phone or other devices crept insidiously into too many corners of your life? Could your relationship with technology use a tune-up? Make any changes that would bring you opportunities for real engagement.

NOVEMBER 13

A pat on the back, a caress of the arm—these everyday, incidental gestures that we usually take for granted, thanks to our amazingly dexterous hands. But after years spent immersed in the science of touch, I can tell you that they are far more profound than we usually realize: They are our primary language of compassion, and a primary means for spreading compassion. —DACHER KELTNER

Last night, I was sitting in the living room of our new home with Alfie lying on top of me. As I stroked his soft, floppy, puppy ears, he began to breathe more slowly and to close his eyes. This gift of touch was a two-way street: we were both enjoying the present.

This moment reminded me of when I was a little child. Most nights, before going to sleep, I would ask my dad for a "stroke-o-back." I used to love the warmth of his hands rubbing my back as I fell asleep. I remember chatting to my dad about it a few years ago. When I was a child, I thought it must have been a chore to come through and stroke my back almost every night. I was surprised when he said that this was one of his favorite parts of the day. He even said that he missed this little family tradition.

It's easy for all of us to overlook the sensations that arise through touch each day, whether it's the feel of your hair in the shower, the heat of your drink in a cup, or the texture of the steering wheel as you drive.

INVITATION

Connect to the present moment through the gift of human touch. For instance, hug or kiss your partner, stroke a pet, or maybe even give your head a little massage.

NOVEMBER 14

Life is grace. Sleep is forgiveness. The night absolves. Darkness wipes the slate clean, not spotless to be sure, but clean enough for another day's chalking. —FREDERICK BUECHNER

Our bodies have a remarkable power to heal. Over the weekend I sliced open the pad of my finger right after I'd sharpened my favorite knife. Thankfully, my body knew what to do. The bleeding eventually stopped, the pain subsided, and soon I could use my finger dexterously again.

Healing is all around us. And thank God for it. Our bodies heal, our relationships heal, and our overstressed minds can heal. Even the scars we bear tell our story of healing—that we were wounded, and now we've recovered. We appreciate the light of a new dawn all the more when we recall the terrible night before.

INVITATION

Think back on times when things were harder for you than they are now—a time you were ill, or facing enormous stress that has resolved, or any other major challenge. Take a moment to notice what it's like having that issue behind you. If you're still in the middle of a big challenge, remember that in this life, healing is available.

NOVEMBER 15

There are two ways of spreading light: to be the candle or the mirror that reflects it. —EDITH WHARTON

When we're with others, we can lift them up or push them down. We can be the light or the darkness. If we choose to be the light, as Edith Wharton suggests, we can be the candle or the mirror that reflects it.

Reflecting on the most joyful and challenging experiences in my life brings back a range of emotions, from appreciation to sadness. A white canvas splattered with different colors of paint captures the essence of mixed emotions. But the common denominator is relationships. My loved ones played an integral role. Whether they were the ones with whom I shared a happy time or who supported me through difficulties, others were at the core.

This type of connection with others brings such joy, meaning, challenge, beauty, depth, and pain. The best and the worst of times are often related to those who mean the most to us.

INVITATION

I'd like to invite you to reminisce with your partner, friend, family member, or colleague over a fond memory you share. When you remind this person of the memory, really tap into the experience of spreading light. Fully engage in the process and feel the words that you speak or type. Imagine being back in that situation and remember how you felt then. Be the candle or the mirror that reflects the light.

NOVEMBER 16

Life is made up of moments, small pieces of glittering mica in a long stretch of gray cement. It would be wonderful if they came to us unsummoned, but particularly in lives as busy as the ones most of us lead now, that won't happen. We have to teach ourselves how to make room for them, to love them, and to live, really live.

—ANNA QUINDLEN

We rarely realize, as time flies by, that we're creating memories we'll look back on years later. In 1995 I was making a memory of the first Thanksgiving with my in-laws, though they weren't yet my in-laws. My wife and I recently reminisced about that period of our lives, when we were studying abroad in Strasbourg and her dad and sister traveled to visit her for the holiday. Marcia and I weren't yet a couple and I had hoped she might like me better if I made a good impression on her family.

It's shocking now to realize that some of my most vivid memories are more than twenty years old—well before marriage, kids, a career. Soon we'll be creating memories of high school graduations, the first time meeting our son- or daughter-in-law, our oldest child's first day of college, the first night of an empty nest. What memories are you creating now that you'll look back on in twenty years?

INVITATION

Pick one activity from your day that you want to experience fully. (It may be helpful to add an alert to your calendar to remind you to pay attention to it.) What do you notice? What emotions are present? What physical sensations? See what it's like to bring your full awareness to an experience you may look back on years from now.

NOVEMBER 17

Some of us think holding on makes us strong, but sometimes it is letting go.　　　　　　　—HERMAN HESSE

Today my dog, Alfie, was stretched out sleepily on the sofa. I stepped away briefly, and when I returned, I noticed him standing by the table. My laptop screen was off, and Alfie had a guilty look. There it was: my charger, in two pieces. His razor-sharp incisors had cut through the wire. The laptop was fine, remarkably, but this little incident threw me. A new charger appeared to be an unnecessary and preventable expense. I really had a bee in my bonnet. It was on my mind for most of the morning. I was frustrated with myself for leaving Alfie alone in the kitchen.

After a couple of hours, I realized that enough was enough. The event had passed and yet it still clouded my thoughts. I went through all the real negative repercussions: I would have to go into town and buy a new charger. I then asked myself, How will I feel about this in one year? The chances are that I'd barely even remember it. I'd probably look back on it and smile. I might even think, *What a cute pup, chewing through the laptop charger—classic Alfie.*

INVITATION

We all experience little frustrations and annoyances throughout the day. Notice if your mind is replaying one over and over, criticizing yourself or someone else. See if you can step back from these thoughts and ask yourself, How will I feel about this in a year? It might just be the nudge you need to let go of little grievances and experience a fresh, new perspective.

NOVEMBER 18

I am always in quest of being open to what the universe will bring me. —JILL BOLTE TAYLOR

As a trauma therapist, I've been struck by the power of memories to haunt us even years after an event. Over a year ago, I was randomly assaulted by someone who outweighed me by about a hundred pounds. Although I wasn't seriously hurt, the episode was etched deeply into my brain and body. I still feel echoes of it when something triggers my memory.

There are other reverberations of that event. It inspired me to write two blog posts about common reactions to trauma, which several people said helped them to understand their own responses to trauma. In the aftermath of the assault, I also became much more aware of the loving support available to me from family, close friends, and my colleagues.

I'm not endorsing an easy platitude like "Everything happens for a reason," but I recognize that the story of my assault is much richer than I knew at first. Our initial "this is bad" reaction can evolve to include positive effects, like my deeper understanding of trauma and of how the nervous system heals over time. As impossible as it may seem at first, good can come even from the lowest points in our lives.

INVITATION

Think of an event in your life that was bad at the time but led to something better. Maybe a job loss opened unexpected opportunities, or a major disappointment forced you to grow. Keep this event in mind today as you practice opening a bit more to the fullness of your experience, bringing greater equanimity to your life as it unfolds.

NOVEMBER 19

Explore the world with an open mind.
—MADELEINE ALBRIGHT

There are often events in our lives that were challenging at the time but which led to something better: the unwanted end of one relationship that gave rise to an even more loving one, or any number of other tough circumstances that resulted in growth and appreciation.

When we're in the middle of a difficult experience, though, it's much trickier to imagine or predict future benefits. Thankfully, there's another option. We can simply pause for a moment. We can pause and create a little sacred space.

In this sacred space, we can become explorers. Whenever something happens that's unexpected or undesirable, it can be incredibly useful to explore aspects of the present moment—our thoughts, emotions, feelings, and the world around us.

As an explorer, it's helpful to approach the situation with a gentle curiosity. We can be inquisitive as to what exists here without presuming we already know the answer.

INVITATION

Notice when you feel frustrated, upset, or irritated today. Use this as an opportunity to explore the current moment. What you discover may surprise you!

NOVEMBER 20

*Action seems to follow feeling, but really action and feeling go together;
and by regulating the action, which is under the more direct control of
the will, we can indirectly regulate the feeling, which is not.*

—WILLIAM JAMES

Our circumstances can have big effects on our emotions. For example, the tenderness we feel toward our loved ones over a relaxing meal is hard to access when we're late and rushing to an appointment.

Back in high school, I learned an important lesson about creating the conditions that enable our best emotions to emerge. My car had a flat tire, and when my dad came home for his lunch break, I showed it to him and asked what I should do. Initially, he seemed annoyed, presumably because he was busy. He said he'd be back in a minute. When he returned, he was wearing clothing more suited to tire changing. He told me he knew he'd be more patient working on the tire if he were in the right clothes for the job. I felt myself relax as I sensed his acceptance of the situation.

That episode has stuck with me in my interactions with my own kids. We don't have to force ourselves to feel patient but can instead behave in ways that allow patience to emerge.

We can't always arrange our lives to foster our preferred emotions, but often we can deliberately create conditions that change our hearts. In the process, we might change someone else's experience.

INVITATION
Think today about the person you want to be—for example, strong, loving, compassionate. Set the stage for being that person, for yourself and for others.

NOVEMBER 21

What we do see depends mainly on what we look for.

—JOHN LUBBOCK

During especially busy times—say, times when you're moving the contents of one house to the next as well as starting a business—it can be easy to focus inward, getting caught up in what we "have to do," overlooking what's going well and forgetting that everyone else has similar amounts on their plates.

When we're busy and feeling the pressures of life, it can be worthwhile to stop and smell the roses. This can be metaphorical, as in pausing to consider those aspects of our life for which we're grateful, but today I mean this quite literally.

A recent study asked nearly four hundred people to notice how nature or human-built objects in their daily surroundings made them feel. As you might expect, those who noticed natural objects experienced higher levels of happiness and connectedness to others, to nature, and to life as a whole. Furthermore, they reported feeling more prosocial, more helpful toward others. Thankfully this research shows we don't have to be walking over rolling hills in the countryside or through an enchanted meadow to reap the benefits of nature. This is about noticing the plant by the window, the bird perched on the roof of a building, the flower growing out of a crack in the pavement, or the tree near your workplace.

It's about stopping, even if for only a moment, to see the natural in our everyday world.

INVITATION

Today, notice nature. Throughout your day, pay attention to natural objects and become aware of any emotions or feelings that are evoked.

NOVEMBER 22

We will always be in the process of remembering how to love ourselves, then forgetting, then remembering again. —GAY HENDRICKS

I hear over and over in my clinical work that it's really hard to love oneself—much harder than loving someone else. There are tremendous benefits to loving oneself—not only in how we feel in our moment-to-moment experience but also in our ability to show love to others. There's nothing selfish about self-love.

But how do we practice self-love when we're not feeling it? Treating ourselves kindlier is a great starting place. There are endless small but meaningful ways we can show ourselves kindness: using a nice clean towel after bathing rather than the slightly damp one hanging on the back of the door; preparing a favorite meal; presenting our food with care; devoting time for a rejuvenating workout; adding a slice of lemon to a glass of water. I've found that setting a cloth napkin at my place when I eat breakfast or lunch makes the meal feel more special than I would have predicted. It brings a sense of self-respect.

These small gestures can improve our experience more than we might expect, and none of them require a lot of time or money. They simply require treating ourselves like someone worth taking care of.

INVITATION
Look for three small ways to show yourself love today. If you find it's hard to think of things, imagine what you might do for another person you care about, or what a friend would do for you. Enjoy the feeling of both giving and receiving kindness.

NOVEMBER 23

Vegetables are a must on a diet. I suggest carrot cake, zucchini bread, and pumpkin pie.
                                                                —JIM DAVIS

We're around the Thanksgiving period! I have fond memories of Thanksgiving in Philadelphia when I was studying at Penn. That year, a member of the society that funded my scholarship invited me to his family home. The house was packed with four generations of family, multiple dogs, and a spread of food on the dining room table that made me wonder if I'd died and gone to carb heaven. I remember feeling privileged to have this experience, while simultaneously missing my own family back in Scotland.

As you may know, Thanksgiving Day has its historical roots in cultural and religious traditions, beginning as a way to give thanks for the blessing of the harvest and the year that had passed. This holiday and time of year remain a wonderful opportunity to consider the blessings in our lives, wherever we are in the world and whomever we're with.

INVITATION

Think of the person or thing you are most grateful for in your own life. Hold that person or thing in your mind and heart for a few moments right now. Truly and fully experience what it feels like to have this blessing in your life. Allow the glow of gratitude to grow. Try this a couple of times throughout the day, wherever you are and whomever you're with.

NOVEMBER 24

Appreciation is a wonderful thing. It makes what is excellent in others belong to us as well. —VOLTAIRE

The individuals who enrich our lives are probably the same people who at times frustrate us to no end. It's easy to appreciate the enjoyable aspects of those we love but find ourselves rejecting their more challenging traits. We might imagine how much better people would be if only they were more like *this* or less like *that*.

I've often found myself appreciating my kids conditionally—admiring their intelligence except when it's used to argue with me; welcoming their displays of love but rejecting strong displays of less agreeable emotions; encouraging them to speak up for themselves but gritting my teeth when their loud voices shock my nervous system.

With time and practice, we can more fully appreciate a person for exactly who they are. We might even find that the things that bother us about people are often the flip side of traits we love about them.

When we let go of the conditions we place on our appreciation for others, we can be open to all the dimensions of the real person in front of us, including the ways they challenge us. Heaven knows we can present our own challenges to others! No doubt we'll continue to have conflicts with the people we care about, but we won't waste our energy trying to make them fundamentally different.

INVITATION

Bring to mind today someone you care deeply about. See if you can open more fully to who they are. Can you embrace even the aspects that annoy you, recognizing them as inextricable parts of this complete being who is unique among all those who have ever existed?

NOVEMBER 25

Everything has beauty, but not everyone sees it. —CONFUCIUS

Yesterday I attended a master class for mindfulness teachers at the University of Oxford. I was surrounded by individuals with varied professions and backgrounds: doctors, business consultants, researchers, and teachers from different parts of the world. Listening to their perspectives was a lovely reminder that we are all unique. No two people are the same, just as no two moments are.

Each moment is unique. Each breath we take is unique. Each bite of food, each bird that flies overhead, each tree, each laugh, each person's face, each piece of art, and each memory is unique. Yet we often approach a person or situation thinking that we know. We think we know what the sky looks like, so we rarely stop to look and admire it. We think we know what the person in front of us is going to say, so we stop truly listening. We think we know what our partner's face looks like, so we stop seeing all its beautiful little details.

INVITATION
Today, let go of what you think you know. Drop the illusion of expectation, and experience reality. Allow yourself to see the beauty that exists all around you.

NOVEMBER 26

In all of living, have much fun and laughter. Life is to be enjoyed, not just endured.　　　　　　　　　　　—GORDON B. HINCKLEY

During a visit to my in-laws' house over the long weekend, I looked out an upstairs window at the bare garden below. The glorious orange cosmos in full bloom at our last visit now felt like a distant memory. Then I realized this house will one day be a memory too—the crepe myrtles in the garden, the foxes and deer, the sunsets over the field, the flocks of birds darkening the sky.

My own grandparents' house nestled in the foothills of the Appalachian Mountains felt so permanent at the time. I had assumed those hundred acres in eastern Kentucky would always be a part of my experience, something I would share with my kids. But my grandparents have been gone for many years, and their house and land now belong to someone else.

The recognition that nothing lasts forever is tinged with sadness, but there's also a terrific lightness to it. In a very real sense, we are all just renting. Nothing we have will be ours forever—not the house and car we own, not our clothes and furniture. Even the molecules that constitute our bodies once belonged to someone else and someday will again. We are part of an endless flow.

The passage of time and eras puts ownership in a different light. We can take ourselves and our troubles less seriously because even those are borrowed. They, too, are passing away. In the meantime, let's live.

INVITATION

Embrace your role as a renter today, recognizing that all you have, even your life, is passing away. While this awareness could be cause for mourning, use it to celebrate instead.

NOVEMBER 27

Life belongs to the living, and he who lives must be prepared for changes. —JOHANN WOLFGANG VON GOETHE

One of my friends is currently trying to lose weight but had reached a plateau. During a chat about a month ago, he expressed feeling demoralized and hopeless. After our discussion, he looked back at the photographs and the weight he was earlier in the year, before he made the decision to become healthier, and was pleasantly surprised. His body shape had changed substantially. Slowly and steadily, he was becoming lighter, leaner, and stronger. Since the results were gradual, he hadn't recognized the full extent of them.

Boosted by a fresh wave of motivation, he adjusted his eating and exercise pattern a little. Last night he let me know that, for the first time in years, he weighed less than 100 kilograms, or 220 pounds. He'd broken this physical and psychological barrier and was feeling enthused. A certain confidence shone through as he shared this with me. I felt delighted for him.

It's easy to think that nothing changes. It's even easier to overlook the progress that we've made, across multiple aspects of our lives.

INVITATION

Today, take stock of all the ways in which you've developed or different areas in your life have advanced. Take a moment to see and appreciate the positive changes that have occurred in the past year, five years, or even ten years. Congratulate yourself and allow yourself to feel proud, happy, and grateful for all the ways, no matter how big or small, in which you've grown.

NOVEMBER 28

The heart is a strange beast and not ruled by logic.
—MARIA V. SNYDER

Momentary shifts in our emotions sometimes give us meaningful information, like when we feel afraid because we're in danger. At other times, however, we give our emotions more significance than they're due. For example, we might feel nervous about something and assume it means things will turn out badly, whereas in reality, we might just be anxious.

In cognitive behavioral therapy, this process is called "emotional reasoning" and is considered a cognitive error. It can be hard to avoid, especially when another cognitive error, the "confirmation bias," leads us to pay attention to things that support our beliefs and ignore the rest. We'll remember the one time we had a bad feeling and something unfortunate happened but forget the countless times our premonitions were false alarms.

Recently I noticed frequent shifts in my feelings about a book I was writing. At times, I felt confident it would turn out well; at others, I was gripped by fear and doubt. I began to see that these ups and downs had essentially nothing to do with whether I would do a good job or not— unless I allowed them to affect my work, of course. When I focused on the plan I'd set and let my emotions do what they would, I avoided getting caught up in them or using them as predictors of the outcome. It was a great relief to step off that roller coaster.

INVITATION

Notice today if emotional fluctuations affect your thinking. If you find you're engaged in emotional reasoning, take a step back and simply observe what you're feeling, perhaps breathing with the emotion. Remind yourself that your feelings don't necessarily reflect something true about the world.

NOVEMBER 29

If you really are thankful, what do you do? You share.

—W. CLEMENT STONE

Yesterday, I took a certified personal trainer exam. I'm delighted to say that the exam went well and that I passed. After finding out the result, I felt very thankful.

The first thing that I wanted to do was share the news. I let Seth, Emma, my parents, and my brothers know. I felt thankful to God and to those around me for all their love and support, which allowed me to do my best today.

There's a lovely and empowering feeling that accompanies willful sharing. When we share, we're favoring abundance over lack. When we share, we're championing confidence over insecurity. When we share, we're showing love rather than envy.

INVITATION

Today my friends, I invite you to share. You might wish to share your time, company, knowledge, food—even a few stories, or a nice compliment. See how creative you can be with what you share. Tap into that place of gratitude and enjoy the gift of giving.

NOVEMBER 30

Learning never exhausts the mind. —LEONARDO DA VINCI

L ife is continually offering us opportunities to learn how to live better. We'll often need to relearn the same lessons repeatedly because we're prone to forgetting. We forget that distress usually comes from stepping out of the present and that working with reality is more effective than fighting it. We forget to take our problems less seriously.

This week I had an opportunity to remember that being late isn't the worst thing in the world. I was watching our kids while my wife went to the doctor, and her appointment ended up running late. I was dismayed to realize that if I couldn't make it back on time, I had no way to contact the patient I was scheduled to see. Typically, in these situations I'll feel my stomach tighten and my irritability rise, and I can get short with my kids.

Despite these tendencies, this time I was somehow able to keep a sense of lightness. I knew it would be unfortunate if I kept the person waiting and wondering where I was. Yet I knew this episode would soon be a memory and in no way would reflect a central defect on my part. I was able to laugh with my kids and stay present for them. It turned out I was five minutes late, which was no big deal.

Even when we're not able to handle a challenge the way we'd like to, we can store up knowledge from it to use later. No situation is a complete loss if we can learn from it.

INVITATION
Spend a few minutes identifying the most important lessons you've learned in life. Set an intention to benefit from that learning today.

DECEMBER 1

Everyone you will ever meet knows something you don't.

—BILL NYE

S omething that I forget time and time again is that the person in front of me is usually trying their best. It can be tempting to judge people based on specific actions. It can be so easy to label someone as bad, selfish, obnoxious, or arrogant—sometimes even evil. We rarely stand in the shoes of others, see through their eyes, and truly understand their perspectives. But if and when we catch ourselves displaying those same behaviors, we have the opportunity to see and understand the context that may have given rise to them.

In a similar way, as we grow in knowledge, experience, and wisdom, we can be lured into thinking that we have all the answers—that we know best. There's something intrinsically dangerous about that rigidity of belief and unwillingness to learn from others. As the Zen proverb goes, "It takes a wise person to learn from his or her mistakes, but an even wiser one to learn from others."

INVITATION

Today, stand in the shoes of others. Throughout the day, as much as possible, try to see situations from the perspective of another person. This could be while you're dressing your children, ordering a coffee, traveling to work, speaking to a friend, working out at the gym, or during any other part of your daily routine. See what insights arise from this new vantage point.

DECEMBER 2

We do as we have been done by. —JOHN BOWLBY

I recently had a therapy session with a very likable young woman who was heartbroken to find herself completely socially isolated at college. In our initial meetings, she had expressed an indifference to relationships outside her family. As we continued to meet, it became clear that this distancing was a well-practiced defense to avoid the pain of rejection.

The woman described several painful experiences from childhood through secondary school—times when she was made to feel weird or defective. As she recounted these events, she also discounted their effects, saying that they really weren't a big deal and that she wasn't sure why she was upset by them now.

As many of us do, she was struggling to take the perspective of a much younger version of herself. I encouraged her to consider the impact those events might have had on the person she was when they occurred—on a five-year-old, for example, in the earliest episode she recalled. She began to see these early learning experiences for what they meant at the time and their likely effects on her attachments as an adult.

Our early relationship experiences can have powerful and lasting effects. As we better understand our relationship patterns, we create the possibility of greater connection with others.

INVITATION

Think about your own early development. How would you describe your interactions with caregivers or peers at a young age? Do any episodes stand out as formative events in your social development—ones that might affect how you relate to others now? Take the perspective of your younger self as you explore these early influences.

DECEMBER 3

I was going to die, sooner or later, whether or not I had even spoken myself. My silences had not protected me. Your silences will not protect you…What are the words you do not yet have? What are the tyrannies you swallow day by day and attempt to make your own, until you will sicken and die of them, still in silence? We have been socialized to respect fear more than our own need for language.

—AUDRE LORDE

I was about five years old. I was sitting at the kitchen table and I had a fantastic story to tell my dad. I began telling it excitedly. My dad's attention drifted. He asked my mom a question. I was a little ashamed my story hadn't engaged him, but I decided to try again. I conjured up the courage and began once more. After a few moments, he asked my brother to pass the salt and then began speaking to my mom again. I didn't try to tell the story a third time.

My dad was probably exhausted after a long day. He might have had a lot on his mind. He may have had an important matter to discuss with my mom. The story that I bought into at the time, however, was that I was boring. The lesson I learned was that it was safer to stay quiet than to speak out.

Fear can hold us back from owning our voice and speaking up. Fear of being judged, laughed at, belittled, or excluded from the group. Part of my journey has been opening to the possibility that my voice is important, worthy, and worth sharing. Where are you on yours?

INVITATION

Share your voice with the world today. Share who you are. Because you are important, you are worthy, and your voice is worth sharing.

DECEMBER 4

Love is the most important and most rewarding investment you can make in another person.   —J. E. B. SPREDEMANN

All of us need to be acknowledged in our relationships. It can be very painful to feel like the most important people in our life don't notice us. For example, I remember as a kid asking my parents questions about the evening news to which they never responded. I recall the surreal feeling that maybe I hadn't actually spoken.

I know now they probably just wanted to watch the news without interruption, but at the time, it was bewildering. Now that I'm a parent, I've found myself doing similar things, like when I'm trying to read a recipe or prepare food. In the midst of life's busyness, it can feel like I don't have time to engage with my kids. Yet I have to wonder what message we give our loved ones when we don't really attend to them.

The only thing that really matters in this life is whether we use it to express our love. Nevertheless, it's easy to treat the activities of our lives as more important than our relationships. I don't know why we get our priorities so backward, focusing on things that pass away and ignoring what endures.

Showing love to others begins by simply acknowledging them—their presence, their perspective, their preferences, their needs. If we've lived out our love, it was a good day.

INVITATION

Consider what gets in the way of showing love to others the way you want to. What kind of day would it be if you gave priority to the people close to you above all else? Turn toward the people who need you as fully as possible today.

DECEMBER 5

We have to learn to be our own best friends because we fall too easily into the trap of being our own worst enemies.

—RODERICK THORP

When someone attacks us, we often feel hurt and retreat or feel offended and attack in return. Rather than wholeheartedly accept their insults, we might question what's happening in that person's life to trigger such vitriolic outbursts. We may realize that it's more about them than it is us.

When our minds hurl torrents of abuse at us, however, we often take these thoughts to be facts! We accept them without question. My mind said I'm lazy, so I must be lazy. My mind said I'm disgusting, so I must be disgusting. We rarely question or interrogate the truth, or usefulness, of these criticisms. We buy into these thoughts and feel low, anxious, insecure, demoralized, and hopeless.

We wouldn't allow the people closest to us to continually speak to us this way—or to speak to themselves in that way! We'd probably find the courage to respond at some point. Yet it's very easy to allow our own internal critics to run loose. We might believe that we need to be tough on ourselves in order to change. But research shows that when we're kinder and speak to ourselves as we would to a good friend, we're more likely to be happier, resilient, and motivated to change for the better.

INVITATION

Be your own best friend! When you notice your mind insulting you, let your mind know that these comments are unhelpful! Talk to yourself the way you would to someone you love and respect. It takes time and practice, but the lifelong benefits of having someone supportive by your side every step of the way are worth it.

DECEMBER 6

Believe something and the Universe is on its way to being changed. Because you've changed, by believing. Once you've changed, other things start to follow. —DIANE DUANE

Our thoughts often fit patterns that are based on the frequency we're tuned to, like a radio. The tracks we hear are predictable and depend on the station—today it might be the "poor me" station; other days, the pessimism, resentment, self-loathing, or worry stations. The more time we spend in a given mind-set, the more we reinforce it.

Identifying a negative frequency provides clues about the underlying beliefs that drive our specific thoughts, feelings, and behaviors. In cognitive behavioral therapy, we call these themes core beliefs because they represent a fundamental way of seeing the world, other people, and ourselves.

So much of our experience will depend on these bedrock assumptions. For example, we might have the core belief "I'm a person of value," leading to habits that serve us well. Unfortunately, we often buy into core beliefs like "I'm not enough"—beliefs that are not only unhelpful but also untrue.

If we discover negative core beliefs, we can practice "changing the station" proactively. We can notice when our minds are prone to unhelpful thoughts, like worrying about the day ahead immediately upon waking. With practice, we can tune in to more adaptive ways of thinking.

INVITATION

Take out your calendar. Think about specific days or times when you're most likely to be at risk of tuning in to unhelpful thoughts. What perspective do you need to adopt that will serve you better? Practice preempting negative thoughts with more adaptive ones and see what the effects are on your actions and emotions.

DECEMBER 7

Life isn't about waiting for the storm to pass. It's about learning to dance in the rain.
                                                            —VIVIAN GREENE

Planning serves us well. We can begin to predict and preempt potential problems, developing solutions to respond more effectively and efficiently. But even when we plan, the unexpected often has, well, other plans. Rain falls when the forecast is for clear skies, traffic accidents occur even if you're driving carefully, keys are misplaced, and belongings are left somewhere unintended. At these times we can feel thrown. We can tumble into a downward spiral of frustration and self-criticism. We start to endure the day, waiting for it to pass.

The key to keeping it together and recovering in these situations is acceptance. Acceptance involves acknowledging without passing judgment or condemnation that this is the way things are right now and that this is how we're feeling. For instance, actually saying out loud:

- "I left my bag on the train, and I'm really annoyed with myself."
- "I can't find my keys, and I feel so frustrated."
- "I don't know what's wrong today, but I just feel so low."

We can tap into how we feel, recognize it, accept it, and then flow with it. If we feel aggravated, we can call it and move with that irritation. If we feel down, we can call it and flow with that feeling. The magical part is that by accepting how we feel, we allow change to take place. We allow life to flow.

INVITATION

Today, flow with life! However you're feeling—whether happy, depressed, excited, disheartened, optimistic, or demoralized—accept the feelings that are there. Call it. And then go with the flow of life.

DECEMBER 8

I can't go on, I'll go on. —SAMUEL BECKETT

I once treated a physically active woman I'll call Sandy. Because of a series of injuries in her midforties, her favorite activities—things like cycling—were no longer possible. As a result, Sandy found herself feeling off-balance and missing the equanimity she had always enjoyed. As she became less available physically and emotionally, her relationships suffered. She deeply desired greater connection with the people she loved.

Responding to another person's disappointments is a balancing act. On one hand, we want to validate strong emotions like sadness and bitterness; on the other, we want to offer something more, something that transcends the difficulties. My work with Sandy emphasized self-compassion in the fullest sense, balancing acceptance of whatever she was feeling with a structured plan to move her toward her goals. Her determination to find a better way through her major difficulties was inspiring.

We never know what the people around us are going through. For some it's physical pain like Sandy's that makes routine activities a challenge. For others it's the daily torment of facing deep depression. For many it's the conviction that "I can't do this anymore," even as they do. It's naming the feeling and continuing to flow with life.

I'm continually amazed by the perseverance of many people I've known—people who manage to find joy and connection in lives that by all accounts are a daily struggle. That ability resides in everyone.

INVITATION

As you encounter any challenges today, tap into the deep well of resolve that is available to each of us. You are strong. Even when we think we've given all we have, we almost certainly have more. Embody strength and resolve throughout this day.

DECEMBER 9

It's all in the mind. —GEORGE HARRISON

We often think we know how strong or weak we are. We all have preconceived ideas of what we're capable of accomplishing. Sometimes in life a storm hits, and somehow we survive. Afterward, we're amazed at what we've come through. We wouldn't have predicted that we could have endured that hardship or recovered from such a blow. We might even be pleasantly surprised. The irony is that, despite this, we often then think, *But I wouldn't be able to go through that again if it happened once more.*

The 40 percent rule is a concept used by Navy SEALs. The principle is simple: even when your mind tells you that you've run out of steam, you need to tap out, and you have nothing left to give, you've only used up 40 percent of your reserve! There's still 60 percent left in the tank to get you home. This could be one reason behind the statistic that 99 percent of people who start a marathon finish it. Even when they hit that "wall" at mile nineteen or twenty and their minds say they're completely out of energy, the body still has enough juice to make it to the finish line six or seven miles later.

How often do we stop short of what we could achieve because our minds tell us that we've reached our limits? In what ways might we grow if we elevate our beliefs about ourselves?

INVITATION

Think about the fundamentals of who you are—those things you're certain you know about yourself. Consider in what ways they're empowering you or holding you back. Today, try to suspend these preconceptions. Let these ideas go, even if just for a day. Be open to new possibilities; feel that freedom and see what's possible.

DECEMBER 10

Appreciating sacredness begins very simply by taking an interest in all the details of your life. —CHÖGYAM TRUNGPA

Our minds often cast about, looking for fulfillment in novelty, distraction, or achievement, as if what we need is somewhere else. During his wedding weekend, Aria and I had a conversation about finding the sacred in our everyday experience. I return again and again to the realization I had at that time: sacred connection is found in what is already in our lives.

Awareness of this connection can catch us off guard. Recently I was chopping vegetables for dinner while the rest of my family read or played together. Suddenly I was hit with a deep appreciation for all aspects of my life, especially for my wife and our three kids, and for the home and food we share.

Joy and beauty are right here, in the people and the details in our lives that we often take for granted. They're in the table where we break bread together, in the silverware we use, in the floors we walk on, the doors we walk through, the sofas and chairs we sit on. They're in *this* meal, *this* conversation, *this* shower, *this* chore. Every day is an invitation to fully inhabit a life that is already yours.

INVITATION

In these final weeks of the year, explore your life intimately. Foster a mind-set of curiosity about things you may take for granted every day—the weight of your favorite kitchen knife, the feel of your refrigerator door handle, the texture of your clothing, the sound of your family members' voices, the color of their eyes.

DECEMBER 11

Life is a challenge, meet it! Life is a dream, realize it! Life is a game, play it! Life is love, enjoy it! —SATHYA SAI BABA

Yesterday I had a surreal moment of profound clarity. Everything that mattered—everything that was truly important—was relational: my wife, our families, our dog, and our friends. These were the foundation stones of my happiness. Everything else—work, money, reputation— seemed like a game. They were fun, but they weren't issues of life or death.

Sometimes we lose ourselves in the game. We become so immersed in the narrative we're spinning that we forget it's just a story. It's like living in the Matrix. The game seems like it's more important than everything else, as though it's the center of our universe. Then, now and again we gain that beautiful, tender, precious thing called perspective and let out a sigh of relief. We breathe softly and deeply, connecting on a deeper level to ourselves and simultaneously to something even greater.

At times, this perspective comes at a cost. The loss of a loved one or something that matters to us may force it upon us. Other times, we're blessed with this insight without the pain of a reality that we don't want to accept. We are given the gift of clarity.

INVITATION

Treat today like it's a computer game! You collect points and coins along the way, moving from one level to the next. It's a game to be played and enjoyed! So collect those coins and move to the next level, remembering that one day it'll come to an end. All that will matter then will be the people who were around you while you played.

DECEMBER 12

Ancient religion and modern science agree: we are here to give praise.
Or, to slightly tip the expression, to pay attention. —JOHN UPDIKE

Our minds are attuned to notice changes in our situation, whereas the status quo is given relatively little attention—particularly if the status quo is good. We're acutely aware of our health when we're sick, for example, and again when we finally feel better. But when we're well, and have been for some time, we rarely give our health a thought.

This tendency makes good sense, on the one hand, as our focus on problems encourages us to fix them. But on the other hand, it's easy to lose sight of all that is right in the world. As we focus on life's difficulties, we might even start to feel a sense of injustice about it all. Yet the difficult times we go through often reveal how much we have to celebrate.

I found myself celebrating life with my family this past week. Our son Lucas had suffered through a double infection that left him lying on the couch for days, exhausted and unable to eat. All the while, he was his usual stoic self, staring blankly and politely declining when I asked if he needed anything. I was heartbroken that I couldn't take away his pain.

It was a joyous Sunday brunch when Lucas finally turned a corner. My wife and I smiled at each other as we watched him devour the food I'd prepared. Suffering is unavoidable, but thankfully not the whole story. When we recall the good that we usually overlook, the best we can do is give praise.

INVITATION

Pay attention today to what this life offers you, and offer back your praise—whatever that means to you.

DECEMBER 13

Circumstances do not make a man, they reveal him.

—JAMES ALLEN

If you squeeze an orange with your hand, what comes out? What about if your friend squeezes the orange? or you use that expensive juicing machine that now stays in your back cupboard because it's an absolute nightmare to clean?

An orange contains orange juice. The juice comes from within the orange. We all know this. Yet when it comes to ourselves and how we feel inside, we often blame external events. We act as if outside agents magically place these emotions within us. You might think it was the driver that tailgated you on your way into work who ruined the rest of your day. The Stoics realized thousands of years ago that what truly influences our feelings, however, is our interpretation of events—our thoughts about what has happened.

Our minds can fall into the traps of dwelling on the negative parts of a situation, jumping to conclusions, and imagining the worst possible outcome. These mental filters can have a profound effect on how we feel, day-in and day-out. With awareness, we can begin to see and bypass these cognitive traps. We can free ourselves from our own minds and begin to experience a little more peace in the present moment.

INVITATION

Today, notice when you're feeling an emotion particularly strongly—for instance anxiety, anger, or frustration. Are you jumping to conclusions or imagining the worst possible outcome? Try to identify the mental filter that's currently in place. Then change your vantage point. Can you give someone the benefit of the doubt or decide to find a silver lining? See how many different ways you can view the same situation and notice how that makes you feel and act.

DECEMBER 14

There is never any need to get worked up or to trouble your soul about things you can't control. —MARCUS AURELIUS

It's remarkable that our minds and bodies can continue to react in a way we know doesn't make sense. For instance, recently I had a 7:00 a.m. medical appointment that had taken six weeks to get. That morning, I overslept until 6:37. I awoke and exclaimed profanely, recalling the doctor's strict cancellation policy for late patients.

When, by a miracle, I got to the hospital at 7:01, I began to relax—until I realized I'd forgotten to complete the forms they'd sent, which clearly read, "If the paperwork is not completed by the time of your scheduled appointment, *the office will have to reschedule.*" Mercifully, they decided I could still be seen.

Even as I felt panicked about being on time and doing the paperwork, I knew there was no real emergency. The worst-case scenario would have been rescheduling. And yet I couldn't shake the intense feeling of urgency as waves of stress continued to wash over me.

When we're in the grip of powerful emotions, we don't have to add to our suffering by struggling uselessly against them. It's like being caught in a riptide—trying to fight it directly only exhausts us, but swimming perpendicular to the tide brings us out of it. In the same way, making our emotional reactions the problem may just intensify them. Once the emotional wave has crested, we can watch it recede as our nervous system returns to equilibrium.

INVITATION

If you experience any emotional upheaval today, despite your best efforts to guard your mind and spirit, allow yourself to breathe with it until it passes. Let your reactions be what they are without labeling them as "excessive" or "unnecessary."

DECEMBER 15

Self-absorption in all its forms kills empathy, let alone compassion. When we focus on ourselves, our world contracts as our problems and preoccupations loom large. But when we focus on others, our world expands. Our own problems drift to the periphery of the mind and so seem smaller, and we increase our capacity for connection—or compassionate action. —DANIEL GOLEMAN

We all have those days when we don't feel happy and the small things seem bigger and little frustrations have a larger effect. Sometimes we just can't seem to pinpoint why we feel this way—there's no obvious rhyme or reason. We just feel "off."

When we're feeling lousy, our minds often criticize us for this. "What's wrong with you? Nothing bad has happened and yet you're feeling low? You're so ungrateful." Ironically, when we judge how we feel, we simply add to our suffering. We feel depressed about feeling depressed, anxious about feeling anxious, and angry that we're feeling angry.

At times like this, salvation can come from shifting our attention off ourselves and onto another person (or fluffy creature). By moving our minds outside ourselves, we can experience a little moment of peace. We can find an opportunity to build up the one thing that we know brings happiness and meaning to our lives: our relationships.

INVITATION

Shift your attention from yourself to others, but in a specific way: by making eye contact with them. We've all ordered a coffee without even seeing what the person serving us looks like. Look into the eyes of the person you're speaking to today and give yourself the chance to appreciate your relationship, and the present moment, a little more.

DECEMBER 16

Never let the future disturb you. You will meet it, if you have to, with the same weapons of reason which today arm you against the present.
—MARCUS AURELIUS

We often want to know how events are going to turn out, so we think through possible scenarios. It's as though we're going for a long drive and planning our every move in advance: *How will I navigate that busy intersection? What if heavy traffic makes it hard to merge? Will my car have any mechanical troubles?* These worries about the future can prevent us from connecting with what's actually happening.

The antidote to this kind of useless worry is trust. Can we trust ourselves to handle each moment of our future? Can we trust that we'll bring to future problems the same abilities we used in past ones?

In reality, all we can manage is the road right in front of us, literally and metaphorically. This kind of trust doesn't preclude planning, of course. But having planned as well as possible, we can take each moment as it comes, trusting that we'll deal with situations as they arise. We will have our faculties at each moment of our lives and will do the best we can. This sense of trust allows us to let go of the future and return to what (or who) is right in front of us.

INVITATION

Resolve today to release worries about what lies ahead, remembering that you're equipped to manage situations as they arise. It may help to adopt a phrase to remind your mind to loosen its grip—for example, "I'll deal with that when the time comes," or "That's something to think about when I get there."

DECEMBER 17

This is the beginning of a New Day…I can waste it or grow in its light and be of service to others. But what I do with this day is important because I have exchanged a day of my life for it…I hope I will not regret the price I paid for it.   —AUTHOR UNKNOWN

Today's opening is from a poem that I read on the desk in my father-in-law's study. I photographed it with my phone and now read it most mornings when I wake up to reorient my outlook.

Some simple truths are easy to forget. We are all blessed to be alive. We are all autonomous beings that truly have the choice of what we do each and every day. What we do is important because our time is one of the most precious commodities we have. The challenge remains finding ways to remember these truths and to act on them today.

INVITATION

Today, carve out the time to find an artifact—a phrase, a quote, a poem, a fortune cookie message, an image, anything—that inspires you to be the best *you* and to connect to what's most important in your life. Write the words or place the image somewhere you will see it each day—somewhere like on the fridge door or by your bed. It takes a little effort, but once it's in place, it's a wonderful way to start your day.

DECEMBER 18

In the depths of winter, I finally learned that within me there lay an invincible summer.
—ALBERT CAMUS

I learned a lot about strength this week from a woman who was raised in India by her grandmother. Each week when they went to the temple, her grandmother would tell her to pray not for things to go well but for strength to face any challenge. Apparently, these prayers have been answered. In the years I've known her, she has been a rock for her family as they have faced several trials. These struggles seem to have strengthened her kindness, generosity, and indefatigable energy.

Her words reminded me of a time when our family income went up for a few months. I had hoped to save half the funds and use the rest for projects we'd been planning. Instead, we had to use the money to cover unexpected expenses: a flood in our basement and a trip to the emergency room. I felt cheated—just when I thought we might finally get a little bit ahead, our savings were wiped out. But then I realized I was looking at it backward. In reality, just when we needed money to cover additional expenses, we had it. It was a gift.

We were never promised a life of ease, but strength is available to face whatever lies before us. We can focus either on how unlucky we are to face a challenge or on how fortunate we are to have the inner strength to deal with it. By focusing on our strength, we take back responsibility for how we answer life's call.

INVITATION

Ask for strength today, opening yourself to any difficulty you encounter. Trust you will have the resources to navigate challenges with grace and skill.

DECEMBER 19

Being the richest man in the cemetery doesn't matter to me. Going to bed at night saying we've done something wonderful, that's what matters to me.　　　　　　　　　　　　　　—STEVE JOBS

An old friend shared recently that the previous couple of days had been rough for him. His wife had opened up and revealed that she felt less happy and less connected to their marriage. She was worried that they'd lost their spark and were drifting apart. We'll call them John and Alice. John confided that he'd noticed they were busier with their careers this year but was surprised to hear the extent of his wife's unhappiness. I was surprised to hear about this too. John and Alice had a marriage that appeared blissfully content on the outside—a seemingly perfect couple. The sobering truth is we never truly know what others are going through. We might look at another husband and wife, or boyfriend and girlfriend, and think that they have it all, without realizing that they're struggling to conceive or are considering separation.

One of the most illuminating things John shared with me is that he and Alice were at a stage in their lives when they had more than ever before: higher salaries; a bigger, nicer house; newer, better cars. It struck me that we can have a beautiful house and fancy cars outside, but if we're sitting with our spouse crying and questioning where it all went wrong, does it really matter?

INVITATION

Ask yourself what truly matters in your life. Take some time to really think about it. Connect with whatever that is today. For instance, if it's a person, listen to them, share with them, kiss them, surprise them with their favorite flowers, or write them a little loving note. Act on what matters to you right now.

DECEMBER 20

Life goes by so very fast, my dears, and taking the time to reflect, even once a year, slows things down. —HILLARY DEPIANO

Our little speck of a planet in this vast cosmos has nearly completed another trip around the sun. As the year draws to a close, it's a good time to consider what the year has brought you. For example, what has changed for you since January? What's kept you busy? Were there any surprises, or regrets? What do you think you'll remember from this year?

As I look back, I'm struck that while it hasn't been an easy year, it's been a good one thanks to my closest relationships. My wife has been unwavering in her love and support, and this partnership with Aria has been immensely helpful. The sweetness of my three children brings tears to my eyes and more than compensates for the stress of parenting. I've also found that my own challenges have given me a deeper understanding as a therapist of what others go through.

We have everything when we have people to love who love us back. This familiar realization is one we return to over and over. Like the earth moving around the sun, we come full circle back to what we know is true.

INVITATION

While we still have more than a week remaining in this calendar year, begin reflecting on what it has brought you. You might talk about these and other things with a partner or friend who shared the year with you. See what stands out as you look back.

DECEMBER 21

Life is available only in the present moment. If you abandon the present moment you cannot live the moments of your daily life deeply.
—THICH NHAT HANH

If you knew everything that was to going to happen in your life, what effect would this have? Would you worry more about upcoming obstacles, or find comfort knowing that you'll navigate the challenges? Would you find this future knowledge liberating or constraining? Personally, I'm happy I don't know. It feels like this would bring an added layer of responsibility. The present moment seems to hold enough on its own.

As we've come back to, over and over, time and time again, all we have is the present moment. The best we can do is live each moment consciously and deeply. Whether the clouds are raining or the sun is shining, whether we're driving along an empty road at night or stuck in the morning traffic, whether we've just eaten the tastiest burrito imaginable or are envying the food of the person sitting next to us, whether our marriage is blossoming or struggling, whether we feel fat or thin, whether we're being kind or harsh to ourselves, all we have is the present moment.

INVITATION

Today, connect to the present moment. Feel your feet on the ground. Notice the air move as you breathe. Hear the sounds around you. This is all you have: the present moment. The best you can do is live it out consciously and deeply.

DECEMBER 22

One of the main discoveries of meditation is seeing how we continually run away from the present moment, how we avoid being here just as we are. That's not considered to be a problem; the point is to see it.

—PEMA CHÖDRÖN

Inhabiting the moment takes care of most anything that could trouble us. And yet, even with this awareness, we reflexively leave the present, often living in fear of an imagined future. I find myself believing it can't be that simple—there must be something I'm supposed to add to presence.

Many of us find the voice of worry, and its suggestion that we think ahead to make sure everything will be okay, very compelling. Even if things are all right at the moment, we want to know if we'll be okay in the future. The answer, of course, is yes, we'll be okay—until we're not. And that will be okay too.

I've had this awareness countless times and then been seduced by the desire to know the end in advance. Rather than letting events unfold one by one, my mind continually skips ahead to think through each one: *How will this one go? And this one? Am I prepared for this event?*

The end of this year brings with it a return to fundamentals. There is much to discover through the most basic of practices. Worries and dread melt away just by being in our experience.

INVITATION

Set a firm intention to be present in your life today. You might adopt a mantra that helps you refind your focus when you notice it's drifted to worries or regrets—for example, "That's not happening now" or "I am here." What happens when you resolve to stay present?

DECEMBER 23

Peace begins when expectation ends. —SRI CHINMOY

Since the Industrial Revolution and the direct link between time and money, Western society has equated busyness with higher status. We want to be seen as working long hours, and we view others as more important when they're constantly on the go. However, there's a difference between being efficient and being busy. If two people both complete the same amount of work to the same standard, why would we glorify the person still in the office at ten o'clock at night rather than the one who leaves at five-thirty to make it home in time for dinner with the family?

We all have mental rule books for life. We often look at what others do and unconsciously internalize rules. For instance, at work it might seem wrong to leave at a certain time, to take the time to enjoy a wholesome lunch away from your desk, or to hold a meeting with someone else by going for a brisk walk.

Most of the rules we internalize are socially constructed. Nature doesn't have a manual with strict instructions. The world doesn't have a universal rule book. Life is freer, more dynamic, and ever changing.

INVITATION

Look out for some of the rules you've taken on. What do you think has to happen to have a "good," "happy," or "productive" day? In what ways is this linked to how you want others to see you? What would be the consequence of breaking, letting go, or changing some of these rules? Give yourself a break from expectations and mental rule books, even for just one day. It might be exactly what you need right now.

DECEMBER 24

Christmas isn't just a day, it's a frame of mind.
—VALENTINE DAVIES

Merry Christmas Eve, my friend! Wherever you are in the world, whomever you're with, and whether you celebrate Christmas or not, I wish you peace, happiness, joy, and connection.

The Christmas season brings a heavy dose of expectation along with it. There's often the social pressure we internalize—that we should have a "perfect" Christmas as well as the limitless expectations we might have for Christmas gatherings, among them perhaps the following:

- What others might say (cue the racist relative)
- How others might act (including thoughtless reactions to our thoughtful presents)
- What others might give us (with usually vain attempts to hide disappointment)
- How the food should taste (after laboring for hours in the kitchen)
- How we should feel (happy, grateful, and upbeat, for instance)

This time of year may also bring back memories of those who are no longer with us. The silver lining is that it may also give us an opportunity to remember and pay homage to those we wish could be with us and to connect to those who are.

We have the power to take each moment as it comes, without expectation or judgment. We can even learn to enjoy the happy, awkward, and unexpected moments of this Christmas season.

INVITATION

Release the expectation of having a perfect Christmas and allow yourself to flow instead with life exactly as it unfolds. Relinquish control over others and be gentle with them and yourself. You might be amazed at what you then appreciate!

DECEMBER 25

This is a place where grandmothers hold babies on their laps under the stars and whisper in their ears that the lights in the sky are holes in the floor of heaven.
—RICK BRAGG

On Christmas Day, more than a decade ago, I became a dad. It's impossible to describe the experience of meeting a brand-new being—a person who moments before had never taken a breath.

For years it had been just my wife and I. Then, for months, her belly was growing, and for two days she was in labor, followed by an hour and a half of pushing with all the strength she had left. And then—joy to the world!—a slimy little baby popped out, I was cutting the umbilical cord, Marcia held him for the first time, and I beheld him. In that moment, we stepped into a timeless space where we had always known and loved our tiny Lucas, our "Bringer of Light," a star from the heavens sent through a portal to eternity.

The relationship of parents with their children is very simple for the first few months: keep them alive and tend to their needs. And then babies become toddlers and develop wills that may not align with our own. Before you know it, you're a parent to a tween, a teen, a college student, an adult. And if we can be open to the being in front of us—with their unique collection of preferences, strengths, and foibles—we'll see a thing of wonder.

INVITATION

Look in wonder today at the people in your life. Let yourself see them as they really are, beholding them as if for the first time, no matter how long you've known them.

DECEMBER 26

We are what we repeatedly do. —WILL DURANT

As I looked around the dining room, four generations of my wife's family were sitting, laughing, and chatting together. Someone then asked everyone at the table, "If you could invite one person to Christmas lunch, who would it be?"

As the conversation progressed, we discussed our selections. This brought another consideration to my mind: if you could be more [*insert adjective here*], what adjective would you choose? How would you know?

Our values are embodied in our actions. If we say that we are charitable, but we do not share our time or resources with others, is it true? If we hold generosity to be important but are continually stingy, which one are we? If you think you're greedy, but an observer has seen plenty of occasions on which you gave to others, whose account is more accurate?

We often think that we *are* a certain way, as if values are inborn or happen to live in each of us to different extents. We view ourselves as fixed entities that differ in *who we are*. Is this the truth, the whole truth, and nothing but the truth? Or do we instead differ more in *what we do*? Are we open to more growth than we might suspect?

INVITATION

If you could embody more of one value, what value would you choose? How would others know? What would they see? Open yourself to the possibility that you can *be* the person you desire and admire, right here, right now. Consider the possibility that if you act it, you become it. You have the potential to be whomever you want to be in the present moment.

DECEMBER 27

To let go means to give up coercing, resisting, or struggling, in exchange for something more powerful and wholesome which comes out of allowing things to be as they are without getting caught up in your attraction to or rejection of them, in the intrinsic stickiness of wanting, of liking and disliking. —JON KABAT-ZINN

Living well seems to involve a never-ending process of releasing that which no longer serves us. Our default position is to cling to things. We're afraid to let go, afraid to trust, afraid to be fully who we are. Letting go is far from easy, so we hang onto the old ways even though it hurts.

As I think back on this year, I realize how I live bound up in many ways—holding onto what I think others expect of me, clinging to expectations of how I want things to go, maintaining narrow definitions of the right way to live. I even find myself bound up physically, holding unnecessary tension in my body, moving slowly, speaking cautiously, not laughing too loud.

Grasping onto what we no longer need seems to be a basic principle of how things work, like entropy in the universe. We collect many things in our lives, things we may have needed at one time but that have outlived their usefulness. When we're willing to loosen our grip, lightness and spaciousness await us.

INVITATION

What are you holding onto that's no longer worth what it costs—a behavior, an addiction, a relationship, an emotion, a memory? Allow your grip to loosen today, letting whatever it is fall away. Feel your load lighten as you make space in your mind and heart.

DECEMBER 28

Nothing in the world is permanent, and we're foolish when we ask anything to last, but surely we're still more foolish not to take delight in it while we have it. —W. SOMERSET MAUGHAM

Recently I watched a brilliant sunrise fill the sky with indescribable pinks and purples and blues. Although it was fleeting, part of me wanted to freeze it in time, to always have it. It was as though after the dazzling colors passed, there would be nothing. In reality, golden sunlight and a beautiful blue sky took its place.

It can be hard when pleasurable experiences come to an end, just as it's painful to imagine giving up the good things in our life. I find myself believing that to lose what I cling to—my health, my ability to work, our house—would be to meet an abyss at the edge of the world.

And yet, every finish line doubles as a starting line: the end of college is the beginning of professional life; the end of pregnancy is the beginning of parenthood; the end of professional life is the beginning of retirement; the end of life, well, it's the beginning of whatever comes next.

The close of this year is another reminder of endings—that nothing lasts forever. And simultaneous with the end of this year will be the start of a brand new one, a perfectly blank canvas.

INVITATION

As we edge closer to the end of the year, notice endings in your own life. If you find yourself trying to hold onto the old, see if you can recognize that life continues to flow. Feel how each ending is the start of something brand-new.

DECEMBER 29

*When one door closes, another opens; but we often look so long and
so regretfully upon the closed door that we do not see the one that has
opened for us.* —ALEXANDER GRAHAM BELL

The time between Christmas and the New Year can be an odd one.
With many people off work or working irregularly, each day can seem
to merge into the next. Without a sense of real purpose during "Chrimbo
Limbo," it seems acceptable to wear pajamas all day and eat chocolate
for breakfast. The day's activities might flit between slowly devouring
the holiday leftovers, watching holiday-themed television programs, and
snacking as though it's a professional sport.

As we approach the New Year, our minds often start to turn toward
resolutions and the changes we'd like to make in our lives. Chances are
we're carrying some extra holiday weight and eating better is beginning
to seem necessary. We might start to feel low, frustrated with our weight
or body shape or where we are in our lives right now. Change can be an
intimidating and daunting prospect.

At times like this, it's important to be gentle with ourselves. You are
where you are. The liberating part is that change is possible—and it can
start whenever we wish.

INVITATION

Today, see if you can view change as an opportunity rather than a burden.
If there are changes you'd like to make in your own life, what benefits
would they bring? Would your life become brighter, happier, and more
joyful as a result? See if you can find the excitement that lives in the opportunity change brings.

DECEMBER 30

*We have all a better guide in ourselves, if we would attend to it, than
any other person can be.* —JANE AUSTEN

T hroughout this year, we have encouraged you to find connection
and peace no matter what life may bring. We've shared parts of
our own stories with you, using these experiences as the inspiration for
daily practices:

- Focusing on your senses

- Feeling your body—your hands, your feet, the breath moving
  through you

- Letting go of the stories we tell ourselves

- Paying attention to the people we care about

- Practicing kindness toward ourselves

- Developing gratitude even amid life's challenges

- Opening to life as it unfolds

- Forgiving both others and ourselves

- Serving others

- Moving through our worries

- Taking responsibility for our own happiness

- Reconnecting with our deepest values and letting our actions flow
  from them

continued on next page

Thank you for coming on this journey with us. I hope it's helped you connect with what you love, even through the challenges you've surely faced this year. As much as anything, I hope you've developed a deeper trust in yourself—your instincts, your tendency toward growth, your basic decency as a person, your fundamental worth.

Although our yearlong journey together ends soon, your relationship with yourself and with your daily practice continues. There will be days that seem impossibly hard and days that are amazingly good. It is enough to be who you are, finding ways to connect, over and over, with presence, your passions, your principles, and the people you love.

INVITATION

I've been offering specific invitations throughout this year; now I'd like to turn things over to you. Trust that *you* know what you need today as you invite yourself to connect. I wish you the very best of life and love.

DECEMBER 31

Awareness. Awareness. Awareness. —ANTHONY DE MELLO

The essence of all the entries and practices that we have shared this year is awareness—awareness of our values, our senses, our bodies, the stories that our minds create, how we view ourselves, and how we act toward others. Awareness is the key to liberation, to happiness, and to loving freely.

A fundamental element lies at the heart of all our feelings of dissatisfaction, unhappiness, and discontent: we are focusing on what we do not have. We dwell on absence—absence of a romantic relationship, of the person who doesn't want to be with us or who is no longer with us, or of the body that we don't have or the house, car, job, career, money, health, etc. We become obsessed with what we do not have. We become fixated with that which does not exist. It may have existed in the past or may exist in the future, but it isn't here right now.

With awareness, we can notice where our attention lies. With awareness, we can become conscious of the thoughts and emotions that pop up in our minds. With awareness, we can choose to leave our heads and live in the now. With awareness, we can feel alive in this rich, vibrant, and glorious present moment.

It's as simple (or as complicated) as that.

INVITATION
Rest in awareness. Wake up to life and connect to this sacred moment.

ACKNOWLEDGMENTS

SETH

I'm grateful for the many connections that brought this book into being. Thank you first to Aria, my dear friend, coauthor, and fellow traveler. You and I couldn't have known where this project would lead us, and it ended up being so much better than I could have hoped for. Thank you for your consistency, day after day, in sending me encouraging and heartfelt posts, even when you were sick in bed and racked by fever or had to scramble to find an internet connection while traveling. The practices you sent were a lifeline on many occasions. I'm so glad we did this!

My parents, the Reverend Charles Gillihan and Carolyn Gillihan, taught me more than they realized about the importance of connection and the imperative of the spiritual life. I appreciate the consistent love we experienced in our home and the stability that provided a haven to return to at the end of each day. It took me a while to appreciate that being raised in a fundamentalist Christian home was a valuable part of my spiritual development as I carry with me the songs and scriptures I learned as a kid. Thank you for teaching your sons to care about others and to value family above material concerns.

I have four brothers: Yonder Moynihan, Malachi Alexander, Timothy Alec, and Charles Whitman. Each of you is a part of me. We've supported one another so many times through the years. As we've all entered adulthood it's pained me to see that suffering is inevitable for all of us, and yet the love we share more than makes up for the difficulties we face.

My parents-in-law, Dr. Lance Leithauser and Cynthia Leithauser, have welcomed me into their family and their home for more than twenty years. Thank you for the encouragement and support you've always given me. I appreciate your providing a place in your home for my early morning writing sessions as I worked on several of my entries for this book.

Dr. Elyssa Kushner introduced me to the practice of mindfulness in the clinic as my postdoctoral supervisor. That introduction quickly led me to my own mindfulness practice, which felt like waking up from sleepwalking through my life. Thank you, Elyssa, not only for enriching my clinical work but for being instrumental in my own journey into mindful awareness.

Many writers and teachers of mindfulness have taught me along the way: the late Chögyam Trungpa wrote a small volume called *Shambhala: The Sacred Path of the Warrior*, which I discovered as if by magic on my bookshelf several years ago. Every page of the book resonated with me as the author seemed to be describing my own personal experience. No other book has influenced my mindfulness practice as much as *Shambhala*.

I have deepened my understanding and application of mindfulness through the writings of Pema Chödrön, one of Chögyam Trungpa's students. Her words are filled with honesty, compassion, and firmness, and I come back to them again and again.

The books and guided meditations of Jon Kabat-Zinn played a crucial role in my introduction to mindfulness. Thich Nhat Hanh's writings deepened my awareness of how we can find the sacred in every micro moment of our lives. I am fortunate to know Michael Baime through our shared affiliation with Penn, and have benefited from our interactions over the years. Zindel Segal introduced me to the role of mindfulness in cognitive behavioral therapy for depression through his writing, conference talks, and at a lunch for graduate students when he gave a talk at Penn.

David Richo expanded my awareness of the role of mindfulness in loving relationships. Eckhart Tolle's books helped me understand that things really are fundamentally okay in this moment, and to recognize the workings of the ego. I've enjoyed Tara Brach's calming words in her many online guided meditations. The work of Sam Harris has deepened my understanding of what mindfulness is and what it means to train the mind.

Thank you to the superb staff at Blackstone Publications: special thanks to Rick Bleiweiss for his enthusiasm about this book from the very beginning; thank you also to Josie Woodbridge, Naomi Hynes, Lauren Maturo, Jeffrey Yamaguchi, Sean Thomas, Mandy Earles, Michael Krohn, and Greg Boguslawski. It was a pleasure to work with editor Nic Albert again, who took this project under his wing and helped us balance the personal and the universal in our writing.

Thank you to Cory Field for his guidance and counsel—you've never steered me wrong.

Over the years, I've treated hundreds of patients in psychotherapy. Your determination to connect with what's most important to you, no matter what you're going through, is inspiring, and many of your insights are captured in these pages. Thank you for sharing your lives and your stories with me.

Finally, my love and gratitude go to my wife, Marcia Leithauser, and our three precious children, Lucas, Ada, and Faye. Words cannot capture how much you mean to me and how deeply I love each of you, but I trust you know. You also know the challenges we faced as I was working on this book, and your steady presence and continual support were life-giving and lifesaving. This book is for you.

ARIA

To my close friend and coauthor Seth: Thank you for your thoughtfulness and compassion throughout this journey to reawaken and reconnect to what matters most. You are an incredible person, and it is a true privilege to walk on this path with you.

To my loving parents: Mum, your joyful spirit and will to celebrate every day is enlivening. Dad, you've taught me that the present moment is precious since the past has gone and the future is yet to come. Thank you both for your ongoing love.

To my dear brothers: Darius, when we shared a bedroom together growing up you pinned a postcard to my noticeboard that read, "Reach for the moon! Even if you miss, you will land among the stars." You've always encouraged me to believe in myself, for which I'm eternally grateful. Cyrus—a.k.a. Top Dog, Tippy Toppy Dog, and C-bomb—you're the man. (I'm glad that we've finally settled this.) You've shaped my life in more ways than I can write here. I know that you're always there for me, and I'm excited about the adventures that lie ahead!

To Hugh and Jayne: I feel blessed to have you as parents-in-law. You were both an amazing support throughout the year. Jayne, your kindness, sense of humor, and home cooking always brightens my day. Hugh, running together, whether along Hadrian's Wall, the River Tyne, or the two oceans in South Africa, reminds me that the present moment is not missing anything and cannot be improved by material possessions. The way that you live each day in line with your values and faith is a constant source of inspiration to me.

To Thich Nhat Hanh and all the monks and nuns at Plum Village: It was at the monastery that I first discovered what it truly means to live mindfully. Thay, you once said that as long as you feel grateful, you can be happy. That has stayed with me since. Your spiritual teachings on mindfulness and peace will always be carried in the hearts of many. A lotus for you.

To Ashley, Conan, and Jack: We carried one another through the peaks and the troughs of the doctorate. The year would not have been the same without you three! Boudoir love. To Gary: the way in which you meet the present moment, whatever it brings, with acceptance, courage, and unremitting optimism has always inspired me. To James, Marcus, Ramin, Kian, David, Callum, Jack (Wolfie), DJ Tank, Ditch, Johnnie, Sean, Dudey, Colin and Robert: You are all legends in your own way. Thank you for your continued support. True friendships are the gifts of life.

To everyone at Blackstone Publishing, especially Rick, Josie, Naomi, Greg, Lauren, Jeff, Sean, Michael, and Mandy: your belief and championing of *A Mindful Year* from start to finish meant a lot to me. Thank you Nic for taking the time to understand the spirit of our collaboration and skillfully edit our entries.

Finally, to my wonderful wife and the love of my life, Emma: You are my best friend and my soul mate. Thank you for your love, honesty, and support, while writing this book and over the past ten years. You are what matters most to me. I love you, Baba.